Next-Gen Backend Development
Mastering Python and Django
Techniques

Contents

1 **Introduction to Python for Backend Development**   **13**

   1.1 Why Python for Backend Development? 13

   1.2 Understanding the Python Ecosystem 15

   1.3 Installing Python and Setting Up the Development Environment 17

   1.4 Python Syntax and Semantics Overview 20

   1.5 Data Types and Variables in Python 21

   1.6 Control Structures: Conditions and Loops 23

   1.7 Functions in Python: Understanding Defining and Calling 25

   1.8 Working with Modules and Packages 27

   1.9 Exception Handling in Python 29

   1.10 Introduction to Object-Oriented Programming in Python   31

   1.11 Understanding Python's Magic Methods 33

   1.12 Virtual Environments and Dependency Management . . 35

   1.13 Introduction to Git for Version Control 37

   1.14 Overview of Python Web Frameworks: Django and Flask   39

   1.15 Setting the Stage for Web Development with Django . . . 42

2 **Setting Up a Django Development Environment**   **45**

   2.1 Overview of Django and its Advantages 45

   2.2 Prerequisites for Django Development 47

3

2.3   Installing Python for Django Development   49

2.4   Setting Up a Virtual Environment   50

2.5   Installing Django and Creating a Django Project   52

2.6   Understanding the Django Project Structure   54

2.7   Configuring Django Settings for Development   56

2.8   Running the Django Development Server   58

2.9   Introduction to Django Applications and Creating an App 60

2.10   Connecting to a Database in Django   61

2.11   Using the Django Shell for Quick Tests   63

2.12   Understanding the Django Migrations System   65

2.13   Version Control for Django Projects with Git   67

2.14   Setting Up a Django Development Workflow   70

2.15   Tools and IDEs for Efficient Django Development   71

3   **Models and Databases in Django**   **75**

3.1   Understanding Models in Django   75

3.2   Defining Django Models: Fields and Relationships   77

3.3   Migrations: Creating and Applying Migrations   79

3.4   Interacting with the Database through Django Models . .   81

3.5   Using the Django ORM for CRUD Operations   83

3.6   Understanding Django QuerySets and Managers   85

3.7   Advanced Model Techniques: Custom Managers and
       Methods   87

3.8   Working with Multiple Databases   88

3.9   Implementing Model Inheritance in Django   90

3.10   Signals in Django Models   92

3.11   Optimizing Database Queries   94

3.12   Integrating with External Databases and APIs   96

3.13   Using Django Models with Forms and Views   98

3.14   Securing Data in Django Models   100

3.15 Best Practices for Designing Django Models 102

4 Django Admin Interface Customization   105

4.1   Introduction to the Django Admin Interface 105

4.2   Registering Models with the Admin Site 107

4.3   Customizing the Model Admin: List Displays, Filters, and Searches 108

4.4   Form Customization in the Admin 110

4.5   Admin Site Customization: Look and Feel 112

4.6   Creating Custom Admin Actions 114

4.7   Securing the Django Admin Interface 116

4.8   Implementing Custom Admin Views 118

4.9   Extending Admin Templates 119

4.10 Django Admin Interface for Related Objects 121

4.11 Integrating Third-Party Tools with Django Admin 123

4.12 Performance Optimization for the Django Admin Interface 125

4.13 Advanced Techniques: Custom Admin Widgets and Form Fields 127

4.14 Deploying and Monitoring the Django Admin Interface . 129

4.15 Best Practices for Django Admin Customization 131

5 Views and URL routing in Django   135

5.1   An Overview of Views in Django 135

5.2   Understanding URL Configuration and Routing 137

5.3   Writing Function-Based Views 139

5.4   Class-Based Views: An Introduction 141

5.5   Advanced Class-Based Views: Customizing and Extending 143

5.6   Using Generic Views for Common Patterns 145

5.7   Managing Forms with Class-Based Views 148

5.8   Implementing Ajax Calls with Django Views 149

5.9   Securing Views: Permissions and User Authentication . . 152

5.10 Handling HTTP Methods and Status Codes 154

5.11 Custom Error Views: Handling 404 and 500 Errors 155

5.12 Optimizing Django Views Performance 157

5.13 Integrating Third-Party Applications into Django Views . 159

5.14 Testing Views: Unit Tests and Integration Tests 161

5.15 Debugging Common Issues with Django Views 163

6   **Templates and Static Files in Django**   **167**

6.1   Introduction to Django Templates 167

6.2   Setting Up Django Template Engine 169

6.3   Template Syntax: Variables, Tags, and Filters 170

6.4   Working with Template Inheritance 172

6.5   Creating Custom Template Tags and Filters 174

6.6   Managing Static Files: Setup and Configuration 176

6.7   Using Static and Media Files in Templates 178

6.8   Template Context Processors 179

6.9   Using Third-Party Template Tags and Filters 181

6.10 Securing Templates Against Injection Attacks 183

6.11 Optimizing Template Rendering Performance 185

6.12 Debugging Template Errors 187

6.13 Internationalization in Templates 189

6.14 Best Practices for Templating and Static Files Management 191

6.15 Combining Templates with Views and Forms 192

7   **Form Handling and File Uploads in Django**   **195**

7.1   Overview of Form Handling in Django 195

7.2   Understanding Django Forms: A Primer 197

7.3   Creating and Using Django Forms 199

7.4   Advanced Form Features: Custom Validation and Cleaning 201

7.5 Working with Django ModelForms 203

7.6 Implementing File Uploads with Django 205

7.7 Handling Multiple Files and Large Uploads 207

7.8 Integrating Third-Party Form Fields and Widgets 209

7.9 Ajax Form Submission and Validation 211

7.10 Securing Django Forms: CSRF Protection and XSS Prevention 213

7.11 Formsets: Managing Multiple Forms on the Same Page . 215

7.12 Styling and Theming Django Forms with CSS and JavaScript 217

7.13 Performance Optimizations for Django Forms 219

7.14 Advanced Techniques: Dynamic Forms and Custom Widgets 221

7.15 Testing and Debugging Django Forms 223

8 **Authentication and Authorization in Django**   **227**

8.1 Introduction to Authentication and Authorization 227

8.2 Setting Up Django's Built-in Authentication System . . . 229

8.3 Custom User Models: Extending the Default User 231

8.4 Creating and Managing User Accounts 233

8.5 Password Management: Hashing, Resetting, and Changing 235

8.6 Implementing Login and Logout Functionality 237

8.7 User Permissions and Groups for Authorization 239

8.8 Customizing Authentication Forms 241

8.9 Integrating Social Authentication 242

8.10 Token-based Authentication for APIs 244

8.11 Using Django Permissions in Views and Templates 247

8.12 Securing Views with Decorators and Middleware 248

8.13 Auditing and Logging User Actions 251

8.14 Testing Authentication and Authorization 253

8.15 Best Practices for Secure Authentication and Authorization255

9   RESTful APIs with Django Rest Framework   257

9.1   Introduction to RESTful APIs and Django Rest Framework257

9.2   Setting Up Django Rest Framework in Your Django Project259

9.3   Serializers: Converting Data for the Web 261

9.4   Handling HTTP Methods: GET, POST, PUT, DELETE . . 264

9.5   Class-Based Views and ViewSets for Efficient API Development 265

9.6   Authentication and Permission in RESTful APIs 267

9.7   Working with Nested Resources and Relationships 269

9.8   Implementing Pagination, Filtering, and Sorting 272

9.9   Versioning Your API for Future Compatibility 274

9.10 Documenting Your API with Tools like Swagger 276

9.11 Testing RESTful APIs with Django Rest Framework . . . 278

9.12 Throttling, Permissions, and Other Security Practices . . 280

9.13 Optimizing API Performance and Response Times 282

9.14 Advanced Topics: Hyperlinked APIs and Custom Fields 284

9.15 Deploying Your API: Best Practices and Considerations . 286

10 Testing and Debugging in Django   289

10.1 Introduction to Testing in Django 289

10.2 Setting Up Your Testing Environment 291

10.3 Writing Your First Test: Unit Tests and Test Cases 293

10.4 Testing Django Models 295

10.5 Testing Views and URL Configuration 296

10.6 Testing Forms and Form Validation 298

10.7 Testing Template Rendering 300

10.8 Integration Testing: Testing the Application as a Whole . 302

10.9 Using Mock Objects and Factories for Efficient Testing . . 304

10.10Testing RESTful APIs with Django Rest Framework . . . 306

10.11 Debugging Techniques in Django 308

10.12 Using Django's Logging Framework for Debugging . . . 311

10.13 Performance Testing: Identifying Bottlenecks 313

10.14 Security Testing: Identifying Vulnerabilities 315

10.15 Best Practices for Testing and Debugging Django Applications 316

11 Performance Optimization in Django Applications   319

11.1 Understanding Performance Bottlenecks in Web Applications 319

11.2 Database Optimization Techniques in Django 321

11.3 Query Optimization: Reducing Database Hits 324

11.4 Caching Strategies for Django Applications 326

11.5 Optimizing Django Views and URL Routing 328

11.6 Template Optimization Techniques 330

11.7 Static Files and Media Management 332

11.8 Using Asynchronous Views and Tasks 334

11.9 API Performance Optimization with Django Rest Framework 336

11.10 Front-end Optimization Techniques for Django Projects . 338

11.11 Securing Your Django Application from Common Performance Issues 340

11.12 Monitoring and Logging for Performance Issues 342

11.13 Tools and Frameworks for Django Performance Testing . 344

11.14 Deploying Django Applications for High Performance . 346

11.15 Case Studies: Real-world Django Performance Optimization 347

12 Deployment and Scaling Django Applications   351

12.1 Overview of Django Application Deployment 351

12.2 Choosing a Deployment Environment: VPS, PaaS, and Serverless 353

12.3 Setting Up a Production Environment for Django 355

12.4 Configuring Django for Production 357

12.5 Deploying Django with WSGI and ASGI Servers 359

12.6 Working with Reverse Proxies and Load Balancers 361

12.7 Static and Media File Management in Production 363

12.8 Database Deployment and Scaling Strategies 365

12.9 Implementing Caching for High Traffic Django Applica-
       tions 367

12.10 Securing Your Django Application for Production 370

12.11 Continuous Integration and Continuous Deployment
       (CI/CD) for Django 372

12.12 Monitoring and Logging Django Applications in Produc-
       tion 374

12.13 Scaling Django Applications Horizontally and Vertically 376

12.14 Using CDN and Edge Computing for Global Scaling . . . 378

12.15 Case Studies: Successful Deployment and Scaling Strate-
       gies 380

Preface

This book, *Next-Gen Backend Development: Mastering Python and Django Techniques*, aims to provide a comprehensive guide for developers aspiring to excel in the fast-paced and ever-evolving field of backend development. By focusing on Python and Django, two foundational pillars of contemporary web development, we intend to offer a structured and in-depth exploration of the techniques, best practices, and advanced features crucial for building robust, scalable, and efficient web applications.

The objectives of this book are multifaceted. Firstly, it seeks to introduce readers to the foundational concepts of Python, particularly as they apply to backend development. This ensures that readers develop a solid grasp of the language's syntax, data structures, and unique features that make it suitable for complex web development tasks. Secondly, it delves into Django, unveiling its architecture, components, and workflows to equip readers with the knowledge necessary to leverage Django's full potential in crafting next-generation web applications. Moreover, the book addresses advanced topics such as RESTful API development, performance optimization, security best practices, modern deployment strategies, and emergent trends, aiming to provide a holistic view of web development within the Python/Django ecosystem.

The content of this book is meticulously curated to offer both breadth and depth. Starting from the essentials of Python programming, it progresses to cover the intricacies of Django's model-view-template (MVT) architecture, examines the nuances of handling forms and implementing user authentication, and ventures into the comprehensive world of Django Rest Framework for API development. Each chapter is thoughtfully designed to build upon the knowledge acquired in previous chapters, synthesizing concepts and practical insights into actionable strategies that developers can apply in real-world scenarios.

This book targets a wide spectrum of readers. Beginners in web development will find foundational chapters that solidify their understanding of Python and Django, while intermediate developers will appreciate the advanced chapters that help to hone their skills and explore new paradigms in backend development. Furthermore, seasoned developers will discover invaluable resources in the chapters on performance optimization, security, deployment, and new trends. These resources support their continuous quest for excellence and innovation.

In essence, *Next-Gen Backend Development: Mastering Python and Django Techniques* aspires to be a vital resource for anyone looking to navigate the intricacies of backend development with confidence and proficiency. By the end of this book, readers will not only have acquired a deep understanding of Python and Django but will also have harnessed the practical expertise necessary to craft state-of-the-art web applications that are resilient and future-proof.

Chapter 1

Introduction to Python for Backend Development

Python has emerged as a leading programming language for backend development due to its readability, efficiency, and comprehensive standard library. Its vast ecosystem of frameworks, notably Django, streamlines web development tasks, making it an ideal choice for building robust and scalable web applications. This chapter presents a primer on Python's core concepts, data structures, and functionalities relevant to backend development, offering a foundation for leveraging Python's capabilities in web application projects.

1.1 Why Python for Backend Development?

Python, a high-level programming language, has seen a meteoric rise in popularity across various fields of software development, especially in backend web development. This surge in popularity can be attributed to its simplicity and readability, making it accessible to newcomers while offering powerful and sophisticated libraries and frameworks for professionals. The purpose of this section is to elucidate the characteristics and capabilities of Python that make it an excellent choice for backend development.

Firstly, Python's syntax is designed to be straightforward and readable. This design philosophy promotes cleaner code and allows developers to express concepts without writing additional code, making Python an ideal language for rapid development. This is particularly beneficial in the realm of backend development, where maintaining and scaling complex web applications can become burdensome.

```
1  def hello_world():
2      print("Hello, World!")
```

In the example above, a function to print "Hello, World!" demonstrates Python's simplicity and readability. Such clarity in syntax reduces the cognitive load on developers, enabling them to focus more on the logic rather than the language intricacies.

Python's extensive standard library is another critical aspect that bolsters its suitability for backend development. These libraries cover a wide range of functionalities, including file I/O, internet protocols, and web services, providing a solid foundation to build upon. Moreover, Python's package management tools, such as pip, facilitate effortless installation and management of external libraries, further expanding Python's capabilities.

```
Successfully installed Django-3.2
```

The output above exemplifies the simplicity of using pip to install Django, a high-level Python web framework that encourages rapid development and clean, pragmatic design.

Moreover, Python's ecosystem is rich with frameworks like Django and Flask, which abstract a lot of the common web development tasks. Django, in particular, offers an ORM (Object-Relational Mapping), authentication support, and an admin panel out-of-the-box, significantly accelerating the development process. Flask, on the other hand, is a micro web framework that provides the essentials for web development, offering developers the flexibility to choose their tools and libraries.

In terms of performance, while Python may not match the speed of compiled languages like C or Java, it is generally more than adequate for most backend development needs. The ability to integrate Python with C through modules allows for performance-critical applications to achieve the necessary speed. Furthermore, with the advent of asynchronous programming through frameworks such as Asyncio, developers can write highly scalable and efficient I/O-bound applications in Python.

```
1  import asyncio
2
```

```
3  async def main():
4      print('Hello ...')
5      await asyncio.sleep(1)
6      print('... World!')
7
8  asyncio.run(main())
```

The above code snippet demonstrates the simplicity of writing asynchronous programs in Python, which can greatly enhance the performance of web applications by handling a large number of concurrent connections.

Finally, Python's vibrant community and the vast array of resources available for learning and problem-solving cannot be overstated. From extensive documentation and tutorials to active online forums and user groups, developers have access to an unparalleled support network. This ecosystem not only makes it easier to solve technical problems but also fosters innovation and collaboration within the field of backend development.

Python offers a perfect blend of simplicity, versatility, and strength for backend development. Its readable syntax, comprehensive standard library, powerful frameworks, and vibrant community create an environment where developers can efficiently develop, deploy, and maintain scalable web applications. Whether for rapid prototyping or building complex, data-driven sites, Python continues to be a premier choice for backend developers worldwide.

1.2   Understanding the Python Ecosystem

The Python ecosystem is a comprehensive infrastructure that encompasses an extensive range of tools, libraries, and frameworks, designed to facilitate various aspects of software development. Central to its appeal for backend development is the richness and diversity of the resources it offers. This ecosystem is built around Python, a versatile and powerful programming language known for its simplicity and readability, making it accessible to newcomers while robust enough for complex development projects.

At the heart of Python's ecosystem is the Python Package Index (PyPI), a repository of software for the Python programming language. PyPI hosts tens of thousands of third-party modules and packages, which can be seamlessly integrated into Python applications. These packages cover a wide array of functionalities, from web development frameworks like Django and Flask, to scientific computing libraries such as NumPy and SciPy, to machine learning toolkits like TensorFlow and scikit-learn.

Python's standard library itself is remarkably comprehensive, offering modules and functions for file I/O, system calls, sockets, and even interfaces to graphical user interface toolkits like Tk. This built-in library serves as the foundation upon which Python developers can build more complex applications, significantly reducing development time by providing a wide variety of high-level functionalities out of the box.

Furthermore, the Python ecosystem is supported by an active and engaged community. This community contributes to the ongoing development of Python by creating and maintaining open-source packages, developing and sharing tools, writing documentation, and offering support through forums and discussion groups. Events such as PyCon, meetups, and hackathons foster collaboration and innovation within the Python community, facilitating knowledge sharing and networking opportunities for developers of all skill levels.

Python's package management tools, such as pip and conda, play a crucial role in managing the installation and versioning of packages. Pip is the Python community's preferred tool for installing packages from PyPI, featuring an easy-to-use command-line interface. Conda, on the other hand, is a cross-platform package manager that can install Python packages as well as the Python interpreter itself. It is particularly favored in the scientific and data analysis communities for its ability to manage complex dependency trees.

In addition to package management, the Python ecosystem encompasses a comprehensive set of development tools aimed at enhancing productivity and code quality. Integrated Development Environments (IDEs) like PyCharm, Visual Studio Code, and Jupyter Notebooks offer sophisticated coding environments tailored to Python development. These tools come equipped with features such as syntax highlighting, code completion, and debugging capabilities. Additionally, Python supports a variety of testing frameworks, such as PyTest, which facilitate rigorous testing practices essential for developing robust applications.

The ecosystem also includes a plethora of resources for learning and professional development. From official documentation and tutorials to books, blogs, and video courses, there is an abundance of materials available for both beginners and experienced developers wanting to deepen their Python knowledge.

The Python ecosystem is a vibrant and comprehensive suite of tools, libraries, and resources, all centered around a programming language celebrated for its ease of use and powerful capabilities. For backend development, this ecosystem provides an unparalleled array of functionalities that can be leveraged to build sophisticated, high-performance web applications. Its extensive package repository, effective management tools, and supportive community ensure that developers have everything they need to bring their projects to life, making Python an ideal choice for modern web development.

1.3 Installing Python and Setting Up the Development Environment

Let's start with the essential step in beginning backend development with Python – installing Python and setting up a suitable development environment. This process involves a few key stages: downloading Python, installing it on your system, and configuring a development environment that can effectively support the development process.

Downloading Python

The first step is to download the latest version of Python. This can be accomplished by visiting the official Python website at https://www.python.org/. It is crucial to download a version of Python that is supported by the Django version you plan to use for your web development projects. Python 3.8 or newer is recommended for most current Django projects, as it provides the latest features and optimizations.

Installing Python

After downloading Python, the next step is the installation process, which slightly varies depending on the operating system.

On Windows:

- Run the downloaded .exe file.

17

- Ensure to check the option 'Add Python 3.x to PATH' before clicking on the 'Install Now' button. This step makes Python accessible from the command line.

- Once the installation is complete, verify the installation by opening the command prompt and typing python --version. The installed Python version should be displayed.

On macOS:

- Open the downloaded .pkg file.

- Follow the installation wizard steps. You might need to enter your administrator password.

- To verify the installation, open the Terminal and type python3 --version. The system should display the Python version you installed.

On Linux:

- Most Linux distributions come with Python pre-installed. To check if Python is installed and determine its version, open the terminal and type python3 --version.

- If Python is not installed or if an upgrade is needed, use your distribution's package manager to install or update Python. For Ubuntu and other Debian-based systems, this can typically be done using sudo apt-get update followed by sudo apt-get install python3.8.

Setting Up the Development Environment

After successfully installing Python, the next crucial task is to set up your development environment. An Integrated Development Environment (IDE) offers a comprehensive facility to programmers for software development. PyCharm and Visual Studio Code are among the most popular IDEs for Python development.

PyCharm:

PyCharm, developed by JetBrains, is a popular IDE specifically designed for Python development. It provides code analysis, a graphical debugger, an integrated unit tester, and supports web development with Django.

- Download PyCharm from
  `https://www.jetbrains.com/pycharm/download/` and follow the installation instructions.

- Once installed, create a new project and select a Python interpreter. You can use the Python interpreter that was installed earlier.

- PyCharm will create a virtual environment by default for your project, which is a recommendable practice for managing project-specific dependencies.

Visual Studio Code (VS Code):

VS Code is a lightweight but powerful source code editor which runs on your desktop. It comes with built-in support for Python development and an extensive ecosystem of extensions.

- Download VS Code from `https://code.visualstudio.com/` and install it.

- Install the Python extension for Visual Studio Code from the marketplace to enhance Python support in VS Code.

- Open a new or existing folder as a project and select the Python interpreter from the command palette. Like PyCharm, you would use the previously installed Python interpreter.

- Consider creating a virtual environment within your project directory to manage dependencies by running `python3 -m venv .venv` in the terminal. Activate the virtual environment by sourcing it (`source .venv/bin/activate` on macOS/Linux, `.venv Scripts activate` on Windows).

Setting up the development environment correctly is as vital as the coding itself for the success of a project. It ensures that developers can work efficiently and manage project dependencies effectively, leading to more manageable and robust applications. With Python installed and your development environment ready, you are well-prepared to embark on backend development projects using Python and Django.

1.4   Python Syntax and Semantics Overview

Python's syntax and semantics are designed with readability in mind, following the principle of "There should be one–and preferably only one–obvious way to do it." This design philosophy simplifies Python code's understanding and maintenance, making it particularly appealing for both newcomers and experienced developers. In this section, we will discuss the basic structures of Python syntax, including variables, operators, control statements, and indentation, which are crucial for backend development.

Variables and Data Types: In Python, variables do not need explicit declaration to reserve memory space. The declaration happens automatically when a value is assigned to a variable. The assignment is done using the equals sign (=). Python is a dynamically typed language, which means that the type of a variable is inferred from the value assigned to it.

```
1  x = 10 # An integer assignment
2  y = "Python" # A string assignment
```

Operators: Python supports a wide range of operators, such as arithmetic operators (+, -, *, /), comparison operators (==, !=, <, >), and logical operators (and, or, not). These operators are fundamental for performing mathematical operations and making decisions in code.

```
1  result = (x + 5) * 10
2  is_greater = x > 5
```

Control Structures: Python's control structures include conditionals and loops, enabling the execution of code blocks based on conditions or repeated execution of a block of code. The if, elif, and else statements are used for conditional executions. For loops, Python provides the for loop, which iterates over the items of any sequence, such as a list or a string, and the while loop, which executes as long as a condition is true.

```
1   if x > 10:
2       print("x is greater than 10")
3   elif x == 10:
4       print("x is exactly 10")
5   else:
6       print("x is less than 10")
7
8   for i in range(5):
9       print(i)
10
11  count = 0
```

20

```
12   while count < 5:
13       print(count)
14       count += 1
```

Indentation: Unlike many other programming languages, Python uses indentation to define blocks or suites of code. This requirement is unique and essential to Python's readability. Other languages often use curly braces or keywords for this purpose. In Python, all statements with the same distance to the right belong to the same block of code, making the structure of the code visually clear.

```
1   if x > 10:
2       print("x is greater than 10")
3       if x > 20:
4           print("x is also greater than 20")
5       else:
6           print("x is less than 20")
```

The elegance and simplicity of Python's syntax and semantics contribute significantly to its suitability for backend development. With a clear understanding of these concepts, developers can write more readable, maintainable, and efficient code, laying a strong foundation for web application projects. Furthermore, adherence to Pythonic principles, such as simplicity and explicitness, promotes best practices in programming and enhances the collaborative development process.

1.5   Data Types and Variables in Python

In the context of backend development, understanding data types and variables is fundamental. Python simplifies working with various kinds of data through its dynamic typing system, automatically identifying the type of data a variable holds. This section will discuss the basic data types in Python, the declaration of variables, and how dynamically typed nature of Python impacts backend development tasks.

In Python, variables do not need explicit declaration to reserve memory space. The declaration happens automatically when a value is assigned to a variable. The assignment operator '=' is used to assign values to variables. For instance, age = 30 assigns the integer value 30 to the variable age. The core data types in Python include integers, floats (decimal numbers), strings (text), and booleans (True or False).

```
1   name = "John Doe" # String
2   age = 30 # Integer
```

```
3  salary = 4500.50 # Float
4  is_active = True # Boolean
```

Additionally, Python has several built-in collection data types that are very useful for backend development: lists, tuples, dictionaries, and sets.

- Lists are ordered and changeable collections which allow duplicate members.

- Tuples are ordered and unchangeable collections which allow duplicate members.

- Dictionaries are unordered, changeable, and indexed collections with no duplicate members.

- Sets are unordered and unindexed collections with no duplicate members.

Here are some examples of how these collection types can be used:

```
1   # List
2   employees = ["John", "Doe", "Smith"]
3
4   # Tuple
5   coordinates = (4, 5)
6
7   # Dictionary
8   employee_record = {"name": "John", "age": 30, "department": "Finance"}
9
10  # Set
11  unique_ids = {1001, 1002, 1003}
```

Type conversion is another aspect of Python's data types that is particularly relevant for backend development. Python provides built-in functions like int(), float(), str(), and bool() for explicit conversion of one data type into another. This is frequently used in backend development when, for example, query parameters from a web request are received as strings but need to be processed as integers or floats.

```
1   str_number = "123"
2   int_number = int(str_number) # Converts string to integer
```

Python's dynamic typing system, while providing flexibility and speeding up the development process, requires developers to be aware of the type of data they are working with, especially when performing operations involving multiple data types. For instance, attempting to concatenate a string and an integer directly will result in a TypeError.

22

```
1  user_age = 30
2  message = "Your age is " + user_age # This will raise a TypeError
3  fixed_message = "Your age is " + str(user_age) # Correct way
```

The simplicity and flexibility of Python's data types and variable declaration significantly contribute to its suitability for backend development. By understanding and utilizing Python's data types, backend
developers can efficiently manage and manipulate data, leading to the
creation of robust and scalable web applications.

This section comprehensively covers the essentials of data types and
variables in Python, emphasizing their relevance and application in
backend development.

1.6 Control Structures: Conditions and Loops

Control structures in Python, comprising conditions and loops, are
fundamental for creating dynamic and interactive backend systems.
They allow developers to execute code blocks based on certain conditions and perform repetitive tasks efficiently. Understanding these
structures is crucial for manipulating data, processing user input, and
implementing the business logic of web applications.

Conditional Statements

Conditional statements in Python are executed through if, elif, and
else keywords. These statements evaluate a condition and execute a
block of code if the condition is true.

```
1  if condition:
2      # Code to execute if condition is true
3  elif another_condition:
4      # Code to execute if another_condition is true
5  else:
6      # Code to execute if none of the above conditions are true
```

It is important to note that Python relies on indentation to define the
scope of a condition block. This design enforces readability but requires developers to be meticulous with their spacing and indentation.

Loops

Python supports two types of loops: `for` and `while`.

The `for` Loop is used to iterate over a sequence (such as a list, tuple, dictionary, set, or string) and execute a block of code for each item in the sequence.

```
for item in sequence:
    # Code to execute for each item
```

The `while` Loop, on the other hand, executes as long as a specified condition is true.

```
while condition:
    # Code to execute as long as condition is true
```

Both loops can use the `break` statement to exit the loop before it completes all iterations and the `continue` statement to skip the current iteration and proceed to the next one.

Looping through Dictionaries

When looping through dictionaries, the `for` loop can be used to iterate over keys, values, or key-value pairs.

```
# Looping through keys
for key in dictionary:
    # Do something with key

# Looping through values
for value in dictionary.values():
    # Do something with value

# Looping through key-value pairs
for key, value in dictionary.items():
    # Do something with key and value
```

List Comprehensions

Python also supports list comprehensions, which provide a concise way to create lists. Common applications include making new lists where each element is the result of some operation applied to each member of another sequence or iterable, or creating a subsequence of those elements that satisfy a certain condition.

```
# Creating a list of squares for integers from 0 to 9
squares = [x**2 for x in range(10)]
```

Exception Handling in Loops

Exception handling can be used within loops to manage errors that occur during iteration. This allows the loop to continue with the next iteration even if an error occurs in the current one.

```
for item in sequence:
    try:
        # Attempt operation that may fail
    except Exception as e:
        # Handle error
```

Nested Loops

Python allows using loops inside loops, known as nested loops. This is particularly useful for iterating through multi-dimensional data structures.

```
for x in outer_sequence:
    for y in inner_sequence:
        # Code to execute
```

Understanding and effectively utilizing conditional statements and loops are essential skills for backend development with Python. They enable developers to write more dynamic, efficient, and responsive applications. Mastery of these control structures will significantly contribute to the robustness and scalability of web applications.

1.7 Functions in Python: Understanding Defining and Calling

Functions in Python are first-class citizens, indicating they can be passed around and used as arguments, just like any other object (e.g., string, int, float). They play a critical role in writing clean, reusable, and modular code. This section will discuss how to define, call, and use functions in Python to enhance backend development practices.

A function in Python is defined using the `def` keyword, followed by a function name with parentheses that may include parameters. The function's body is indented under the definition and usually contains a `return` statement. The syntax for defining a function is as follows:

```
def function_name(parameters):
    # function body
    return value
```

Consider a simple function `add`, which takes two parameters and returns their sum:

```
1  def add(x, y):
2      return x + y
```

To call this function, you simply use the function name followed by parentheses enclosing the arguments:

```
1  result = add(5, 3)
2  print(result)
```

8

Functions can also take default arguments, making the corresponding parameters optional during the function call. If the argument is omitted, Python uses the default value:

```
1  def add(x, y=10):
2      return x + y
```

Calling the add function without the second argument uses the default value of 10 for y:

```
1  result = add(5)
2  print(result)
```

15

Python also supports variable-length argument lists, which allow you to pass an arbitrary number of arguments to your function. These arguments can be accessed within the function as a tuple. To define such a function, you prepend the parameter name with an asterisk (*):

```
1  def add(*args):
2      return sum(args)
```

This add function can handle any number of arguments:

```
1  result = add(1, 2, 3, 4)
2  print(result)
```

10

Python functions can return multiple values. This is achieved by returning the values as a tuple, which can then be unpacked into separate variables:

```
1  def arithmetic_operations(x, y):
2      return x+y, x-y, x*y, x/y
```

26

Calling `arithmetic_operations` and unpacking the results:

```
1  add, sub, mult, div = arithmetic_operations(10, 5)
2  print(f"Addition: {add}, Subtraction: {sub}, Multiplication: {mult}, Division: {div
       }")
```

```
Addition: 15, Subtraction: 5, Multiplication: 50, Division: 2.0
```

Leveraging functions efficiently can significantly improve code read-ability and reusability, essential aspects of sustainable backend de-velopment. Furthermore, understanding how to define and manip-ulate functions is fundamental for utilizing many of Python's more advanced features, including decorators and lambdas.

Functions are a pivotal feature of Python, facilitating the creation of modular and maintainable code. Mastery of Python functions en-hances a developer's ability to abstract and encapsulate code logic, fostering better backend development practices.

1.8 Working with Modules and Packages

In this section, we will discuss the organization of code into modules and packages in Python, which is crucial for structuring backend ap-plications in a scalable manner. A module in Python is simply a file containing Python definitions and statements. The file name is the module name with the suffix `.py` added. Modules can define functions, classes, and variables that can be imported and utilized in other Python programs, thereby encouraging code reusability and modularity.

Python's package management allows for an even higher level of or-ganization, enabling the structuring of Python's module namespace using "dotted module names". A package is essentially a directory that contains a special file named `__init__.py`. This file can be empty but indicates that the directory it resides in is considered a Python package, thus allowing modules within that directory to be imported into scripts or other modules.

Importing Modules: To use the functionality of a module in your script or application, it must first be imported. A module can be imported using the `import` statement. For example, to import a module named math, you would simply write:

```
1  import math
```

Once imported, you can access variables, functions, and classes defined in the module using the dot notation, as follows:

```
1   result = math.sqrt(25)
```

This would set `result` to 5.0, the square root of 25, using the `sqrt` function from the `math` module.

Importing Specific Attributes: It's also possible to import specific attributes from a module directly into the importing module's symbol table:

```
1   from math import sqrt
2   result = sqrt(25)
```

This approach eliminates the need for dot notation at the cost of potentially masking similarly named items in the importing module's scope.

Renaming Imports: For convenience or to avoid naming conflicts, imported modules or symbols can be renamed using the as keyword:

```
1   import math as m
2   result = m.sqrt(25)
```

This allows you to refer to the `math` module as m throughout your code.

Packages: Packages allow for a hierarchical structuring of the module namespace using dot notation. As an example, imagine a package named `mypackage` that has two submodules: `submodule1` and `submodule2`. To import a specific function from `submodule1`, you would use:

```
1   from mypackage.submodule1 import myfunction
```

This structure makes it easier to organize and find modules related to similar functionality or belonging to the same domain.

The __init__.py Files: Packages in Python utilize __init__.py files to enable importing of modules from packages. This file can also be used to execute initialization code for a package or to define a list of modules to be imported when import * is used on the package.

Finding Modules: When you import a module, Python searches for it in the following locations, in order:

- The directory from which the input script was run or the current directory if the interpreter is being interacted with interactively.

28

- The list of directories contained in the `PYTHONPATH` environment variable, if it is set.

- The installation-dependent list of directories configured at the time Python was installed.

Understanding and effectively utilizing modules and packages is fundamental to developing scalable and maintainable Python applications, especially when dealing with large codebases. By compartmentalizing functionalities into well-organized modules and packages, developers can greatly enhance code readability and reuse, thereby making back-end development more efficient and robust.

1.9 Exception Handling in Python

Exception handling in Python is a critical aspect of writing reliable, robust, and user-friendly software applications. In essence, exception handling allows a programmer to anticipate and manage errors that may occur during the execution of a program. In Python, exceptions are triggered by errors in an application's logic or when the Python interpreter encounters an unexpected situation. The advantage of employing exception handling is the prevention of program crashes by gracefully responding to errors.

Python adopts a straightforward syntax for exception handling, utilizing the try, except, else, and finally blocks. The primary mechanism involves placing the potentially error-prone code within a try block, followed by one or more except blocks designed to catch and handle specific exceptions when they occur.

```
1  try:
2      # Code which might raise an exception
3      result = 10 / 0
4  except ZeroDivisionError:
5      # Handling of specific exception
6      print("Attempted to divide by zero.")
7  finally:
8      # Code that is executed regardless of exception occurrence
9      print("This code block is always executed.")
```

The above example illustrates the basic structure of exception handling in Python. When the Python interpreter encounters the division by zero operation, it raises a ZeroDivisionError. The except block that catches this specific exception then executes, resulting in the print statement being executed, thus informing the user of the error in a controlled manner. The finally block is optional and used for clean-up actions that must be executed under all circumstances, such as releasing external resources.

Python supports catching multiple exceptions in a single except block using a tuple. This approach streamlines the handling of different exceptions using the same block of code, enhancing the code's readability and maintainability.

```
1  try:
2      # Risky operation
3  except (ZeroDivisionError, ValueError):
4      # Handling multiple exceptions
5      print("Caught an exception that could be either ZeroDivisionError or ValueError.
          ")
```

For a more refined control over exception handling, Python enables the association of an exception with a variable. This grants access to the exception object itself, offering insights into the error details, such as the error message or the error code.

```
1  try:
2      # Failing operation
3  except Exception as e:
4      print(f"An error occurred: {str(e)}")
```

The use of predefined Python exceptions, classified broadly into built-in exceptions (like IOError, ImportError, ValueError, etc.) and user-defined exceptions, tailors the handling mechanism to the specific error context. User-defined exceptions are particularly useful for signaling application-specific errors, fundamentally enhancing the error reporting and debugging processes.

Defining a custom exception in Python involves inheriting from the built-in Exception class or from one of its subclasses. This capability to extend the exception hierarchy allows programmers to create a structured and intuitive error handling mechanism that is bespoke to their application's requirements.

```
1  class CustomError(Exception):
2      """Base class for other custom exceptions"""
3      pass
```

In essence, exception handling in Python equips developers with a powerful set of tools for predicting and managing errors effectively. This promotes the creation of fault-tolerant applications that can resolve or report errors in a graceful and user-friendly manner. Employing these practices ensures that applications are not only more stable but also easier to maintain and debug, thereby significantly enhancing the overall quality of the software.

1.10 Introduction to Object-Oriented Programming in Python

Object-Oriented Programming (OOP) is a programming paradigm that uses objects and classes in programming. It aims to implement real-world entities like inheritance, polymorphism, encapsulation, and abstraction in programming. The concept of OOP in Python focuses on creating reusable code. This paradigm is essential in Python and facilitates tasks in backend development by allowing the creation of modular and scalable web applications.

In Python, everything is an object, and classes are the blueprints for objects. A class encapsulates data for the object. This section will discuss how Python implements OOP principles and how you can use them to enhance your backend development projects.

Classes and Objects:

In Python, classes are created using the `class` keyword. Objects are instances of classes. When a class is defined, a new namespace is created, and used as the local scope — thus, all assignments to local variables go into this namespace.

Example of class definition and object instantiation:

```
1  class Person:
2      def __init__(self, name, age):
3          self.name = name
4          self.age = age
5
6  # Creating an instance of the Person class
7  person1 = Person("John Doe", 30)
```

In the above example, the `__init__` method is called a constructor and is automatically invoked when an object of the class is instantiated. The `self` parameter refers to the instance of the class itself.

Inheritance:

Inheritance allows a class (child class) to inherit attributes and methods from another class (parent class), facilitating reusability and a hierarchical structure among classes.

Example of inheritance in Python:

31

```
1  class Employee(Person):
2      def __init__(self, name, age, employee_id):
3          super().__init__(name, age)
4          self.employee_id = employee_id
```

Here, the `Employee` class inherits from the `Person` class. The `super()` function allows us to call the `__init__` method of the parent class, enabling the child class to inherit the parent's attributes.

Polymorphism:

Polymorphism in Python allows functions to use objects of different types at different times. This is often achieved through method overriding, where a method in a child class has the same name as a method in its parent class but is implemented differently.

Example demonstrating polymorphism:

```
1  def get_info(self):
2      return "Name: " + self.name + ", Age: " + str(self.age)
3
4  # Method overriding in the child class
5  class Employee(Person):
6      def get_info(self):
7          return "Employee ID: " + str(self.employee_id) + ", " + super().get_info()
```

Encapsulation:

Encapsulation is the concept of bundling data (attributes) and methods (functions) that operate on the data into a single unit, or class, and restricting access to some of the object's components. This is usually achieved using private and protected members.

Example demonstrating encapsulation:

```
1  class Account:
2      def __init__(self, owner, balance=0):
3          self.owner = owner
4          self.__balance = balance # private attribute
5
6      def deposit(self, amount):
7          if amount > 0:
8              self.__balance += amount
9              return "Deposit successful"
10         else:
11             return "Deposit amount must be positive"
```

Abstraction:

Abstraction involves hiding the complex implementation details and showing only the essential features of the object. In Python, abstraction can be achieved by using abstract classes and methods.

Example of creating an abstract class in Python:

```
1  from abc import ABC, abstractmethod
2
3  class Shape(ABC):
4      @abstractmethod
5      def area(self):
6          pass
7
8  class Circle(Shape):
9      def __init__(self, radius):
10         self.__radius = radius
11
12     def area(self):
13         return 3.14 * self.__radius ** 2
```

In the Shape class, the area method is decorated with @abstractmethod, indicating it's an abstract method and must be implemented by any subclass of Shape.

Understanding and implementing the principles of Object-Oriented Programming in Python can greatly enhance your productivity and efficiency in backend development. By encapsulating data, inheriting properties, polymorphism, and using abstraction, you can write more modular, scalable, and maintainable code.

1.11   Understanding Python's Magic Methods

Magic methods in Python, also known as dunder methods (from the double underscores that encompass their names), are special methods that start and end with double underscores, such as __init__ or __str__. They are implicitly invoked by the Python interpreter to perform basic operations. For instance, when adding two objects using the + operator, the __add__ method is automatically called. Understanding these methods is crucial for harnessing the full potential of Python, especially in backend development where creating classes that integrate seamlessly with Python's built-in operations can significantly enhance the efficiency and readability of the code.

The first and perhaps the most well-known magic method is __init__, which acts as the constructor for a class. It is called when an instance of a class is created, allowing for the initialization of its attributes. Let's consider a simple class that uses __init__:

```
1  class Book:
2      def __init__(self, title, author):
3          self.title = title
4          self.author = author
```

Moving beyond object creation, magic methods can define how objects should be represented as strings, managed in contexts of boolean evaluation, or how arithmetic and comparison operations should be handled. The __str__ and __repr__ methods, for example, control how objects are presented as strings, with __str__ being more user-friendly and __repr__ aimed at developers.

```
class Book:
    def __init__(self, title, author):
        self.title = title
        self.author = author
    def __str__(self):
        return f"{self.title} by {self.author}"
    def __repr__(self):
        return f"Book({self.title}, {self.author})"
```

When two objects are added using the + operator, the __add__ method is called. Similarly, other arithmetic operations like subtraction (__sub__), multiplication (__mul__), and division (__truediv__) have their respective magic methods. Implementing these methods provides a way to use these operators with instances of custom classes.

```
class Point:
    def __init__(self, x, y):
        self.x = x
        self.y = y
    def __add__(self, other):
        return Point(self.x + other.x, self.y + other.y)
```

Container types can leverage magic methods to mimic the behavior of built-in types like lists and dictionaries. The __getitem__, __setitem__, and __delitem__ methods allow objects of the class to use indexing and slicing operations or to iterate over items.

```
class Library:
    def __init__(self):
        self.books = []
    def __getitem__(self, index):
        return self.books[index]
    def __setitem__(self, index, value):
        self.books[index] = value
    def __delitem__(self, index):
        del self.books[index]
```

Exception handling can be customized using magic methods like __enter__ and __exit__, which define a class's behavior within a context manager (using the with statement). This is particularly useful for managing resources like file streams or network connections in a safe and predictable manner.

```
class ManagedFile:
    def __init__(self, name):
```

```
3        self.name = name
4    def __enter__(self):
5        self.file = open(self.name, 'w')
6        return self.file
7    def __exit__(self, exc_type, exc_value, traceback):
8        if self.file:
9            self.file.close()
```

Magic methods provide a powerful way to leverage Python's built-in behaviors and operations for custom objects, making code more Pythonic and integrating objects more deeply into Python's syntax and operational model. By understanding and implementing these methods, backend developers can create more readable, maintainable, and efficient applications that make full use of Python's capabilities.

1.12 Virtual Environments and Dependency Management

Virtual environments and dependency management are critical components of a modern Python development workflow, particularly in backend development where the complexity of projects often involves working with multiple packages and frameworks such as Django. This section will discuss the importance of virtual environments, how to create and manage them, and effectively handle project dependencies.

A virtual environment in Python is an isolated environment that allows Python packages to be installed for use by a particular application, without interfering with the packages of other Python projects. This is crucial in ensuring that dependencies required by different projects do not clash and that the development environment closely mirrors the production environment, thereby reducing the chances of encountering unforeseen issues.

Creating a virtual environment in Python is straightforward. The module used for this purpose is venv, which is included in the Python Standard Library from Python 3.3 onwards. To create a virtual environment, navigate to your project directory and run the following command in your terminal:

```
1  python -m venv myprojectenv
```

This command will create a new directory named myprojectenv within your project directory, which will contain the Python executable files, and a copy of the pip tool to install other Python packages.

Activating the virtual environment is necessary to isolate your project's Python environment from the global environment. Activation can be achieved using the following commands, which vary depending on the operating system:

- On Windows:

```
1   .\myprojectenv\Scripts\activate
```

- On Unix or MacOS:

```
1   source myprojectenv/bin/activate
```

Upon activation, you will notice that the command prompt now includes the name of the virtual environment, indicating that any Python or pip commands will now operate within this isolated environment.

Dependency management is another essential aspect to consider. As projects grow, they might require various external packages. Keeping track of these dependencies and ensuring that they are consistent across all development and production environments is vital. This is where the `pip` tool plays an essential role.

To install a package using `pip`, simply run:

```
1   pip install package-name
```

To handle project dependencies more effectively, it is standard practice to maintain a `requirements.txt` file in your project's root directory. This file contains a list of all the packages your project depends on, possibly specifying versions to ensure consistency across different environments. You can generate this file by running:

```
1   pip freeze > requirements.txt
```

The above command will list all installed packages in your current virtual environment and save them to `requirements.txt`. To install all the dependencies from this file, run:

```
1   pip install -r requirements.txt
```

Virtual environments and dependency management are indispensable in Python backend development. They help in creating a clean and controlled working environment by managing project-specific dependencies separately. This practice not only facilitates easier collaboration between developers but also plays a significant role in deploying applications efficiently by ensuring that the right versions of project dependencies are installed. Understanding and utilizing these tools effectively is crucial for successful Python projects.

1.13 Introduction to Git for Version Control

Version control systems play a critical role in the lifecycle of software development, enabling developers to manage changes to source code over time. Git, a free and open-source distributed version control system, is among the most popular and widely used systems due to its flexibility, performance, and security. Git facilitates tracking modifications, coordinating work among multiple developers, and maintaining a history of all changes to a project. This section will discuss the significance of Git for backend development, particularly with Python and Django, and provide a comprehensive guide on its installation, basic operations, branching, merging, and collaboration workflows.

Git's distributed nature allows each developer to have a local copy of the entire repository, including its history, making operations like commit, revert, and branch fast and independent of network access. This feature also enhances the redundancy and resilience of project data. The fundamental concepts underlying Git include commits, branches, merges, and remotes, each playing a vital role in the version control process.

To commence using Git, installation on your system is the preliminary step. For Windows, Mac, and Linux operating systems, specific installation packages are available. After installation, configuring user information using the Git command line is essential for proper attribution of work:

```
1  git config --global user.name "Your Name"
2  git config --global user.email "youremail@example.com"
```

This global configuration sets the name and email address for all Git transactions on the system. Following this, initializing a new Git repository or cloning an existing one from a remote server is typically the next step. For initializing a new repository, navigate to the project's directory and execute:

```
1  git init
```

This command creates a new .git subdirectory in your project, establishing it as a Git repository. To clone an existing repository, the command is:

```
1  git clone https://github.com/username/repository.git
```

'Git clone' copies all the data from the remote repository to your local machine, including all versions of every file and branch.

The day-to-day operations in Git primarily involve creating, editing, staging, and committing files. The workflow usually follows this pattern:

1. Make changes to your project files.

2. Stage the changes, preparing them for a commit:

```
1    git add <filename>
```

or, to stage all modified files:

```
1    git add .
```

3. Commit the staged changes to the repository's history:

```
1    git commit -m "Commit message describing the changes"
```

Branching and merging are powerful features of Git, allowing multiple developers to work concurrently on different features or fixes. Creating a new branch is achieved with:

```
1  git branch <branchname>
```

Switching to your new branch is done via:

```
1  git checkout <branchname>
```

Merging incorporates the changes from one branch into another, typically into the main or master branch after the feature is completed or the fix is verified:

```
1  git merge <branchname>
```

In collaborative projects, it is common to work with remote repositories. Pushing local changes to a remote repository is done with:

```
1  git push origin <branchname>
```

Fetching updates from the remote repository and merging them into your local branch are essential for staying up-to-date with the team's progress:

```
1   git pull
```

Mastering Git is indispensable for developers working on backend systems with Python and Django or any software development project. Its distributed nature supports a collaborative environment, enhances productivity, and secures the project's codebase integrity. Proper use of Git commands, branching, merging, and collaborating through remotes ensures efficient version control, critical for managing complex projects and fostering team collaboration.

1.14   Overview of Python Web Frameworks: Django and Flask

In this section, we will discuss the Python web frameworks, Django and Flask, which are essential tools for backend development. Understanding these frameworks is crucial for developing efficient, scalable web applications. Python's rich ecosystem offers various frameworks, but Django and Flask stand out due to their unique features and widespread adoption.

Django is a high-level Python web framework that encourages rapid development and pragmatic design. It is known for its "batteries-included" approach, providing an extensive set of libraries out of the box. This approach saves developers time by avoiding the need to select and integrate various third-party libraries. Django's components are reusable and can be configured to suit the needs of any web project. Its architecture follows the Model-View-Template (MVT) pattern, which separates data handling, business logic, and presentation layers, thereby promoting clean and maintainable code.

The core features of Django include:

- An ORM (Object-Relational Mapping) that abstracts database operations using Python classes.

- A powerful URL routing system that allows for designing clean, SEO-friendly URLs.

- An automatic admin interface, generated dynamically through introspection, that provides a convenient interface for managing application content.

- A built-in authentication system supporting user accounts, permissions, cookie-based user sessions, and more.

- Scalability to handle heavy traffic requirements, with tools to optimize performance and caching mechanisms.

Flask, on the other hand, is a microframework for Python based on Werkzeug and Jinja2. It is lightweight and modular, making it ideal for small to medium-sized projects or as a component in larger applications. Unlike Django, Flask provides the bare minimum to get a simple app up and running, giving developers the flexibility to choose their tools and libraries. This "micro" in microframework means Flask aims to keep the core simple but extensible.

Features of Flask include:

- A built-in development server and a fast debugger.

- Integrated support for unit testing.

- RESTful request dispatching which uses HTTP methods as guidelines for CRUD operations.

- Flexible application configuration and environment management.

- Secure cookie support for creating and reading client-side sessions.

- The ability to scale up to complex applications with a variety of available extensions.

Choosing between Django and Flask depends on the requirements of the project at hand. Django is well suited for developers looking for a full-featured framework that can handle everything from web development basics to advanced features like content administration, user authentication, and RSS feeds. Flask is more appropriate for projects that require a minimalistic approach, or when integrating with front-end technologies for a microservices architecture.

To illustrate the difference in how these frameworks are used, consider a simple example of creating a "Hello, World!" application in both Django and Flask.

In Flask, a "Hello, World!" application looks like this:

```
from flask import Flask
app = Flask(__name__)

@app.route('/')
def hello_world():
    return 'Hello, World!'

if __name__ == '__main__':
    app.run(debug=True)
```

The simplicity of Flask is evident in this example. Here, we import the Flask class, create an instance of it, and define a route to serve our function that returns the "Hello, World!" response.

Conversely, creating a "Hello, World!" application in Django involves more steps, reflecting its "batteries-included" philosophy. You would need to set up a project, create an application, define a view, map the view to a URL, and finally run the development server.

To sum up, Django and Flask cater to different needs and preferences in web development. Django's extensive feature set is designed to meet the needs of developers looking for an all-in-one solution, while Flask appeals to those seeking simplicity and flexibility. Both frameworks play a significant role in the Python ecosystem, and choosing between them depends on specific project requirements, complexity, and development philosophy.

1.15 Setting the Stage for Web Development with Django

Django is an open-source web framework that adheres to the "Don't Repeat Yourself" (DRY) principle, aiming to streamline the development of complex, database-driven websites by emphasizing reusability of components. It simplifies the process of building web applications by providing a standard method for web development, enabling developers to focus on the unique aspects of their applications without having to reinvent the wheel.

The initial step in leveraging Django for web development involves setting up a Django project. A project in Django context refers to the entire application and its components, including settings, databases, and application-specific modules. The creation of a Django project can be initiated with the following command, assuming Django is already installed:

```
1    django-admin startproject myproject
```

This command creates a `myproject` directory in your current directory containing:

- A management script (`manage.py`) that assists in various Django-related tasks.

- A `myproject` subdirectory, which includes the project's settings, URLs, and additional configurations.

After setting up the project, the next crucial step is to start a Django application, which is a web application within the project designed to do something specific (e.g., a web blog, a database of public records, or a simple poll application). To create an application, navigate to the directory where `manage.py` resides and run:

```
1    python manage.py startapp myapp
```

This command generates a `myapp` directory with numerous files pre-configured for app development, including models, views, and tests. An understanding of these components is essential:

- Models.py: Defines the data model—essentially, the database layout with additional metadata.

- Views.py: Handles the request-response cycle for your web application. A view retrieves data from the model and renders it with a template.

- Tests.py: Contains test classes for your application.

Models are a critical aspect of Django applications. They define the structure of the database, with each model mapping to a single table in the database. Models in Django are defined by Python classes; Django provides an Object-Relational Mapper (ORM) to map these classes to database tables. The following is an example model definition:

```
1    from django.db import models
2
3    class MyModel(models.Model):
4        title = models.CharField(max_length=100)
5        description = models.TextField()
```

Once a model is defined, it can be used to perform database operations without having to write SQL queries manually. Django's ORM abstracts the database layer, offering a Pythonic way to create, retrieve, update, and delete records.

To apply the model to the database, migrations are used. Migrations in Django are a way of propagating changes made to models (adding a field, deleting a model, etc.) into the database schema. The following commands generate and apply migrations:

```
1    python manage.py makemigrations
2    python manage.py migrate
```

Django also emphasizes the DRY principle through its template system, allowing for the definition of HTML templates for the frontend. Templates can inherit from base templates, fostering reuse and reducing code duplication across pages.

Lastly, Django includes a powerful URL dispatcher that allows you to design clean, elegant URLs. Unlike many web frameworks, Django encourages beautiful URL design with no framework limitations.

By setting up a Django project, creating an application, defining models, applying migrations, and understanding the template system and URL dispatcher, developers can establish a solid foundation for web development with Django. The framework's comprehensive nature, combined with its emphasis on reusable components and DRY principles, makes it an exemplary tool for modern backend development.

Chapter 2

Setting Up a Django Development Environment

Setting up a proper development environment is crucial for efficient Django project development. This involves installing Python, setting up Django, configuring a database, and ensuring the development server runs correctly. The goal is to create a seamless workflow that supports best practices in Django development, enabling developers to focus on writing application logic rather than wrestling with configuration issues. This chapter guides through establishing a robust Django development environment, including virtual environments, database connections, and debugging tools, paving the way for successful Django projects.

2.1   Overview of Django and its Advantages

Django, a high-level Python web framework, enables rapid development of secure and maintainable websites. Developed by experienced developers, it takes care of much of the hassle of web development, so developers can focus on writing their app without needing to reinvent the wheel. It's free and open source, has a thriving and active community, great documentation, and many options for free and paid-for support.

Django adheres to the DRY (Don't Repeat Yourself) principle, aiming to reduce the amount of redundant code. This not only helps in making the development process faster but also facilitates easier maintenance and upgrades of the application. The framework is designed on the model-template-view (MTV) architecture, a variation of the widely-used model-view-controller (MVC) architecture. The MVC pattern separates the data access, business logic, and presentation layers of an application, a crucial aspect that Django simplifies with its own interpretation, enhancing the development process.

One of the key advantages of using Django is its robust security features. It is engineered to help developers avoid common security mistakes by providing a framework that has been designed to "do the right things" to protect the website automatically. For instance, Django provides a secure way to manage user accounts and passwords, preventing common attacks such as SQL injection, cross-site scripting, cross-site request forgery, and clickjacking. Its user authentication system provides a secure way to manage user accounts and session.

Another significant feature is Django's built-in admin interface, one of the most celebrated features. It is dynamically generated and provides a ready-to-use interface for administrative activities, which reduces development time and enables quick project progress. This can be especially useful in the early stages of development, where you can quickly create models and have an interface to interact with them without having to write any additional code.

Django also excels in handling high traffic websites, with its ability to scale to meet the heaviest traffic demands. Websites like Instagram, Pinterest, and Mozilla are some of the most notable examples of Django's capability to manage massive traffic efficiently. Its scalability is partly achieved through its caching framework, which can use a variety of caching methods to fit the needs of your project, from file-based caching to cache frameworks like Memcached.

The framework supports a wide range of databases and includes a powerful ORM (Object-Relational Mapping) to map project objects with database tables. This abstraction layer allows developers to perform database operations without having to write raw SQL, reducing errors and increasing productivity. Furthermore, Django has a unique

46

migration system which automatically applies changes to the database schema whenever models are updated, without losing data.

For Django to be truly effective, it is crucial to mention its ecosystem comprising an extensive array of reusable apps, sites, tools, and libraries. The Django Packages repository is a comprehensive directory of reusable apps, sites, frameworks, and distributions available to assist in your Django web development projects.

Lastly, Django's documentation stands out for its completeness, clarity, and utility. It is often hailed as exemplary documentation in the world of open source projects. Alongside, there is substantial material available in the form of tutorials, guides, and forum discussions which are accessible to developers of all skill levels.

Django is an excellent choice for developing complex web applications rapidly and efficiently. Its comprehensive feature set, including the robust security mechanisms, scalable architecture, versatile ORM, and the dynamic admin interface, cater to the needs of developers looking for a high-level web framework that minimizes web development challenges. The vibrant community and wealth of documentation further support the framework's position as a preferred tool for web developers worldwide.

2.2   Prerequisites for Django Development

Before diving into Django development, several foundational tools and knowledge bases are essential to set up an effective development environment. These prerequisites will ensure that developers have the necessary groundwork to leverage Django's capabilities fully. This section discusses the critical components required before beginning Django development, ranging from basic Python knowledge to understanding web development concepts and installing Python on your development machine.

First, a solid understanding of Python is crucial. Django is a high-level Python web framework that encourages rapid development and clean, pragmatic design. Therefore, familiarity with Python's syntax, data structures, control flow, functions, and object-oriented programming concepts is necessary. Developers should be comfortable with writing Python scripts and understanding Python's package management system, pip, which plays a significant role in setting up Django projects.

Next is the installation of Python. Django is compatible with various Python versions, but it is recommended to use the latest Python version that Django supports to take advantage of the latest features and improvements in Python. Installation instructions vary depending on the operating system. It involves downloading Python from the official Python website and running the installer for Windows or using package managers for Linux and macOS.

Understanding the basics of web development is another essential prerequisite. Knowledge of how the web works, including familiarity with the client-server architecture, HTTP protocol, HTML, CSS, and JavaScript, is beneficial. This foundational knowledge helps in understanding Django's design principles and how it handles web requests, templates, and static files.

Version control systems, particularly Git, play a crucial role in modern software development practices, including Django development. Knowledge of version control is a must for managing code changes, collaboration, and deploying Django applications. Familiarity with basic Git operations such as cloning a repository, committing changes, pushing to remote repositories, and branching is important.

Working with databases is a significant part of Django development, given Django's robust ORM (Object Relational Mapper). Basic understanding of databases, SQL (Structured Query Language), and data modeling concepts will greatly aid in designing Django models and manipulating data through Django's ORM. While Django supports multiple database backends, familiarity with at least one of the databases supported by Django, such as PostgreSQL, MySQL, or SQLite, is required.

Setting up a virtual environment is crucial for managing project-specific dependencies without affecting the global Python installation. A virtual environment allows you to create a self-contained directory that contains all the necessary executables to run your project. Knowledge of creating and managing virtual environments using tools like venv or virtualenv is important before starting with Django projects.

Lastly, an integrated development environment (IDE) or a code editor that supports Python and web development can significantly enhance productivity. While Django projects can be developed using any text editor, IDEs like PyCharm or Visual Studio Code offer advanced features like syntax highlighting, code completion, debugging tools, and Django-specific support, which can be beneficial.

Preparing for Django development involves a multi-faceted approach that includes both technical and conceptual preparation. By ensuring a solid foundation in Python, web development basics, version control, database management, virtual environments, and selecting an appropriate development tool, developers can pave the way for a smooth and efficient Django development experience.

2.3 Installing Python for Django Development

To begin developing with Django, the first requirement is to have Python installed on your system. Django is a Python web framework; thus, Python is a fundamental prerequisite. This section will guide you through the process of installing Python, ensuring it is properly set up to support Django development activities.

Python can be downloaded from the official Python website (python.org). It is important to download a version that is compatible with the Django version you plan to use. As of this writing, Django 3.2 and newer versions support Python 3.6 and above. Therefore, downloading the latest version of Python 3 ensures compatibility with the most recent Django releases and takes advantage of the latest features and security enhancements of the Python language.

Once the appropriate Python version is identified:

```
1  1. Navigate to python.org in your web browser.
2  2. Hover over the `Downloads` tab and select the version of Python you wish to
      install based on your operating system (Windows, MacOS, or Linux/UNIX).
3  3. Click the download button to start the download of the Python installer.
```

After downloading the installer, proceed with the following steps to install Python on Windows:

```
1  1. Run the downloaded installer.
2  2. Ensure to check the box labeled `Add Python 3.x to PATH` before clicking `
      Install Now`. This action makes Python available from the command line across
      the system.
3  3. Follow the on-screen instructions to complete the installation.
```

For MacOS and Linux/UNIX, Python is often pre-installed. However, the pre-installed version might not be the latest or the one best suited for Django development. To install or update Python on MacOS, you can use Homebrew, a popular package manager. On Linux/UNIX, the package manager provided by your distribution (such as apt for

49

Ubuntu/Debian or yum for Fedora) can be used. Here is an example of installing Python using Homebrew on MacOS:

```
1   brew install python3
```

And an example for Ubuntu/Debian systems:

```
1   sudo apt-get update
2   sudo apt-get install python3
```

After installing Python, it is crucial to verify the installation. Open a terminal or command prompt and enter:

```
1   python --version
```

This command should output the version of Python that was installed, confirming that Python is properly installed and accessible.

Additionally, ensure that the Python Package Installer (pip) is installed. Pip is used to install Python packages from the Python Package Index (PyPI) and is essential for setting up a Django development environment. To check if pip is installed:

```
1   pip --version
```

If pip is installed, the command will display the version of pip currently installed.

In summary, installing Python is a straightforward process, but taking the time to ensure it is correctly set up is critical for a hassle-free Django development experience. With Python installed and verified, the next step in setting up your Django development environment is creating a virtual environment where Django and its dependencies can be installed.

2.4   Setting Up a Virtual Environment

Setting up a virtual environment is a fundamental step in creating a Django project. A virtual environment is an isolated environment that allows Python packages to be installed for use by a specific project without affecting other Python projects or the system Python installation. This isolation ensures that each project can have its own dependencies, regardless of what dependencies every other project has.

To create a virtual environment for a Django project, the following steps should be taken:

First, ensure that Python 3 is installed on your system. Django requires Python 3.6 or newer. You can verify your Python version by running the command 'python –version' in the terminal.

Next, install the virtual environment package if it is not already installed. This can be done by running the command:

```
1  pip install virtualenv
```

After the installation is complete, navigate to the directory where you want to create your Django project. Then, create a new virtual environment in this directory by running:

```
1  python -m venv myenv
```

In the command above, 'myenv' is the name of the virtual environment. You can choose any name you prefer for your environment.

Once the virtual environment is created, you need to activate it. Activation of the virtual environment will change your shell's prompt to show what virtual environment you are currently using, and it can ensure that all Python commands refer to the Python and pip located in your virtual environment, thus isolating your project's dependencies from the global Python installation.

To activate the virtual environment on Windows, run:

```
1  myenv\Scripts\activate
```

On macOS and Linux, run:

```
1  source myenv/bin/activate
```

After activation, your command line prompt will change to indicate that your virtual environment is active. At this point, any Python or pip commands you issue will use the versions in your virtual environment and not any system-wide Python installation.

It is also crucial to ensure that your virtual environment is ignored by version control systems like git. This can be achieved by adding the virtual environment directory (e.g., 'myenv') to your '.gitignore' file. Isolating the environment ensures that each developer working on the project can set up their own virtual environment without interfering with the project setup.

When you are done working within the virtual environment and wish to return to the system-wide Python installation, you can simply deactivate the virtual environment by running:

```
1  deactivate
```

This command will exit the virtual environment and return your terminal to its normal state, where it uses the system's default Python interpreter.

To summarize, the creation and activation of a virtual environment are integral steps in setting up a Django project. They ensure that projects are encapsulated with their dependencies, making it easier to manage project specifics and avoid conflicts between projects. With a virtual environment, the development workflow becomes more streamlined and focused, aligning well with best practices in Python development.

2.5   Installing Django and Creating a Django Project

Installing Django and creating a new Django project are pivotal steps in setting up a development environment tailored for Django development. This process involves several commands executed within a Python virtual environment. The virtual environment ensures that dependencies for different projects are kept isolated from each other and from the global Python installation. This section will discuss the installation of Django using pip, the Python package manager, and the creation of a Django project using the Django command-line tools.

To begin, ensure that a virtual environment is activated in the terminal or command prompt. Activation of the virtual environment is usually indicated by the name of the virtual environment appearing in parentheses at the beginning of the command line prompt. If you have not activated a virtual environment, refer to the previous section on setting up a virtual environment for guidance.

With the virtual environment activated, the next step is to install Django. This is done using pip, the Python package manager. To install the latest version of Django, run the following command:

```
1  pip install django
```

This command fetches the latest version of Django from the Python Package Index (PyPI) and installs it in the active virtual environment. To verify the successful installation of Django, you can use the following command:

```
1  django-admin --version
```

This should output the installed version of Django, confirming that Django has been successfully installed in your virtual environment.

After installing Django, the next step is to create a new Django project. A Django project is essentially a collection of settings for an instance of Django, including database configuration, Django-specific options, and application-specific settings. To create a new Django project, navigate to the directory where you want to create your project and run the following command:

```
1  django-admin startproject myproject
```

Replace myproject with the desired name of your Django project. This command creates a new Django project directory structure, which includes the following items:

- A manage.py file, a command-line utility that lets you interact with this Django project in various ways.

- An inner directory named after your project, which contains the actual Python package for your project.

- A settings.py file, which contains settings for your Django project.

- A urls.py file, which is responsible for URL declarations for your project.

- A wsgi.py file, which serves as an entry-point for WSGI-compatible web servers to serve your project.

- An __init__.py file, an empty file that tells Python that this directory should be considered a Python package.

It is worth noting that the manage.py script is a command-line utility that allows you to interact with your Django project in various ways, such as starting a web server, creating database migrations, and much more.

To verify that your Django project has been created successfully and that the development environment is correctly set up, navigate to the root directory of your project (where manage.py is located) and run the following command:

```
1  python manage.py runserver
```

This command starts the Django development server, a lightweight web server written purely in Python, designed for development and testing. Once the server is running, you can visit http://127.0.0.1:8000/ in your web browser. You should see the Django welcome page, indicating that your project has been created successfully and the development server is running correctly.

Installing Django within a virtual environment and creating a new Django project forms the foundational step in setting up a Django development environment. This process involves using pip to install Django, utilizing Django's command-line tools to create a new project, and verifying the installation through the Django development server. This sets the stage for further development tasks and the creation of Django applications within the project.

2.6 Understanding the Django Project Structure

Django projects follow a specific structure that, while flexible enough to accommodate various types of web applications, adheres to a standard pattern that Django developers should become familiar with. This structure promotes modularity, reusability, and a clean separation of concerns, which is essential for the maintenance and scalability of web applications.

When a new Django project is created using the django-admin startproject command, a project directory is set up containing several files and subdirectories. The initial structure looks something like this:

```
myproject/
    manage.py
    myproject/
        __init__.py
        settings.py
        urls.py
        asgi.py
```

```
wsgi.py
```

Let's dissect these components to understand their purpose and how they fit into the Django framework.

- `manage.py`: This is a command-line utility that lets you interact with this Django project in various ways. It is essentially a thin wrapper around the `django-admin` command. You will use `manage.py` to run development tasks such as making database migrations, starting the development server, and creating app-specific files.

- The inner `myproject/` directory is the actual Python package for your project. Its name is the Python package name you'll use to import anything inside it (e.g., `myproject.urls`).

  - `__init__.py`: An empty file that tells Python that this directory should be considered a Python package.
  - `settings.py`: Contains settings for the Django project, including database configurations, static file locations, middleware settings, and more. It is where you will configure the behavior of your Django project.
  - `urls.py`: The URL declarations for this Django project; a "table of contents" of your Django-powered site. You will map URLs to Django views here.
  - `asgi.py` and `wsgi.py`: These modules help your Django project communicate with web servers using the ASGI and WSGI standards, respectively. The WSGI module is used for traditional, synchronous web applications, while ASGI supports asynchronous web applications along with synchronous ones.

Understanding this structure is crucial for Django developers because it is the foundation upon which Django applications are built. The modular design means that while the `settings.py`, `urls.py`, `asgi.py`, and `wsgi.py` files manage project-wide configurations and URL mappings, the actual application logic resides within apps.

Creating a Django app within your project is done using the `python manage.py startapp <app_name>` command. Each application you create will have a similar but distinct structure tailored for developing a particular feature or module of the project. An app typically contains models, views, tests, migrations, and static and template directories. This separation allows for the development of reusable apps that can be plugged into this or other Django projects.

In summary, the Django project structure facilitates good software design principles such as the Don't Repeat Yourself (DRY) principle. It encourages splitting the project into logical components, thus making it easier for developers to understand, maintain, and scale Django projects. As developers work with Django, they will appreciate the framework's consistency and the straightforward nature of its project structure, which simplifies the development of complex web applications.

2.7 Configuring Django Settings for Development

Configuring Django settings for development is an important step to optimize the development process and ensure that the Django server operates correctly and securely. Django settings control the behavior of various components of a Django project. These settings are specified in the settings.py file located inside the project directory. This section will discuss how to properly configure development-specific settings including database configurations, debug mode, static and media files, and allowed hosts.

Firstly, setting DEBUG to True is critical during development. This enables Django's debug mode, providing detailed error pages whenever an exception is raised. This feature is invaluable for developers to trace back errors. However, it's important to ensure that DEBUG is set to False in a production environment to avoid leaking sensitive information.

```
1  DEBUG = True
```

Next, the database configuration is a key component. During the development phase, using SQLite as the database is common due to its ease of setup and use. However, Django supports various database backends through the DATABASES setting. For instance, to configure a PostgreSQL database, the configuration in settings.py would look as follows:

```
1  DATABASES = {
2      'default': {
3          'ENGINE': 'django.db.backends.postgresql',
```

```
4          'NAME': 'your_db_name',
5          'USER': 'your_db_user',
6          'PASSWORD': 'your_db_password',
7          'HOST': 'localhost',
8          'PORT': '5432',
9      }
10  }
```

Managing static files in Django involves correctly setting STATIC_URL and MEDIA_URL for development. Static files include CSS, JavaScript, and image files associated with Django apps, whereas media files are typically user-uploaded content. During development, it is common to serve these files directly from the Django server. For this purpose, the configuration should look as below:

```
1  STATIC_URL = '/static/'
2  MEDIA_URL = '/media/'
```

Further, in settings.py, specifying the directories where Django looks for static files is necessary:

```
1  STATICFILES_DIRS = [
2      BASE_DIR / "static",
3  ]
```

Similarly, for media files, setting up the location where those files are stored is required:

```
1  MEDIA_ROOT = BASE_DIR / "media"
```

Moreover, setting ALLOWED_HOSTS is a security measure to prevent HTTP Host header attacks. During development, this can be set to allow all hosts by including an asterisk:

```
1  ALLOWED_HOSTS = ['*']
```

However, for production, this should list the fully qualified domain name(s) of your Django server.

Finally, integrating email functionality for error logging or user registration features can be configured in the development settings. During development, setting up Django to use a console backend to print the email output to the console is useful. This avoids the need for setting up an SMTP server for testing purposes.

```
1  EMAIL_BACKEND = 'django.core.mail.backends.console.EmailBackend'
```

In a nutshell, configuring Django settings for development involves setting debug mode on, setting up the database, configuring static and media file settings, specifying allowed hosts, and optionally configuring email backends for development. Accurately configuring these settings paves the way for a smoother development experience by reducing potential issues and allowing developers to focus on building application logic. It is crucial to adjust these settings based on the environment to maintain the application's security and performance. This process of environment-specific configuration management is a best practice in Django development, ensuring that settings are optimized for the conditions under which the application is running.

2.8   Running the Django Development Server

Running the Django development server is a fundamental step in the development process, enabling immediate access to the project for testing and debugging purposes. Django comes equipped with a lightweight web server specifically designed for developmental use. This server is not intended for production environments but offers a convenient way for developers to view their progress in real-time within a localized setting.

To initiate the Django development server, one must first ensure that they are within the root directory of their Django project. This is typically the directory containing the manage.py file, a command-line utility that allows interaction with the Django project in various ways. The command to start the server is executed in the terminal as follows:

```
1   python manage.py runserver
```

Upon execution, the server starts and listens for incoming requests on the default port, which is 8000. However, developers can specify a different port by appending the desired port number to the command, as demonstrated below:

```
1   python manage.py runserver 8080
```

The output in the terminal will indicate the IP address and port where the server is running, typically http://127.0.0.1:8000/ for the default setting. This output is crucial for accessing the Django project through a web browser.

```
Watching for file changes with StatReloader
Performing system checks...

System check identified no issues (0 silenced).
```

```
Django version 3.2, using settings 'myproject.settings'
Starting development server at http://127.0.0.1:8000/
Quit the server with CONTROL-C.
```

It is important to understand that the development server automatically reloads the python code of the project upon any modification to the files. This means there is no need to restart the server manually after making changes to the source code, enhancing the workflow efficiency. However, changes to templates do not always trigger a reload, so occasionally a manual server restart may be necessary to see template updates reflected.

The Django development server is equipped with a debug mode, activated by default. This mode provides detailed error pages when exceptions occur within the application, aiding in the debugging process. While these detailed error pages are invaluable during development, exposing such information in a production environment can pose security risks. Therefore, it is crucial never to use the development server for production purposes.

In scenarios requiring the server to be accessible over a network, developers can use the following command to listen on all public IPs:

```
1  python manage.py runserver 0.0.0.0:8000
```

This modification enables other devices on the same network to access the development server using the host device's IP address, further facilitating collaborative development efforts or cross-device testing.

Throughout the development process, the terminal will display HTTP request logs, providing insight into the traffic received by the server. These logs include details such as the request method, URL, response status code, and request processing time. Monitoring these logs can offer valuable debugging information and insights into the application's performance characteristics.

In summary, the Django development server is a critical tool in the Django ecosystem, offering a convenient and efficient way for developers to run and test their projects in a real-time, web-accessible environment. Its ease of use, coupled with automatic code reloading and detailed error reporting, significantly streamlines the development workflow, allowing developers to focus on building and refining their applications.

2.9 Introduction to Django Applications and Creating an App

Django applications are the building blocks of any Django project. An application in Django is a self-contained package that performs a specific service or includes a set of related features. Applications are reusable and can be integrated into other Django projects with minimal effort. This modular approach promotes reusability and reduces development time by allowing developers to use pre-built apps for common functions instead of creating everything from scratch.

To begin creating a Django app, it is assumed that Django has been successfully installed in a virtual environment and a Django project has been initialized. The creation of a Django app can be accomplished through the command line interface by running a management command provided by Django. The command to create a new app within a Django project is as follows:

```
1  $ django-admin startapp <app_name>
```

where <app_name> is the name of the application to be created. This name should be concise and descriptive, reflecting the app's functionality. For example, if the app is designed to handle user profiles, an appropriate name could be user_profiles.

Executing the above command creates a new directory with the specified <app_name> within the Django project's root directory. This directory contains several files and subdirectories that make up the scaffold of a Django app, including:

- migrations/ - A directory for storing migration files, which are used to evolve the database schema over time as models are created and modified.

- __init__.py - An empty file that signifies to Python that this directory should be considered a Python package.

- admin.py - A file for registering models with the Django admin interface, making it easier to perform CRUD operations on the database through a web interface.

- apps.py - Contains settings specific to this application, including configuration options and application-specific settings.

- `models.py` - Defines the models of the application, which are Python classes that are mapped to database tables.

- `tests.py` - Contains test cases for the application, allowing for automated testing of app functionality.

- `views.py` - Contains the views for the application, which handle requests and return responses. Views interact with models and templates to serve the application's web pages.

After creating a new app, it is necessary to inform the Django project of its existence. This is done by adding the app to the `INSTALLED_APPS` setting in the project's `settings.py` file. `INSTALLED_APPS` is a list of strings specifying the names of all Django applications that are active for this Django project. To include the newly created app, add its configuration class, typically found in the `apps.py` file of the app and named `<AppName>Config`, to the list. For example:

```
1  INSTALLED_APPS = [
2      ...
3      'myapp.apps.MyAppConfig',
4      ...
5  ]
```

Adding the app to `INSTALLED_APPS` enables Django to recognize the app and include it in various command line operations such as database migrations. It also allows the app to utilize Django's rich ecosystem of reusable apps, middlewares, and context processors.

Creating a Django app is the first step in developing functional components for a Django project. By adhering to Django's conventions and utilizing its built-in tools and libraries, developers can efficiently build, integrate, and maintain applications, significantly enhancing the modularity and scalability of their projects.

2.10 Connecting to a Database in Django

Connecting to a database is an integral part of setting up a Django project as it enables the persistence and retrieval of application data. Django supports multiple databases out of the box, including SQLite, PostgreSQL, MySQL, and Oracle. This section will discuss how to configure a Django project to connect to these databases, focusing on setting up a database connection, modifying the settings file, and understanding Django's Object-Relational Mapping (ORM) system for database interactions.

Django uses the settings found in the `settings.py` file of a Django project to establish a connection with the specified database. This file contains a `DATABASES` dictionary, which provides configurations for the default database. By default, Django is configured to use SQLite, a lightweight database engine suitable for development and testing but less so for production environments.

To illustrate, the default `DATABASES` setting in `settings.py` looks like this:

```
1  DATABASES = {
2      'default': {
3          'ENGINE': 'django.db.backends.sqlite3',
4          'NAME': BASE_DIR / 'db.sqlite3',
5      }
6  }
```

For many applications, a more robust database such as PostgreSQL is preferred. To connect a Django project to a PostgreSQL database, the configuration in `settings.py` would need to be modified accordingly. First, ensure that the `psycopg2` package, a PostgreSQL adapter for Python, is installed in the project's virtual environment.

```
1  pip install psycopg2
```

After installing psycopg2, modify the `DATABASES` setting in `settings.py` to something similar to the following:

```
1   DATABASES = {
2       'default': {
3           'ENGINE': 'django.db.backends.postgresql',
4           'NAME': 'your_database_name',
5           'USER': 'your_database_user',
6           'PASSWORD': 'your_database_password',
7           'HOST': 'localhost',
8           'PORT': '5432',
9       }
10  }
```

This configuration specifies the database engine, the name of the database, the user, the password, and the connection details such as the host and port.

To interact with the database, Django uses its ORM, which provides a high-level API that abstracts away the specifics of the SQL language. Django models, defined in the `models.py` file of each application within the Django project, serve as the single, definitive source of information about data. They contain the essential fields and behaviors of the stored data. Once models are defined, Django provides a rich set of tools to automate the creation of database schemas (migrations), interact with the data (the Django admin and shell), and integrate with Django's automatically-generated web admin.

Here is a simple example of a Django model:

```
1   from django.db import models
2
3   class Book(models.Model):
4       title = models.CharField(max_length=100)
5       author = models.CharField(max_length=100)
6       published_date = models.DateField()
```

After defining models, execute the following commands to create the corresponding table in the database:

```
python manage.py makemigrations
python manage.py migrate
```

The first command, `makemigrations`, creates migration files based on the changes detected in the models. The second command, `migrate`, applies these migrations to the database, creating the tables and fields accordingly.

Connecting a Django project to a database involves configuring the `DATABASES` setting in `settings.py` according to the requirements of the selected database engine. The ORM system of Django then facilitates interaction with this database through models, migrations, and other high-level operations. With the database properly connected and configured, a Django project is well-poised to manage application data effectively.

2.11   Using the Django Shell for Quick Tests

Django's shell is an invaluable tool for developers, offering a powerful interface for interacting with the Django project's code and models directly. This feature leverages the interactive capabilities of the Python shell and extends them within the Django context, allowing for quick tests, data queries, and experimentation without the need for deploying or running the full development server. Understanding and utilizing the Django shell effectively can significantly enhance productivity and debugging speed during development.

To initiate the Django shell, the developer must execute the following command in the terminal from the root directory of the Django project:

```
1  $ python manage.py shell
```

This command launches an interactive Python shell session, within which the Django environment is fully loaded and accessible. Once inside the Django shell, developers can import models and execute Django ORM (Object-Relational Mapping) queries directly, simplifying tasks such as inspecting the database, creating or modifying data, or testing model methods.

For instance, to interact with a Django model named Post, one would start by importing the model:

```
1  from myapp.models import Post
```

Following the import, developers can perform database queries. For example, to fetch all objects from the Post model, the command would be:

```
1  posts = Post.objects.all()
2  print(posts)
```

The output, illustrating a query's result set, may resemble:

```
<QuerySet [<Post: Post Title 1>, <Post: Post Title 2>]>
```

The Django shell can also be used for creating new entries in the database. This capability is particularly useful for quickly testing model behaviors or adding test data. To create a new Post instance, the following sequence might be used:

```
1  new_post = Post(title='Sample Post', content='This is a test post.')
2  new_post.save()
```

Upon executing the above commands, a new Post object is created and saved to the database, with its fields populated as specified.

Moreover, Django's shell supports the Django ORM's rich querying capabilities, enabling complex queries involving filtering, ordering, and aggregation. This feature is crucial for optimizing database interactions and ensuring that data manipulation logic behaves as intended.

To demonstrate a filtered query, consider retrieving a subset of Post objects based on a condition:

```
1  filtered_posts = Post.objects.filter(title__contains='Sample')
```

```
2   for post in filtered_posts:
3       print(post.title)
```

This command would print titles of all Post instances containing the word 'Sample' in their title, illustrating the ease of performing and iterating over filtered query sets within the Django shell.

Besides model interaction, the Django shell can execute any Python code; hence, it serves as an excellent platform for testing snippets of Django-specific or generic Python logic.

Leveraging the shell effectively requires an understanding of the Django ORM and Python syntax, but once mastered, it becomes a core part of a Django developer's toolkit for rapid development and debugging. Additionally, Django offers an enhanced shell experience via the ipython and notebook packages, offering features such as auto-completion and in-browser code execution, which further empower developers in their tasks.

The Django shell is a potent feature for conducting quick tests, data manipulations, and exploratory coding within a Django project. Its direct access to the Django ORM and project settings, combined with the interactive nature of the Python shell, makes it an indispensable tool for efficient Django development.

2.12 Understanding the Django Migrations System

Django's migration system is a powerful and integral part of the Django web framework, designed to evolve the database schema over time in a consistent and easy-to-manage manner. A schema is essentially the structure of the database, which includes tables, columns, and their relationships. As the development progresses, changes to the database schema are almost inevitable, whether it be adding new models, altering existing fields, or removing unused tables. Manually applying these changes to the database can be error-prone and tedious. The Django migrations system automates this process, allowing for smooth transitions and minimizing the risk of data loss.

At its core, the migrations system works by generating scripts known as migrations. These migrations are Python files that describe the changes to be applied to the database schema. Each migration file consists of one or more operations that Django will execute on the database. These operations could be creating a new table, adding a field to an existing table, or even changing a field's type.

To generate a migration, Django examines the current set of models against the last migration applied to the database and figures out the changes that need to be made. To illustrate, consider that a developer decides to add an 'email' field to a 'User' model. Django will recognize this change and create a migration file that defines an operation to add the 'email' column to the corresponding table in the database.

```
1   python manage.py makemigrations
```

After running this command, Django will autodetect the changes made to the models and create a new migration file in the 'migrations' directory of the app. The name of the file will be a timestamp followed by a description of the changes, ensuring a linear history of modifications. It's worth noting that migrations need to be explicitly applied to update the database schema:

```
1   python manage.py migrate
```

Executing the 'migrate' command will apply all unapplied migrations, in order, to the database. Django tracks which migrations have already been applied using a special table in your database, so it knows exactly which migrations it needs to apply.

One of the brilliant aspects of Django's migrations system is its ability to handle backward migrations. This means developers can revert changes made by migrations if the need arises. For example, if a field was added to a model and later it was decided that the field is no longer required, Django can generate a migration to remove that field:

```
1   python manage.py makemigrations --empty yourappname
```

The above command generates an empty migration file, in which custom backward or forward operations can be manually specified. However, for most common operations, Django automatically generates both forward and backward operations.

Another important feature to mention is Django's ability to handle dependencies between migrations. In projects with multiple applications, changes in one application might depend on changes in another. Django's migrations system intelligently calculates these dependencies and ensures migrations are applied in an order that respects these dependencies, thereby maintaining data integrity and the overall consistency of the database schema.

For environments where manual oversight is required before applying changes to the database schema, Django supports generating SQL statements for migrations:

```
1  python manage.py sqlmigrate yourappname migrationname
```

This command takes the name of an app and a migration name (which is the filename of the migration without the '.py' extension) and returns the SQL statements that Django will execute for that migration. This is particularly useful for reviewing the exact changes Django intends to make or for applying those changes manually if required.

In summary, Django's migration system is a robust feature designed to facilitate the evolution of database schemas in a manageable, systematic, and safe manner. It not only reduces the potential for human error but also provides a clear and ordered history of changes, supporting both development and maintenance phases of project lifecycle. The system's support for automatic and manual migrations, backward operations, and dependency management makes it a critical tool for Django developers aiming for efficient and reliable database schema management.

2.13 Version Control for Django Projects with Git

Version control systems play a pivotal role in the development of any software project by tracking and managing changes to the codebase. Among these systems, Git has emerged as a preeminent tool due to its powerful features and widespread adoption. When it comes to Django projects, leveraging Git for version control is indispensable for efficient collaboration, code management, and deployment. This section will delve into the essentials of using Git in the context of Django development, covering initial repository setup, common Git workflows, and best practices for managing Django-specific files.

To start, ensure that Git is installed on your development machine. Installation procedures vary by operating system, but once installed, Git allows for the seamless initiation, tracking, and synchronization of project changes. A Django project, like any other software project, consists of a collection of files that include source code, configuration files, templates, and static assets. By placing a Django project under Git version control, developers can maintain a comprehensive history of their project's evolution, facilitate collaboration among team members, and streamline the deployment process.

To initialize a Git repository within a Django project, navigate to the project's root directory and execute the following command:

```
1  git init
```

This command creates a new Git repository by initializing a hidden '.git' directory in the project root, which will store all version control information. Following the initialization, it is crucial to define which files and directories should be tracked by Git and which should be ignored. This is accomplished through a '.gitignore' file placed in the project root. For a Django project, certain files and directories such as '__pycache__', virtual environment directories (e.g., 'venv' or '.venv'), and database files (usually 'db.sqlite3' for development) should be excluded from version control to avoid cluttering the repository with unnecessary or sensitive information.

A typical '.gitignore' file for a Django project might include:

```
__pycache__/
venv/
.env
db.sqlite3
*.pyc
media/
```

After configuring the '.gitignore' file, the next step is to add the existing project files to the repository and make an initial commit. This can be achieved by running:

```
1  git add .
2  git commit -m "Initial commit"
```

The 'git add .' command stages all changes (excluding those specified in '.gitignore'), while 'git commit' creates a snapshot of the project at its current state, annotated with a descriptive message.

For Django developers working within a team or even for solo developers intending to maintain a comprehensive project history, adopting a consistent branch strategy is beneficial. A common approach is to use the main branch for stable releases and feature branches for developing new features or bug fixes. Before starting work on a new feature or fix, a developer should create and switch to a new branch using:

```
1  git checkout -b feature/some-feature
```

Once development on the feature is complete and tested, it can be merged back into the main branch:

```
1  git checkout main
2  git merge feature/some-feature
```

Frequent commits throughout the development process with meaningful messages afford a granular history of the project, allowing developers to track changes, revert to previous versions if necessary, and understand the reasoning behind code modifications.

For collaborative projects, pushing local git repositories to a remote server like GitHub, GitLab, or Bitbucket is standard practice. This requires setting up a remote repository on the chosen platform and linking it with the local repository using:

```
1  git remote add origin <repository-URL>
```

Subsequently, pushing the local commits to the remote repository can be done via:

```
1  git push -u origin main
```

This command synchronizes the local and remote repositories, facilitating collaboration among developers and securing a backup of the project's codebase on the remote server.

Integrating Git into Django project development is essential for managing the source code, enhancing collaboration among team members, and ensuring a smooth deployment process. By understanding and applying the basic concepts and workflows of Git version control, Django developers can maintain a well-organized, versioned, and collaborative codebase, paving the way for successful project outcomes.

2.14 Setting Up a Django Development Workflow

Setting up a Django development workflow involves several crucial steps that ensure a smooth and efficient process for developing Django projects. These steps are designed to optimize development time, adhere to best practices, and facilitate a team-oriented approach to

Django development. This section will discuss the establishment of a virtual environment, the integration of version control, configuration management, the use of development servers, and the adoption of tools and IDEs that enhance productivity.

Establishing a virtual environment is the first critical step in creating a Django development workflow. A virtual environment is a self-contained directory tree that contains a Python installation for a particular version of Python, plus a number of additional packages. The use of a virtual environment ensures that each Django project has its dependencies managed separately, reducing the risk of conflicts between project requirements. To set up a virtual environment, one can use the following command:

```
1  $ python -m venv myprojectenv
```

Once created, the virtual environment must be activated with:

```
1  $ source myprojectenv/bin/activate # On Unix or MacOS
2  $ myprojectenv\Scripts\activate # On Windows
```

With the virtual environment activated, all Python packages installed using pip will be placed in the 'myprojectenv' directory, isolated from the global Python environment.

Integration of version control is a pivotal part of the development workflow. Version control systems like Git allow developers to track changes to the codebase, collaborate with others, and revert to previous states of the project if needed. Initializing a Git repository in the Django project directory can be achieved with:

```
1  $ git init
```

Following initialization, a '.gitignore' file should be created to exclude certain files and directories (e.g., bytecode files, media files, and the virtual environment directory) from version control. This prevents unnecessary files from being committed to the repository, keeping it clean and manageable.

Configuration management in Django development involves the separation of environment-specific settings from the codebase. The 'settings.py' file in a Django project contains numerous configurations that might need to be different across development, testing, and production environments. A common practice is to use environment variables to manage these configurations and to keep sensitive information out of version control.

70

Running the Django development server is an integral part of the workflow. It allows developers to test their applications in a local environment that simulates the production setup. The development server can be started with the following command:

```
1  $ python manage.py runserver
```

Upon execution, the server will be available at 'http://127.0.0.1:8000/', and developers can interact with their application through a web browser.

Finally, the adoption of tools and Integrated Development Environments (IDEs) plays a significant role in enhancing the Django development workflow. IDEs like PyCharm or VS Code provide features such as syntax highlighting, code completion, debugging tools, and direct integration with version control systems. These tools support developers in writing efficient and error-free code, quickening the development process.

Setting up a Django development workflow involves the thoughtful integration of several components: virtual environments for dependency management, version control for codebase tracking and collaboration, configuration management for environment-specific settings, the use of development servers for local testing, and the adoption of productivity-enhancing IDEs and tools. Together, these elements form a robust workflow that supports the efficient development of Django applications.

2.15 Tools and IDEs for Efficient Django Development

The choice of tools and Integrated Development Environments (IDEs) can significantly influence the productivity and efficiency of a Django developer. Hence, selecting the right set of tools that align with one's development workflow is paramount. This section will discuss the most prominent IDEs and tools that cater to Django development, focusing on their features, benefits, and how they integrate within Django's ecosystem.

Firstly, PyCharm is a popular IDE among Django developers, provided by JetBrains. Its Professional version offers full-fledged Django support, including project templates, a rich debugger, and a visual database tool. PyCharm facilitates Django template editing with code completion for template tags and filters and provides specific run configurations for Django servers. The IDE also integrates with Django's test framework, simplifying the process of writing and running tests.

```
1   # Example of Django server run configuration in PyCharm
2   import os
3   import sys
4   from django.core.management import execute_from_command_line
5
6   if __name__ == "__main__":
7       os.environ.setdefault("DJANGO_SETTINGS_MODULE", "myproject.settings")
8       execute_from_command_line(sys.argv)
```

Visual Studio Code (VS Code) is another highly extensible editor that has gained popularity among Django developers. With the Python extension for VS Code, developers can leverage features like IntelliSense, linting (PEP 8), debugging, and unit testing. The Django template support is not as comprehensive as in PyCharm, but it can be improved with third-party extensions. Configuring VS Code for Django development requires some setup, such as defining the appropriate Python interpreter and installing Django-specific extensions.

```
# Sample output after configuring Django in VS Code
Selected Python interpreter for Django project: /path/to/virtualenv/bin/python
Django extension activated. Ready for development!
```

Another notable IDE is Atom, which, with the right set of packages, can be turned into a powerful environment for Django development. Atom's hackable nature allows for customization to fit any developer's needs. The 'atom-django' package, for instance, provides basic Django template tag autocompletion. However, compared to PyCharm and VS Code, Atom requires more manual configuration to achieve a fully integrated Django development setup.

In addition to IDEs, several command-line tools and utilities can enhance Django development. One of these is Django Extensions, a third-party package that adds custom management commands to the Django project. Commands such as `runserver_plus`, `shell_plus`, and `show_urls` are invaluable for increasing development efficiency.

```
1   # Installation of Django Extensions
2   pip install django-extensions
```

Another vital tool in a Django developer's arsenal is Docker. Containerizing Django applications with Docker simplifies dependency management, ensures consistent environments across different stages of development, and streamlines deployment processes. A Dockerized

Django setup typically involves creating a 'Dockerfile' for the Django application and a 'docker-compose.yml' file for defining services, including the web application and database.

```
1  # Sample Dockerfile for a Django project
2  FROM python:3.8
3  ENV PYTHONUNBUFFERED 1
4  RUN mkdir /code
5  WORKDIR /code
6  COPY requirements.txt /code/
7  RUN pip install -r requirements.txt
8  COPY . /code/
```

Finally, Git plays a central role in version control for Django projects. Its vast ecosystem of tools and services, such as GitHub and GitLab, supports collaborative development and CI/CD pipelines, which are integral to modern Django development workflows.

To conclude, the productivity of Django development is heavily dependent on the tools and IDEs chosen by the developer. Whether it's a fully-featured IDE like PyCharm, a versatile editor such as VS Code, or command-line tools and utilities, incorporating these tools into the development workflow can significantly enhance efficiency and focus on high-quality Django application development.

Chapter 3

Models and Databases in Django

In Django, models play a central role in structuring the application's data layer, interfacing with the database through an intuitive Object-Relational Mapping (ORM) system. This chapter delves into defining models, database relationships, and handling migrations, essential for representing and manipulating application data efficiently. It further explores advanced model features, database optimization techniques, and integrating external databases, equipping developers with the skills to design a performant and scalable database schema within Django projects.

3.1   Understanding Models in Django

In Django, models are the single, definitive source of information about your data. They contain the essential fields and behaviors of the data you're storing. Essentially, each model maps to a single database table. The basics of Django models hinge on this concept, where each model class represents a database table, and each field of the model represents a database column.

Let's illustrate the definition of a simple model. This model represents a 'Book', with a title, author, and publication date.

```
1   from django.db import models
```

```
2
3   class Book(models.Model):
4       title = models.CharField(max_length=100)
5       author = models.CharField(max_length=100)
6       publication_date = models.DateField()
```

Django models offer a wealth of options for defining these fields' attributes to match exactly the database structure intended. For instance, 'CharField' is used for character fields and requires a 'max_length' parameter that translates into the SQL definition to define the column size. 'DateField' is another example, optimized for dates. This modeling capability extends far beyond simple types, offering comprehensive support for a wide range of data types and database relationships.

In addition to field definitions, Django models encapsulate metadata for fine-tuning the model's interaction with the database. This is facilitated through the 'Meta' inner class. Attributes such as database table name ('db_table'), ordering of records ('ordering'), and verbose names for the model ('verbose_name' and 'verbose_name_plural') are defined in this class.

```
1   class Book(models.Model):
2       ...
3       class Meta:
4           db_table = 'library_books'
5           ordering = ['publication_date']
6           verbose_name = 'book'
7           verbose_name_plural = 'books'
```

Database relationships, including many-to-one, many-to-many, and one-to-one, are a cornerstone of relational database design, and Django models adeptly manage these relationships. Relationships in Django are defined using 'ForeignKey', 'ManyToManyField', and 'OneToOne-Field' fields.

```
1   class Author(models.Model):
2       name = models.CharField(max_length=100)
3
4   class Book(models.Model):
5       title = models.CharField(max_length=100)
6       authors = models.ManyToManyField(Author)
7       publication_date = models.DateField()
```

In the example above, a many-to-many relationship is created between the 'Book' and 'Author' models, permitting a book to have multiple authors and an author to write multiple books.

Migrations in Django are an integral component of models, facilitating the creation and modification of database tables through elegant version control. Django automatically generates migrations for model

76

changes, ensuring the database schema evolves smoothly alongside the application code. Migrations are applied using the Django command line interface, which executes the necessary SQL commands to update the database schema accordingly.

```
$ python manage.py makemigrations
$ python manage.py migrate
```

Interacting with the database through models is achieved via the Django ORM, a powerful bridge between the model definitions and the database. This ORM enables developers to perform database queries without writing raw SQL. Operations such as creating, retrieving, updating, and deleting records are implemented through the model's API, ensuring an intuitive, pythonic way of database manipulation.

```
1   # Creating a new book
2   book = Book(title='Django for Professionals', author='William S. Vincent',
        publication_date='2023-01-01')
3   book.save()
4
5   # Retrieving all books
6   all_books = Book.objects.all()
7
8   # Updating a book's title
9   book.title = 'Learn Django'
10  book.save()
11
12  # Deleting a book
13  book.delete()
```

In summary, Django models are a pivotal feature of Django, encapsulating both the data structure and the behavior of the application's data layer. Through models, Django abstrates the complexities of database interactions, providing a clear, efficient path for database design, manipulation, and querying within the framework's ecosystem.

3.2 Defining Django Models: Fields and Relationships

Let's start by discussing the foundation of Django's ORM system: models. A Django model is a Python class that defines the structure of an application's data. It includes fields and metadata describing how the data should be stored in a database. The fields you define in a model represent the database table columns.

In defining a model, the first step is to specify its fields. Django supports a wide range of field types, from basic text and numbers to dates and file uploads. Each field class you add to your model will typically correspond to a specific database column type. For instance, a models.CharField is often used for short strings and corresponds to VARCHAR in SQL, while models.IntegerField is used for integers.

Consider the following example of a simple model representing a blog post:

```
from django.db import models

class BlogPost(models.Model):
    title = models.CharField(max_length=200)
    content = models.TextField()
    publish_date = models.DateTimeField('date published')
```

In this model, BlogPost has three fields: title, content, and publish_date. Each field instance requires certain arguments. For CharField, max_length is mandatory, indicating the maximum string length. DateTimeField takes an optional human-readable name. If you do not specify an argument for the database column name, Django uses the field's name.

Relationships between different models are a core aspect of relational databases and are equally important in Django. The ORM supports three main types of relationships: "many-to-one", "many-to-many", and "one-to-one".

Let's explore these relationships in detail.

- A **many-to-one** relationship can be defined using models.ForeignKey. It implies that multiple instances of a model are linked to a single instance of another model. For example, multiple blog comments can be linked to a single blog post.

- A **many-to-many** relationship, denoted by models.ManyToManyField, indicates that instances of a model can be associated with multiple instances of another model. For example, a book model could have a many-to-many relationship with an author model, as books can have multiple authors and authors can write multiple books.

- **One-to-one** relationships are represented by models.OneToOneField. This relationship signifies that one record in a database is linked to exactly one record in another

78

database. For instance, a user profile could be linked to a user account with a one-to-one relation.

Below is an example illustrating a **many-to-one** relationship between a Comment model and the BlogPost model:

```
class Comment(models.Model):
    blog_post = models.ForeignKey(BlogPost, on_delete=models.CASCADE)
    content = models.TextField()
    commenter_name = models.CharField(max_length=100)
    date_posted = models.DateTimeField('date posted')
```

Here, models.ForeignKey is used to create a many-to-one relationship, linking multiple comments to a single blog post. The on_delete parameter specifies the behavior to adopt when the referenced object is deleted. In this case, models.CASCADE is used to indicate that when a BlogPost is deleted, its associated Comments should also be deleted.

Understanding how to define models and their relationships is crucial for leveraging Django's ORM to effectively interact with the database. By carefully designing your models and their interconnections, you can ensure the integrity and efficiency of your application's data layer.

3.3 Migrations: Creating and Applying Migrations

Migrations are a critical component of Django's ORM system, facilitating changes in the model's schema without losing data. Django migrations allow for version control of the database schema, which helps in developing applications collaboratively and in altering the database structure as the application evolves. This section will discuss the process of creating and applying migrations, alongside best practices for handling schema changes.

Creating migrations in Django is a straightforward process, achieved by running a specific management command. When a developer makes changes to a Django model, such as adding a new field or modifying an existing one, these changes don't automatically reflect in the database schema. Instead, Django requires the changes to be translated into migrations - files containing Python code that Django uses to alter the database schema to match the current state of models.

To generate these migration files, the command python manage.py makemigrations is used. Running this command prompts Django to inspect all models for changes since the last migration and to package these changes into new migration files. The output of this command might look as follows:

```
Migrations for 'app_name':
  app_name/migrations/0002_auto_20201123_1712.py
    - Add field new_field to example_model
```

This output indicates that Django has detected changes in the example_model inside the application 'app_name' and has created a migration file named '0002_auto_20201123_1712.py' to apply these changes.

The content of a migration file details the operations to be performed on the database. Here is an example using 'lstlisting' to display a simplified migration file structure:

```
1  # Generated by Django 3.1 on 2020-11-23 17:12
2
3  from django.db import migrations, models
4
5  class Migration(migrations.Migration):
6
7      dependencies = [
8          ('app_name', '0001_initial'),
9      ]
10
11     operations = [
12         migrations.AddField(
13             model_name='example_model',
14             name='new_field',
15             field=models.CharField(max_length=100, default=''),
16             preserve_default=False,
17         ),
18     ]
```

In this migration file, Django has included an operation to add a new field new_field to the model example_model. The dependencies attribute lists prior migrations that this migration depends on, ensuring migrations are applied in the correct order.

Applying migrations is the next step, executed with the command python manage.py migrate. This command looks for all unapplied migrations and applies them in sequence to update the database schema. The process is intelligent enough to skip any migrations that have already been applied, ensuring that each migration is executed exactly once. Successful application of migrations would result in output similar to:

```
Operations to perform:
  Apply all migrations: app_name
```

```
Running migrations:
  Applying app_name.0002_auto_20201123_1712... OK
```

It's worth mentioning that migrations can be applied to specific apps or even specific migration files by specifying the app label or migration name as an argument to the `migrate` command.

In practice, managing migrations includes not just creating and applying them but also knowing how to roll back changes, resolve conflicts, and optimize migration files for performance. Rolling back a migration is achieved by specifying the migration you want to revert to. This is especially useful during development when changes to the database schema are frequent and might require adjustment.

Furthermore, when working with a team, migrations might conflict if multiple developers make schema changes simultaneously. Django handles this by requiring that all migrations have a unique name and sequence in the migration history. In case of conflict, developers must 'rebase' their migrations by recreating them based on the latest version of the database schema after pulling changes from the version control system.

Lastly, it is advisable to periodically squash migrations. Squashing is the process of condensing many migrations into a single one, which can significantly speed up setup time for new instances of the application and reduce clutter in the migrations directory.

In summary, understanding and properly managing migrations are key to a healthy Django project. Migrations facilitate a smooth workflow for evolving the database schema, enabling developers to focus on designing robust, flexible models without worrying about the underlying database operations.

3.4 Interacting with the Database through Django Models

Interacting with the database is a fundamental aspect of backend development, and Django models provide a robust interface for creating, retrieving, updating, and deleting database records. This section will discuss the mechanisms provided by Django for database interaction, focusing on the Django Object-Relational Mapping (ORM) system. The Django ORM abstracts the complexities of SQL into Python objects, allowing developers to perform database operations without writing raw SQL queries.

Firstly, let's explore how to create new records in the database. Django models are defined in the 'models.py' file of a Django app. Once a model is defined, you can create a new instance of this model and save it to the database. Here is an example:

```
1  from myapp.models import MyModel
2
3  # Create a new instance of MyModel
4  new_record = MyModel(field1='value1', field2='value2')
5
6  # Save the new record to the database
7  new_record.save()
```

The 'save()' method tells Django to perform an INSERT SQL statement behind the scenes. If the model instance already exists in the database (determined by a primary key field), Django will instead perform an UPDATE SQL statement.

Retrieving records from the database is done through the model's manager, typically accessed via 'ModelName.objects'. Django provides a rich API for querying the database. For example, to retrieve all records from 'MyModel', you would use:

```
1  records = MyModel.objects.all()
```

For more refined queries, Django's ORM allows for filtering, ordering, and chaining querysets. An example of a more specific query could look like this:

```
1  filtered_records = MyModel.objects.filter(field1='value').order_by('-field2')
```

This retrieves records where 'field1' is equal to 'value', ordered in descending order by 'field2'.

Updating and deleting records follow a similarly intuitive syntax. To update all records matching a certain condition:

```
1  MyModel.objects.filter(field1='value').update(field2='new value')
```

And to delete these records:

```
1  MyModel.objects.filter(field1='value').delete()
```

It is essential to highlight that Django's ORM is designed to be efficient and prevent common pitfalls such as SQL injection. However, when interacting with the database, especially in the case of bulk operations, developers must be aware of the performance implications. Django provides tools such as 'select_related' and 'prefetch_related' for optimizing database queries, which are critical for maintaining performance in database-heavy applications.

Moreover, the ORM system supports complex queries, including joins and subqueries, via the 'annotate', 'aggregate', and 'F' expressions, enabling sophisticated data analysis directly from Django models without resorting to raw SQL.

Finally, database transactions are a crucial aspect of ensuring data integrity. Django models come with support for transactions, allowing developers to group database operations in a way that they are either all successfully executed or all rolled back in case of an error.

```
from django.db import transaction

with transaction.atomic():
    # Perform one or more database operations
    record1.save()
    record2.save()
    # If any of the operations fail, all changes will be rolled back
```

Django models provide a powerful and intuitive interface for interacting with the database. Through carefully designed abstractions, Django allows developers to perform CRUD operations, complex queries, and maintain data integrity with minimal effort, making it an excellent choice for developing database-driven applications.

3.5   Using the Django ORM for CRUD Operations

Django's Object-Relational Mapping (ORM) system provides a powerful means for executing Create, Read, Update, and Delete (CRUD) operations on the database. These operations are the cornerstone of data management in web applications, enabling developers to interact with the database in a Pythonic way. This section will discuss the specifics of implementing CRUD operations using Django's ORM, illustrating each operation with concrete examples.

Create Operations: To create a new record in the database using Django's ORM, one must first instantiate a model instance with the desired field values, and then call the save() method on the instance. For example, given a model Book with fields title and author, creating a new Book record can be achieved as shown below:

```
1  from app.models import Book
2
3  # Create a new book instance
4  new_book = Book(title='Django for Professionals', author='William S. Vincent')
5  # Save the instance to the database
6  new_book.save()
```

Read Operations: Django's ORM enables the querying of database records in a concise manner. The objects attribute of a model class provides a QuerySet object, which allows for the retrieval of instances from the database. To fetch all records of a model, the all() method is used. To filter records based on certain criteria, the filter() method is employed. For example, retrieving all books by a specific author:

```
1  # Fetch all books by author 'William S. Vincent'
2  books_by_william = Book.objects.filter(author='William S. Vincent')
```

Update Operations: To update existing records, Django ORM allows for the modification of model instance fields followed by calling the save() method. Alternatively, the update() method can be used on a QuerySet to update records in bulk. For example, updating the title of a specific book:

```
1  # Update the title of a specific book
2  book = Book.objects.get(id=1)
3  book.title = 'Django for Beginners'
4  book.save()
5
6  # Bulk update example
7  Book.objects.filter(author='William S. Vincent').update(title='Updated Title')
```

Delete Operations: Deleting records can be achieved by calling the delete() method on a model instance or a QuerySet. For instance, deleting a single book or all books by a certain author can be done as follows:

```
1  # Delete a single book
2  book = Book.objects.get(id=1)
3  book.delete()
4
5  # Delete all books by 'William S. Vincent'
6  Book.objects.filter(author='William S. Vincent').delete()
```

In addition to these basic CRUD operations, Django's ORM supports a range of advanced querying capabilities, including chainable filters, aggregation functions, and complex lookups. This allows for the efficient execution of sophisticated database queries crucial for developing feature-rich applications.

Django's ORM abstracts away the complexities of raw SQL, offering an intuitive interface for database manipulation. By leveraging its full capabilities, developers can perform CRUD operations efficiently, contributing to the development of robust applications. The elegance and simplicity of Django's ORM syntax facilitate rapid application development, adhering to the DRY (Don't Repeat Yourself) principle and enhancing code maintainability.

3.6 Understanding Django QuerySets and Managers

In this section, we will discuss Django's QuerySets and Managers, two fundamental components that form the backbone of Django's ORM (Object-Relational Mapping) system. Understanding these components is crucial for efficient data retrieval and manipulation in Django applications.

A QuerySet in Django is a collection of database queries to retrieve objects from your database. It is capable of executing a variety of complex queries to filter, order, and group data in a database table. QuerySets are lazy, meaning they are only evaluated when they're needed. This lazy evaluation allows for efficient use of resources and ensures that only necessary data is fetched from the database.

Let's examine basic operations with QuerySet. Consider a Django model named `Article`. To retrieve all instances of `Article` from the database, Django provides the following syntax:

```
1  from my_app.models import Article
2  all_articles = Article.objects.all()
```

This query, `Article.objects.all()`, returns a QuerySet containing all articles in the database. It is important to note that at this point, the database query has not been executed. The query will be run once the QuerySet is evaluated, for example, by iterating over it or forcing its evaluation by calling a method like `list()`.

In addition to retrieving all objects, QuerySets allow for complex queries using methods like `filter()`, `exclude()`, and `order_by()`. Here is an example that demonstrates filtering and ordering:

```
1   recent_tech_articles = Article.objects.filter(category='Tech').order_by('-
        publish_date')
```

This query fetches articles categorized under 'Tech', ordered by their publication date in descending order.

QuerySets are chainable, allowing the construction of queries piece by piece. For instance, consider the need to refine the previous query to exclude articles tagged as 'Draft'. This can be achieved with:

```
1   final_articles = recent_tech_articles.exclude(tags__name='Draft')
```

Moving onto managers, every Django model has at least one Manager instance, which is the interface through which database query operations are provided to Django models. By default, Django adds `objects` as the default manager for every model, but custom managers can be defined to extend or modify the default querying behavior.

Defining a custom manager involves creating a subclass of `django.db.models.Manager` and overriding its methods or adding new ones. For example, to create a custom manager that includes a method to retrieve only published articles, we could define:

```
1   from django.db import models
2
3   class PublishedArticleManager(models.Manager):
4       def get_queryset(self):
5           return super().get_queryset().filter(status='Published')
```

And then assign this manager to the `Article` model:

```
1   class Article(models.Model):
2       # Model fields omitted for brevity
3       objects = models.Manager() # The default manager.
4       published = PublishedArticleManager() # Our custom manager.
```

With this setup, `Article.published.all()` will return a QuerySet of articles that have `status` set to 'Published', demonstrating how custom managers offer a way to encapsulate common query patterns.

In summary, understanding and effectively using QuerySets and managers are pivotal for interacting with the database in a Django application. They provide a powerful, flexible, and intuitive mechanism for retrieving and manipulating data, which, when used judiciously, can lead to more maintainable, efficient, and expressive code.

3.7 Advanced Model Techniques: Custom Managers and Methods

In this section, we will discuss the implementation and usage of custom managers and methods within Django models, essential for encapsulating business logic, enhancing code reusability, and simplifying database queries. Django models come with a default manager that handles basic query operations. However, when dealing with complex queries or operations that are frequently used across the application, defining custom managers and methods becomes invaluable.

Custom Managers

A manager in Django is the interface through which database query operations are provided to Django models. Every Django model has at least one manager, and by default, it is named `objects`. Custom managers are created by extending the `models.Manager` class and adding extra methods to it.

To define a custom manager, create a new class that inherits from `models.Manager`. Inside this class, define any method that encapsulates the complex operations or queries you want to reuse. For instance, suppose you have a blog application where you frequently need to query for published posts. You could define a custom manager for this operation as follows:

```
from django.db import models

class PublishedManager(models.Manager):
    def get_queryset(self):
        return super().get_queryset().filter(status='published')
```

This custom manager `PublishedManager` has a method `get_queryset` that returns the queryset of objects that have `'published'` as their status. To attach this manager to a model, you simply add an instance of it to the model class:

```
class Post(models.Model):
    status = models.CharField(max_length=100)
    published = PublishedManager() # Custom manager
```

Now, in addition to the default `objects` manager, the `Post` model also has a `published` manager that allows fetching published posts directly, bypassing the need for filtering every time the operation is performed.

Custom Methods

Custom methods in Django models are used to add functionality to model instances. These methods operate on a single model instance and are useful for instance-specific operations that do not fit into the scope of managers.

Define custom methods by simply adding functions to the model class. For example, in the context of a blog application, consider adding a method to the Post model that checks whether a post can be published based on certain conditions:

```
class Post(models.Model):
    status = models.CharField(max_length=100)

    def is_publishable(self):
        return self.status not in ['draft', 'banned']
```

This is_publishable method can be called on any instance of the Post model to determine if the post meets the criteria to be considered publishable.

Both custom managers and methods are powerful features of Django's ORM, allowing developers to abstract and encapsulate common patterns and operations into reusable components. By leveraging these advanced techniques, developers can significantly reduce code redundancy, maintain a clean separation of concerns, and improve the overall maintainability of Django applications.

3.8 Working with Multiple Databases

Working with multiple databases in a Django application introduces a layer of complexity but is essential for scenarios where data separation is necessary, or scalability concerns dictate the need for distributing database load. Django offers a robust framework to handle multiple databases elegantly, allowing developers to designate specific models to specific databases, route database queries to the appropriate database, and manage database migrations across multiple databases.

To configure an application to use multiple databases, the first step involves defining the databases in the DATABASES setting in your Django project's settings.py file. An example configuration is provided below:

```
DATABASES = {
```

```
 2    'default': {
 3        'ENGINE': 'django.db.backends.sqlite3',
 4        'NAME': BASE_DIR / 'db.sqlite3',
 5    },
 6    'users': {
 7        'ENGINE': 'django.db.backends.postgresql',
 8        'NAME': 'users_db',
 9        'USER': 'your_username',
10        'PASSWORD': 'your_password',
11        'HOST': 'localhost',
12        'PORT': '',
13    }
14 }
```

This configuration specifies two databases: the default SQLite database
and a PostgreSQL database for user-related data. Each database is
identified by a key in the DATABASES dictionary, with the database
settings as the value.

Once multiple databases are configured, the next step is to route models to the correct database. Django does not automatically determine
which database to use for a given model. Instead, you have to explicitly
direct where models should live using database routers. A database
router is a class that implements four methods: db_for_read(),
db_for_write(), allow_relation(), and allow_migrate(). These
methods determine the database for reading, writing, the possibility of
relationships between models across databases, and where migrations
should be applied, respectively.

Here is an example of a simple database router:

```
 1  class UserRouter:
 2      def db_for_read(self, model, **hints):
 3          if model._meta.app_label == 'auth':
 4              return 'users'
 5          return None
 6
 7      def db_for_write(self, model, **hints):
 8          if model._meta.app_label == 'auth':
 9              return 'users'
10          return None
11
12      def allow_relation(self, obj1, obj2, **hints):
13          if obj1._meta.app_label == 'auth' or \
14             obj2._meta.app_label == 'auth':
15              return True
16          return None
17
18      def allow_migrate(self, db, app_label, model_name=None, **hints):
19          if app_label == 'auth':
20              return db == 'users'
21          return None
```

The `UserRouter` class directs all read and write operations for the auth app (typically used for user management in Django) to the 'users' database. It also allows for relationships within the auth app models by always returning `True` in `allow_relation()` if one of the models belongs to the auth app.

After defining a router, it must be added to the `DATABASE_ROUTERS` setting in `settings.py`, like so:

```
1   DATABASE_ROUTERS = ['path.to.UserRouter']
```

Handling migrations with multiple databases requires careful consideration. By default, migrations apply to the 'default' database. However, using the `allow_migrate()` method in a router, you can specify which database a particular app's migration should be applied to. When running migrations, you can also use the `--database` flag to specify the target database:

```
python manage.py migrate --database=users
```

This command applies migrations for the 'users' database. It is crucial to ensure that migrations are correctly applied to the appropriate database to avoid schema inconsistencies.

Working with multiple databases in Django provides a flexible and powerful mechanism to manage data across different databases within a single application. Through the effective use of database settings, routers, and migration management, developers can ensure data is correctly routed, accessed, and maintained across multiple databases, providing a scalable solution for complex applications.

3.9   Implementing   Model   Inheritance   in Django

In Django, model inheritance is a powerful feature that allows developers to define new models by reusing, extending, or modifying existing ones, facilitating DRY (Don't Repeat Yourself) principles in database schema design. Implementing model inheritance in Django can be accomplished in several ways, each serving different use cases and having its unique considerations. This section will discuss three primary forms of model inheritance supported by Django: abstract base classes, multi-table inheritance, and proxy models.

Abstract Base Classes allow you to define common information for a set of models. When you create a model that inherits from an abstract base class, Django constructs a model that is a combination of the base class and the child class. The key characteristic of abstract base classes is that Django does not create a table for them; they are merely used as a foundation for other models. To designate a model as an abstract base class, you include 'abstract = True' in the model's Meta class. Here is an example:

```
1   from django.db import models
2
3   class CommonInfo(models.Model):
4       name = models.CharField(max_length=100)
5       age = models.PositiveIntegerField()
6
7       class Meta:
8           abstract = True
9
10  class Student(CommonInfo):
11      home_group = models.CharField(max_length=5)
```

In the example above, 'CommonInfo' model will not have a database table. Instead, the fields defined in 'CommonInfo' will be integrated into the 'Student' model table.

Multi-table Inheritance is used when each model in the hierarchy is considered a complete model by itself and needs to be queried and used independently. In this case, Django creates a separate database table for each model in the inheritance chain and uses a One-to-One link to join the child model with its parent. Here is how you can define models to implement multi-table inheritance:

```
1   from django.db import models
2
3   class Place(models.Model):
4       name = models.CharField(max_length=50)
5       address = models.CharField(max_length=80)
6
7   class Restaurant(Place):
8       serves_hot_dogs = models.BooleanField(default=False)
9       serves_pizza = models.BooleanField(default=False)
```

In this multi-table inheritance example, Django creates a separate table for both 'Place' and 'Restaurant', with the latter having an implicit One-to-One link to the former.

Proxy Models provide a way to modify the behavior of a model, including the default managers or adding new methods, without creating a new database table. Proxy models are declared by setting 'proxy = True' in the model's Meta class.

91

```
1   from django.db import models
2
3   class Person(models.Model):
4       first_name = models.CharField(max_length=30)
5       last_name = models.CharField(max_length=30)
6
7   class MyPerson(Person):
8       class Meta:
9           proxy = True
10          ordering = ['last_name']
11
12      def do_something(self):
13          # Custom method
14          pass
```

In this example, 'MyPerson' does not cause the creation of a new table in
the database, but instead, you can use it to provide a custom interface
to the 'Person' model.

Implementing model inheritance in Django effectively requires understanding the database design implications, performance considerations, and the specific use cases each form of inheritance is best suited
for. Abstract base classes are ideal for eliminating redundancy without
affecting the database schema. Multi-table inheritance is suitable when
distinct entities share common characteristics yet need to be treated
as separate entities. Proxy models are perfect for cases where the
underlying data structure is adequate, but you need to alter the model's
behavior or appearance in the admin.

In summary, model inheritance in Django provides a robust mechanism for reusing, extending, and modifying existing models. By leveraging abstract base classes, multi-table inheritance, and proxy models,
developers can design a clean, maintainable, and efficient data layer.

3.10   Signals in Django Models

Signals in Django models provide a powerful mechanism for decoupling various parts of a Django application. This feature facilitates
the execution of custom logic whenever certain actions occur in the
database, such as the creation, update, or deletion of model instances.
Signals are an essential tool in implementing event-driven programming within Django, allowing developers to attach additional behaviors to model events without modifying the core logic of model classes.

Django's signal dispatcher mechanism uses a sender-receiver pattern
where signals are sent by model actions and received by connected

handlers. The framework includes a set of built-in signals for common database events, including `pre_save`, `post_save`, `pre_delete`, `post_delete`, among others. These signals are dispatched by Django's ORM at various points in the lifecycle of a model instance, providing hooks for developers to plug in custom behaviors.

To connect a signal to a receiver function, the `receiver()` decorator from the `django.dispatch` module is commonly used. This decorator takes a signal and an optional sender and connects the decorated function to the signal for the specified sender. The sender specifies which model class should trigger the signal, allowing for more granular control over signal handling.

```
from django.db.models.signals import post_save
from django.dispatch import receiver
from .models import MyModel

@receiver(post_save, sender=MyModel)
def my_model_post_save(sender, instance, created, **kwargs):
    if created:
        print(f"New instance of {sender.__name__} created: {instance}")
    else:
        print(f"Instance of {sender.__name__} updated: {instance}")
```

The example above demonstrates how to connect a `post_save` signal to a receiver function that prints a message whenever an instance of `MyModel` is saved. The receiver function receives several arguments from the signal dispatcher, including the `sender` (the model class), the `instance` (the model instance being saved), and a flag `created` indicating whether the instance is being created or updated.

Signals can also be used for more complex scenarios, such as clearing cache, sending notifications, or automatically creating or updating related records. However, it's important to use signals judiciously. Overuse of signals can lead to hard-to-debug code and performance issues due to the implicit nature of signal connections.

Custom signals can be defined for application-specific events. Creating a custom signal involves instantiating a `Signal` object from `django.dispatch` and connecting receiver functions to it as demonstrated with built-in signals.

```
from django.dispatch import Signal, receiver

# Define custom signal
my_custom_signal = Signal(providing_args=["arg1", "arg2"])

# Connect receiver to the custom signal
@receiver(my_custom_signal)
def my_custom_signal_handler(sender, **kwargs):
```

```
9      print(f"Custom signal received from {sender} with args: {kwargs['arg1']}, {
           kwargs['arg2']}")
10
11   # Dispatching custom signal
12   my_custom_signal.send(sender='MySender', arg1='value1', arg2='value2')
```

In practice, signals offer a robust extensibility point for Django models, enabling applications to maintain clean separation of concerns and enhance functionality with minimal intrusion into model definitions. However, developers should balance the use of signals against direct model method overrides or middleware to maintain clarity and performance of the application. By understanding and leveraging Django signals appropriately, developers can build dynamic, efficient, and maintainable applications.

3.11   Optimizing Database Queries

Optimizing database queries is crucial for enhancing the performance of a Django application. Efficient database interaction ensures that the application can handle higher loads with minimal delays, thereby improving the user experience. This section will discuss strategies and techniques to optimize database queries in Django.

Firstly, it is essential to understand the nature of the queries being executed by Django's ORM. Django provides a rich API for database operations, which, if used judiciously, can lead to significant performance improvements. The use of select_related and prefetch_related methods is foundational in optimizing database queries for related objects.

The select_related method is used when the goal is to reduce the number of database queries through join operations. For instance, consider a model Author that has a ForeignKey relationship to a model Book. When querying for books and their corresponding authors, using select_related will fetch related Author objects in a single database query.

```
1   books = Book.objects.select_related('author').all()
```

On the other hand, prefetch_related is utilized for fetching many-to-many or reverse ForeignKey relationships. This method performs separate queries for each relationship and does the joining in Python, which can be more efficient than complex join operations in some scenarios.

```
1  libraries = Library.objects.prefetch_related('books').all()
```

Another vital aspect of query optimization is the judicious use of the only and defer methods to control the fields that are loaded from the database. This is particularly useful for models with many fields, where only a subset is required for processing. The only method instructs Django to load only a specific set of fields, reducing memory usage and potentially decreasing load times.

```
1  authors = Author.objects.only('name', 'birth_date').all()
```

Conversely, the defer method allows deferring the loading of certain fields until they are specifically accessed. This approach can be advantageous when working with large text fields or binary data that is not always needed.

```
1  authors = Author.objects.defer('biography').all()
```

Indexing plays a pivotal role in query optimization. Properly indexed fields can drastically reduce query execution times, especially for large datasets. Django allows for the specification of indexes at the model level, enabling developers to hint the database on how data access patterns will occur.

```
1   from django.db import models
2
3   class Book(models.Model):
4       title = models.CharField(max_length=100)
5       publication_date = models.DateField()
6
7       class Meta:
8           indexes = [
9               models.Index(fields=['title'], name='title_idx'),
10              models.Index(fields=['publication_date'], name='pub_date_idx'),
11          ]
```

Query optimization also involves avoiding N+1 query problems, reducing unnecessary database hits, and employing database functions and aggregates judiciously for data computation. The use of Django's annotate and aggregate methods can offload computation to the database, which is often more efficient than processing data in Python.

```
1   from django.db.models import Count
2
3   author_books = Author.objects.annotate(num_books=Count('book')).all()
```

Finally, continuous monitoring and analysis of query performance are essential. Django's database query logging and the use of third-party tools like Django Debug Toolbar can help identify inefficient queries and areas for optimization.

In summary, optimizing database queries within Django involves a combination of strategic model querying methods, intelligent field selection, appropriate use of indexing, avoidance of common performance pitfalls, and continuous performance monitoring. By following these practices, developers can significantly enhance the responsiveness and scalability of Django applications.

3.12 Integrating with External Databases and APIs

Integrating with external databases and Application Programming Interfaces (APIs) expands the capabilities of Django applications by allowing them to communicate with other systems and services, thereby enhancing functionality and enabling the integration of diverse data sources. This section discusses the methods and considerations for effectively connecting Django projects with external databases and consuming third-party APIs.

To integrate an external database, Django's database settings need to be configured to include the external database's connection parameters. Django supports multiple databases, and each can be defined in the DATABASES setting in the settings.py file. An example configuration for connecting to an external MySQL database is as follows:

```
DATABASES = {
    'default': {
        # default database configuration
    },
    'external': {
        'ENGINE': 'django.db.backends.mysql',
        'NAME': 'external_db_name',
        'USER': 'external_db_user',
        'PASSWORD': 'external_db_password',
        'HOST': 'external_db_host',
        'PORT': 'external_db_port',
    }
}
```

Once the external database is configured, Django's ORM can be used to define models that map to the tables in the external database. However, to ensure that queries against these models target the correct database, it is necessary to use Django's .using() method when performing queries, specifying the database alias defined in the DATABASES setting.

Integrating third-party APIs involves sending HTTP requests to the API endpoints and processing the responses. Django does not include built-in support for making HTTP requests, so developers typically use libraries such as Requests. The following example demonstrates how to make a GET request to a third-party API and process the JSON response:

```
1  import requests
2
3  def get_external_data():
4      response = requests.get('https://api.example.com/data')
5      if response.status_code == 200:
6          data = response.json()
7          # Process the data
8      else:
9          # Handle request error
```

When integrating external APIs, it is also important to handle API authentication, rate limiting, and error responses gracefully. Most APIs require an API key or token for authentication, which can be included in request headers or query parameters. Rate limiting needs to be respected by implementing retry mechanisms or respecting the API's rate limit headers. Processing error responses correctly ensures that the application can gracefully recover or inform the user accordingly.

For a seamless integration of external databases and APIs into Django applications, several best practices should be followed:

- Keep sensitive information such as API keys and database passwords out of source code by using environment variables or Django's SECRET_KEY mechanism.

- Utilize Django's database routers to cleanly separate read and write operations among different databases.

- Employ caching to reduce the number of requests made to external APIs and decrease load times.

- Monitor and log API requests and responses to quickly identify and troubleshoot issues.

In summary, integrating external databases and APIs into Django applications extends their functionality by allowing them to communicate with other software and services. By carefully configuring database connections, making HTTP requests to external APIs, and adopting best practices, developers can create powerful, integrated Django applications.

3.13 Using Django Models with Forms and Views

In the context of Django, models define the structure of the database, and forms and views facilitate the interaction between the user and the application's data. This section will discuss the seamless integration of Django models with forms and views, a vital aspect of developing dynamic web applications that interact robustly with a database.

Django forms provide a mechanism for generating HTML forms, validating submitted data, and converting them into Python data types that can be processed or stored. Django views, on the other hand, control what data is presented to the user and the response to user actions. The integration of models, forms, and views is pivotal for the creation and manipulation of database records through user interfaces.

ModelForm: Bridging Models and Forms

The 'ModelForm' class is Django's solution for converting model instances into form counterparts and vice versa. Using 'ModelForm' saves a considerable amount of code by avoiding the need to define form fields manually, as it auto-generates them based on the model.

To use 'ModelForm', one must declare a subclass of 'ModelForm' that specifies which model it is related to:

```
1  from django.forms import ModelForm
2  from .models import YourModel
3
4  class YourModelForm(ModelForm):
5      class Meta:
6          model = YourModel
7          fields = ['field1', 'field2']
```

In this example, 'YourModelForm' automatically inherits form fields for 'field1' and 'field2' from 'YourModel'. This form can now be used within views to create or update instances of 'YourModel'.

Creating and Editing Model Instances with ModelForms

Integrating 'ModelForm' in views permits the handling of both GET and POST requests efficiently. A typical pattern for creating or updating model instances involves defining a view that instantiates a form in the case of a GET request or processes submitted data in the case of a POST request.

```
from django.shortcuts import render, redirect
from .forms import YourModelForm

def model_create_or_update_view(request, id=None):
    instance = None
    if id:
        instance = YourModel.objects.get(id=id)
    if request.method == 'POST':
        form = YourModelForm(request.POST or None, instance=instance)
        if form.is_valid():
            form.save()
            return redirect('success_url')
    else:
        form = YourModelForm(instance=instance)
    return render(request, 'your_template.html', {'form': form})
```

This view accommodates both the creation of new instances and the editing of existing ones, determined by the presence of an 'id' parameter.

Integrating Models with Views and Templates

Django views bridge the gap between models and templates. They query the database for model instances and pass them to templates for rendering. For example, to display all instances of a model, a view can retrieve all records using the model's 'objects.all()' method and send them to a template using Django's context mechanism.

```
from django.shortcuts import render
from .models import YourModel

def model_display_view(request):
    instances = YourModel.objects.all()
    return render(request, 'display_template.html', {'instances': instances})
```

In 'display_template.html', one can iterate over 'instances' to display each record's information.

The integration of Django models with forms and views is a cornerstone of Django's design, enabling developers to construct complex web applications with rich user interfaces that interact with database-backed models. By leveraging 'ModelForm' and understanding the patterns for handling form submission and model instance rendering, developers can effectively implement create, read, update, and delete (CRUD) functionality in their applications. This approach not only streamlines development by reducing boilerplate code but also ensures consistency and security in data handling.

3.14   Securing Data in Django Models

Securing data within Django models is a critical aspect of developing secure web applications. Django, a high-level Python web framework, provides several mechanisms to help safeguard sensitive data. This section elucidates on techniques and practices to enhance data security in Django models, including field encryption, user authentication, and permission controls.

Field encryption is vital for storing sensitive information such as passwords, personal user data, or financial information. Django does not provide built-in field encryption, necessitating the use of third-party packages such as `django-fernet-fields` or `django-cryptography` that implement encryption at the field level. These packages typically use symmetric-key encryption to secure data before it is saved to the database and decrypt data when it is retrieved.

Implementing field encryption with `django-cryptography` can be demonstrated as follows:

```
1  from django.db import models
2  from django_cryptography.fields import encrypt
3
4  class SecureInfo(models.Model):
5      user = models.ForeignKey('auth.User', on_delete=models.CASCADE)
6      encrypted_data = encrypt(models.TextField())
```

In the example above, the `encrypted_data` field ensures that any data stored in this field is automatically encrypted before being saved to the database and decrypted upon retrieval.

User authentication and session management are another cornerstone of security in Django models. Django's built-in authentication system provides methods for securely managing user accounts and sessions. It is imperative to manage user authentication and session data securely to prevent unauthorized access and session hijacking. Developers should ensure that Django settings for session security, such

100

as SESSION_COOKIE_SECURE and CSRF_COOKIE_SECURE, are enabled for HTTPS sites.

To further secure user data, Django permissions should be meticulously implemented. Permissions allow developers to specify who can access, add, change, or delete data. Django offers a robust permission system, integrated with its authentication system, enabling developers to assign permissions to groups and individual users. Ensuring proper use of permissions protects sensitive data from unauthorized access or alterations.

For example, to restrict access to a model to only authenticated users, you can use Django's LoginRequiredMixin as follows:

```
1  from django.contrib.auth.mixins import LoginRequiredMixin
2  from django.views.generic import DetailView
3  from .models import SecureInfo
4
5  class SecureInfoDetailView(LoginRequiredMixin, DetailView):
6      model = SecureInfo
```

In the example, SecureInfoDetailView will only be accessible to authenticated users, thus enforcing a basic level of access control.

Furthermore, careful management of querysets and managers in Django models can contribute to data security. By customizing managers and querysets, developers can ensure that data is only accessible to users with the appropriate permissions or roles. This technique prevents unauthorized access to data through indirect means, such as manipulated query parameters or URL exploration.

Securing data in Django models requires a multifaceted approach, incorporating field-level encryption, secure authentication and session management, meticulous permission controls, and the judicious use of customized querysets and managers. By adhering to these practices, developers can significantly enhance the security of their web applications, protecting sensitive data from unauthorized access, alteration, or exposure.

3.15   Best Practices for Designing Django Models

Designing efficient models is pivotal for the performance and maintainability of Django applications. This section will discuss guidelines and best practices for structuring models in Django to maximize efficiency, scalability, and readability.

Firstly, it is crucial to carefully plan and define the data schema. Each model should represent a single, coherent dataset, following the principle of Single Responsibility. Models should be designed to minimize redundancy and ensure data normalization to reduce data duplication and inconsistencies.

When defining fields on models, opting for the most appropriate field types is essential. Django offers a rich selection of field types, such as CharField, IntegerField, and DateTimeField, among others. Proper use of these field types, including leveraging ForeignKey for relationships, promotes data integrity and database performance. Additionally, setting the max_length attribute where applicable, such as on a CharField, helps optimize database storage.

```
1  from django.db import models
2
3  class Author(models.Model):
4      name = models.CharField(max_length=100)
5      biography = models.TextField()
6
7  class Book(models.Model):
8      title = models.CharField(max_length=200)
9      publication_date = models.DateField()
10     author = models.ForeignKey(Author, on_delete=models.CASCADE)
```

Regarding relationships, understanding the relationship types (One-to-One, One-to-Many, and Many-to-Many) and when to use them is key for structuring related data efficiently. One-To-Many relationships are implemented by adding a ForeignKey field to the model that represents the "many" side of the relationship. Many-to-Many relationships are represented using ManyToManyField, which Django manages through an automatically generated intermediate join table.

Indexing is another important aspect of model design. Adding indexes to fields that are frequently used in filters or order_by clauses can significantly improve query performance. However, excessive indexing can lead to increased storage requirements and slower write operations, so indexes should be used judiciously.

```
1  class Book(models.Model):
2      title = models.CharField(max_length=200, db_index=True)
3      publication_date = models.DateField()
4      author = models.ForeignKey(Author, on_delete=models.CASCADE)
```

In terms of model inheritance, Django offers three ways to achieve it: abstract base classes, multi-table inheritance, and proxy models. Each method has its use case, but abstract base classes are particularly useful for when you want to put some common information into a number of other models.

For managing model instances, custom managers and model methods can be defined to encapsulate common operations. This promotes code reusability and keeps business logic within models, enhancing the maintainability of the application.

```
1   class PublishedBookManager(models.Manager):
2       def get_queryset(self):
3           return super().get_queryset().filter(status='published')
4
5   class Book(models.Model):
6       title = models.CharField(max_length=200)
7       status = models.CharField(max_length=10)
8
9       objects = models.Manager() # The default manager.
10      published = PublishedBookManager() # Our custom manager.
11
12      def publish(self):
13          self.status = 'published'
14          self.save()
```

Data validation is crucial for maintaining data integrity. Django models provide a clean method to add validation logic by overriding the clean method. This method is called before saving an instance and is where one should place their custom validation logic.

To facilitate future migrations and changes, it is advisable to use Django's built-in migration system effectively. Keeping migrations backward compatible and squashing migrations periodically can help maintain a clean migration history and reduce application startup time.

Lastly, securing sensitive information is paramount. Fields containing sensitive data should be properly encrypted, or measures should be taken to restrict their access both in the Django application and at the database level.

By adhering to these best practices, developers can design Django models that are efficient, reliable, and scalable, leading to more maintainable and performant Django applications.

Chapter 4

Django Admin Interface Customization

The Django admin interface stands out as a highly customizable tool allowing developers to quickly create a powerful interface for managing application content. Through customization, it can be fine-tuned to meet specific project requirements, enhancing productivity and data management capabilities. This chapter explores strategies for extending and modifying the default behavior and appearance of the Django admin, including model registration, form customization, and creating custom actions, thereby transforming the admin interface into a tailored, efficient, and user-friendly resource.

4.1 Introduction to the Django Admin Interface

The Django admin interface is a remarkable feature of the Django web framework that enables developers and administrators to create, read, update, and delete the content of a website or application directly through a web-based interface. By default, the Django admin translates Python models into a dynamic interface, configured with minimal code. This capability significantly accelerates the development process, especially during the early stages of a project, by providing a ready-to-use interface for interacting with the application's data models.

At its core, the Django admin interface is automatically generated from the Python models defined in a Django project. This involves a process where Django introspects the model definitions, deriving the structure and relationships present within them. Consequently, it renders a user-friendly web interface that corresponds to the defined data models, allowing for an intuitive manipulation of the database records represented by these models.

The inclusion of the Django admin interface in a project is straightforward. It begins with activating the admin app, a step usually completed during the initial setup of a Django project. Following this, individual models must be registered with the admin to make them available through the interface. The registration process involves creating an instance of `admin.ModelAdmin` for each model and using the `admin.site.register()` function to associate the model with its admin representation. Listing 4.1 provides an example of model registration with the Django admin.

Listing 4.1: Example of model registration with Django admin

```
1  from django.contrib import admin
2  from .models import MyModel
3
4  class MyModelAdmin(admin.ModelAdmin):
5      pass
6
7  admin.site.register(MyModel, MyModelAdmin)
```

Once models are registered, the Django admin interface offers multiple features out of the box. These include the ability to navigate through the database tables corresponding to registered models, create new database entries, edit existing ones, and delete entries where necessary. The interface supports filtering and searching of records, which can be customized to fit the specific needs of the project.

Advanced customization of the Django admin interface is achievable through a variety of means. The appearance and functionality can be modified extensively to cater to the requirements of individual projects. Customizations range from simple changes, such as adjusting which fields are displayed in the list view, to more complex enhancements like integrating custom forms for data entry and manipulation.

The Django admin's extensibility does not end with visual and functional tweaks. It extends to security features as well, offering mechanisms for restricting access to parts of the admin based on user permissions. Further, developers can extend the admin with custom views, override templates, and integrate third-party tools to enhance its capabilities.

In summary, the Django admin interface serves as a powerful tool for web application development, dramatically simplifying the process of content management. Its ease of use, combined with extensive customization options, makes it an invaluable feature for both developers and administrators. The following sections will delve deeper into strategies for extending and customizing the Django admin, showcasing how it can be adapted to serve the unique needs of various projects.

4.2   Registering Models with the Admin Site

Registration of models with the Django admin site is a preliminary step to take full advantage of Django's built-in administrative interface. This process makes the models accessible via the admin interface, enabling CRUD (Create, Read, Update, Delete) operations directly through the browser. This capability significantly accelerates development workflows and facilitates rapid data management and testing.

To register a model, the Django framework provides a straightforward decorator-based approach. This involves utilizing the @admin.register decorator, followed by the model class definition. Below is an example demonstrating how to register a simple model named Product:

```
1  from django.contrib import admin
2  from .models import Product
3
4  @admin.register(Product)
5  class ProductAdmin(admin.ModelAdmin):
6      pass
```

In the above example, Product is a model class that has been defined in the models.py file of the application. By decorating the ProductAdmin class with @admin.register(Product), the Product model is registered with the admin site. The ProductAdmin class inherits from admin.ModelAdmin, which provides numerous options for customization. However, in its simplest form, the class is declared with a pass statement, indicating no additional customization is applied at this stage.

Alternatively, models can be registered without the decorator by explicitly calling the admin.site.register() method, passing in the model and the corresponding model admin class. For instance, if for some reason the decorator approach is not suitable, the following syntax achieves the same result:

```
1  from django.contrib import admin
2  from .models import Product
3
4  class ProductAdmin(admin.ModelAdmin):
5      pass
6
7  admin.site.register(Product, ProductAdmin)
```

Both methods ensure the Product model appears in the admin site, yet the decorator method is generally preferred for its readability and succinctness.

Once a model is registered, it appears in the Django admin interface, under an automatically generated section that matches the application name. From the interface, users can add new records, edit existing ones, and delete them, leveraging Django's forms to ensure data integrity and enforce validation rules defined in the model.

It is crucial to understand that, by default, all fields on a model are editable in the admin unless configured otherwise. This behavior can be altered by specifying the fields or exclude attributes of the model admin class, thereby providing finer control over which fields are displayed and editable through the admin interface.

To summarize, registering models with the Django admin site is a simple yet powerful process, essential for leveraging the full capabilities of the Django admin interface. It not only facilitates direct manipulation of database records through a web interface but also serves as a foundation upon which further customizations and enhancements can be built.

4.3 Customizing the Model Admin: List Displays, Filters, and Searches

In this section, we will discuss the customization of the Model Admin interface in Django's admin panel, focusing on three main areas: list displays, filters, and searches. These features are paramount in enhancing the user interface, making data management tasks more efficient and user-friendly. Customizing model admin involves configuring the

108

ModelAdmin class, which provides a rich set of attributes and methods for customization.

List Displays

The list display configuration allows you to control which fields are displayed on the change list page of the admin for a given model. By default, Django will display only the __str__() representation of each object. However, for a more informative and useful overview, displaying additional fields is often necessary.

To customize the fields displayed, you can modify the list_display attribute of your ModelAdmin class. This should be a list or tuple containing the names of the fields you wish to display.

```
1  class BookAdmin(admin.ModelAdmin):
2      list_display = ('title', 'author', 'publish_date')
3
4  admin.site.register(Book, BookAdmin)
```

Aside from field names, list_display can also include callable objects that accept one parameter (the model instance) and return a value to be displayed.

Filters

Filters provide a way to narrow down querysets based on field values. They can significantly enhance the usability of the admin interface by allowing users to filter the displayed records on predefined criteria.

To add filters, you utilize the list_filter attribute in your ModelAdmin class. This attribute can be filled with names of fields on the model, which automatically creates filter interfaces in the sidebar of the change list page.

```
1  class BookAdmin(admin.ModelAdmin):
2      list_filter = ('publish_date', 'author')
3
4  admin.site.register(Book, BookAdmin)
```

Django supports various types of filters, from simple choices filters to custom filters for dealing with more complex filtering logic.

Searches

Implementing search functionality enables users to quickly find records without having to navigate through pages of data. The `search_fields` attribute of the `ModelAdmin` class allows specifying fields on the model that should be searched to match the user's query.

```
1  class BookAdmin(admin.ModelAdmin):
2      search_fields = ['title', 'author__name']
3
4  admin.site.register(Book, BookAdmin)
```

Notice the use of double underscores to denote a search that spans related objects, such as finding books by their author's name. The search functionality is performed using a LIKE query on the underlying database, and for best performance, it is advisable to index these fields in your database schema.

Customizing the list display, filters, and search capabilities of the Django admin interface can dramatically improve the efficiency and user experience of managing data within your Django application. By leveraging the `ModelAdmin` attributes such as `list_display`, `list_filter`, and `search_fields`, developers can provide a powerful and bespoke admin interface tailored to the needs of their project.

4.4   Form Customization in the Admin

Form customization in the Django admin interface provides a powerful means to enhance the usability and functionality of admin forms. Through careful adjustments, developers can tailor the admin interface to better fit the specific needs of their applications, ensuring a smoother user experience for administrators managing site content. This section will discuss various techniques for customizing forms within the Django admin, namely through the use of form classes, field overrides, and custom widgets.

Firstly, utilizing custom form classes in the admin allows for a fine-grained control over the presentation and functionality of model forms. To define a custom form for use in the admin, one must create a subclass of `django.forms.ModelForm` and specify the desired customizations. Once the form class is defined, it can be integrated with the admin by setting the `form` attribute in the model's `admin.ModelAdmin` class.

```
1  from django.contrib import admin
```

```
2   from django import forms
3   from .models import MyModel
4
5   class MyModelForm(forms.ModelForm):
6       class Meta:
7           model = MyModel
8           fields = '__all__'
9           widgets = {
10              'my_field': forms.Textarea(attrs={'cols': 80, 'rows': 20}),
11          }
12
13  class MyModelAdmin(admin.ModelAdmin):
14      form = MyModelForm
15
16  admin.site.register(MyModel, MyModelAdmin)
```

In this example, the custom form class `MyModelForm` specifies a custom widget for the `my_field` field. This simple yet powerful technique enables developers to influence both the appearance and behavior of form fields, which can significantly improve the data entry process.

Another method of form customization in the Django admin is through field overrides in the `ModelAdmin` class. By defining the `formfield_for_*` family of methods, developers can customize how individual model fields are represented within the admin. These methods provide an opportunity to adjust a field's representation dynamically based on the context.

```
1   class MyModelAdmin(admin.ModelAdmin):
2       def formfield_for_choice_field(self, db_field, request, **kwargs):
3           if db_field.name == 'my_choice_field':
4               kwargs['choices'] = (
5                   ('option1', 'Option 1'),
6                   ('option2', 'Option 2'),
7               )
8           return super().formfield_for_choice_field(db_field, request, **kwargs)
```

In this snippet, the `formfield_for_choice_field` method is overridden to dynamically set the choices for a specific field, thereby offering a contextual customization based on either the request object or other logical conditions you may impose.

Lastly, the utilization of custom widgets is crucial in achieving a high degree of customization in admin forms. Widgets in Django are responsible for rendering the HTML of form fields and handling input data on submission. By creating a custom widget and associating it with a form field, developers can significantly alter both the look and feel and the interaction patterns of form fields.

```
1   from django import forms
2   from django.contrib import admin
3   from django.db import models
```

```
4    from .models import MyModel
5
6    class MyCustomWidget(forms.widgets.Textarea):
7        template_name = 'custom_templates/my_custom_widget.html'
8
9    class MyModelAdmin(admin.ModelAdmin):
10       formfield_overrides = {
11           models.TextField: {'widget': MyCustomWidget},
12       }
13
14   admin.site.register(MyModel, MyModelAdmin)
```

Here, a custom widget MyCustomWidget is defined with a custom template for rendering, providing an unprecedented level of control over the field's presentation. This mechanism not only enhances the visual aspect of the admin forms but also allows for the incorporation of interactive client-side functionality, such as rich text editors or advanced file upload mechanisms.

In summary, form customization in the Django admin interface is an essential technique for refining the administrative user experience. Through the use of custom form classes, field overrides, and custom widgets, developers can tailor the admin interface to meet the specific needs of their projects. These customizations not only improve the aesthetics and usability of admin forms but also empower administrators to manage application data more effectively.

4.5   Admin Site Customization: Look and Feel

Customizing the look and feel of the Django admin interface significantly enhances the user experience, aligning it more closely with your project's branding and design guidelines. The Django admin interface's default appearance is pragmatic but might not fit every project's aesthetic requirements or branding. This section will discuss strategies for modifying the admin interface's templates, static files, and incorporating custom CSS and JavaScript to transform the admin's appearance and functionality.

The customization of the Django admin interface's look and feel primarily involves overriding default admin templates and static files (CSS, JavaScript). Django admin templates are responsible for rendering the admin interface, while static files manage its styling and interactive features.

Overriding Admin Templates: Django's admin uses a consistent templating system. Customizing these templates allows for modifications in the layout and presentation of the admin site. To override an admin template, first identify the template you wish to change. Then, replicate the template's directory structure in your project's `templates` directory, maintaining the original template's name. For example, to customize the main dashboard of the admin site, you would create a custom template at `templates/admin/index.html` in your Django project.

Customizing Static Files: Static files like CSS and JavaScript can be customized to alter the appearance and behavior of the admin interface. To override the default admin CSS, for instance, place a custom CSS file in your project's `static` directory, following the path convention used by the admin. This approach typically involves creating a file at `static/admin/css/custom.css`. After creating your custom CSS file, you need to ensure it is loaded by the admin site, which usually involves modifying an existing template to include the custom stylesheet.

Integrating custom CSS and JavaScript requires modifying the admin templates to include these files. This might include adding `<link rel="stylesheet">` and `<script>` tags in the `<head>` section of an overridden admin template. For instance, to include a custom CSS file, the following line should be added to the overridden template:

```
<link rel="stylesheet" type="text/css" href="{% static 'admin/css/custom.css' %}">
```

Similarly, to incorporate custom JavaScript, you would add:

```
<script type="text/javascript" src="{% static 'admin/js/custom.js' %}"></script>
```

It's important to note that when customizing the look and feel of the Django admin, careful attention should be paid to maintaining the usability and accessibility of the interface. Changes should enhance the admin interface's functionality and aesthetic appeal without detracting from its usability.

In addition to modifying templates and static files, the Django admin's look and feel can be further customized through the use of third-party packages. These packages can offer pre-built themes and additional functionalities that can be easily integrated into your project, saving development time and ensuring a professional appearance.

Lastly, remember to test your customizations across various devices and browsers to ensure compatibility and responsiveness. This ensures a consistent and professional experience for all users of the Django admin interface, regardless of how they access it.

Customizing the look and feel of the Django admin requires a combination of overriding default templates, modifying static files, and possibly integrating third-party tools. By following these steps, developers can create a more engaging and branded experience for admin users, making data management tasks more efficient and pleasant.

4.6   Creating Custom Admin Actions

Creating custom admin actions in Django allows for the implementation of bulk operations that can be applied to multiple records simultaneously. This feature is particularly useful for tasks such as updating several records at once, exporting data to external files, or even performing more complex operations that are specific to the application's requirements. This section will discuss the steps required to create and integrate custom actions within the Django admin interface, leveraging Django's built-in functionalities to enhance administrative efficiency.

To begin with, custom admin actions are defined as functions within the admin model. Each action function takes three parameters: the model admin instance ('self'), the current HttpRequest object ('request'), and a QuerySet containing the set of selected objects that the action will be applied to ('queryset'). The basic structure of a custom admin action is illustrated in the example below:

```
1  from django.contrib import admin
2
3  def make_published(modeladmin, request, queryset):
4      queryset.update(status='published')
5
6  make_published.short_description = 'Mark selected stories as published'
```

In the above example, 'make_published' is a custom action for a hypothetical model that manages stories, which updates the status of all selected stories to "published". The 'short_description' attribute provides a display name for the action in the Django admin interface.

After defining the action, it must be registered with the model admin. This is done by adding the action function to the 'actions' list attribute of the model admin class, as shown below:

```
1  class StoryAdmin(admin.ModelAdmin):
2      list_display = ['title', 'status']
3      actions = [make_published]
```

```
4
5  admin.site.register(Story, StoryAdmin)
```

With these steps, the 'make_published' action will be available in the admin interface for the 'Story' model. When selected from the actions dropdown and applied, it will update the status of all selected story records to "published".

To further customize the behavior of custom actions, conditional enabling or disabling based on request or the queryset can be implemented. For instance, an action might only be applicable to certain records based on their current state or the permissions of the user. The enabling condition can be integrated directly into the action function or managed through the model admin's 'get_actions' method, providing a dynamic mechanism for controlling action availability.

Custom admin actions can also interact with the user, for example, by displaying messages using Django's messaging framework. This allows for feedback about the outcome of an action, enhancing the interactive experience. Below is an enhanced version of the 'make_published' action, which includes success messaging:

```
1  from django.contrib import admin
2  from django.contrib import messages
3
4  def make_published(modeladmin, request, queryset):
5      updated = queryset.update(status='published')
6      modeladmin.message_user(request, f"{updated} stories were successfully marked
            as published.", messages.SUCCESS)
7
8  make_published.short_description = 'Mark selected stories as published'
```

In this enhanced version, 'message_user' is used to notify the user about the number of stories that were successfully updated, providing immediate feedback within the admin interface.

Furthermore, creating custom admin actions goes beyond modifying model fields. Actions can generate files, redirect to specific URLs, or perform virtually any server-side task. This flexibility makes custom admin actions a powerful tool for extending the functionality of the Django admin interface, enabling administrators to perform complex operations efficiently directly from the admin panel.

Custom admin actions in Django provide a mechanism for extending the functionality of the admin interface, allowing for bulk operations on selected records. By defining actions as functions and registering them with model admins, developers can enhance the administrative capabilities of their Django applications, improving both productivity and user experience. Whether it's updating status fields, exporting data, or performing more sophisticated tasks, custom admin actions offer a customizable and powerful feature for managing application data effectively.

4.7 Securing the Django Admin Interface

Securing the Django admin interface is paramount for any web application, as it contains sensitive functionality that can affect the whole application. The default configuration of the Django admin is not designed for a production environment. Without proper security measures, it can become a significant vulnerability. This section will discuss strategies and practices to enhance the security of the Django admin interface, focusing on authentication and authorization, securing data transmission, and monitoring and logging access.

Firstly, it's crucial to limit access to the Django admin interface. This is achieved by enforcing strong authentication mechanisms. One should start by ensuring that the default superuser account has a strong, unique password. Django supports integrating with more sophisticated authentication mechanisms, such as two-factor authentication (2FA) and Single Sign-On (SSO), through third-party packages like `django-allauth` and `django-otp`. Implementing 2FA adds an additional layer of security by requiring a second form of verification beyond just a password.

```
1  # Installation of django-allauth for SSO
2  pip install django-allauth
```

After enhancing authentication, you should focus on authorization. It involves defining and enforcing what authenticated users can and cannot do. Django's built-in groups and permissions system can be leveraged to assign roles and restrict access to certain parts of the admin interface based on a user's group. It is advisable to adhere to the principle of least privilege, meaning users should be granted only the permissions necessary to perform their duties.

```
1  from django.contrib.auth.models import Group, Permission
2  from django.contrib.contenttypes.models import ContentType
3  from myapp.models import MyModel
4
5  # Create a new group for specific users
6  new_group, created = Group.objects.get_or_create(name='Special Access Group')
7
8  # Assign model-specific permissions to the group
```

```
9   ct = ContentType.objects.get_for_model(MyModel)
10  permission = Permission.objects.create(codename='can_access_special_model',
11                                         name='Can Access Special Model',
12                                         content_type=ct)
13  new_group.permissions.add(permission)
```

Securing data transmission is another critical aspect. Ensuring that all traffic to and from the admin interface is encrypted using HTTPS is essential for protecting sensitive information from being intercepted. This can be enforced by setting the SECURE_SSL_REDIRECT setting to True in your Django settings, which redirects all HTTP requests to HTTPS.

```
1   # Enforcing HTTPS in Django settings
2   SECURE_SSL_REDIRECT = True
```

Monitoring and logging access to the Django admin interface is indispensable for security. Keeping detailed logs of who accessed the admin, when, and what actions they performed can help in detecting unauthorized access and understanding user behavior. Django does not log admin actions by default, but one can extend the ModelAdmin class to include logging functionality.

```
1   from django.contrib import admin
2   from django.contrib.auth.models import LogEntry
3
4   class LogEntryAdmin(admin.ModelAdmin):
5       list_display = ('action_time', 'user', 'content_type', 'object_id', '
              object_repr', 'action_flag', 'change_message')
6
7   admin.site.register(LogEntry, LogEntryAdmin)
```

Finally, regularly updating Django and its dependencies is crucial for security. Vulnerabilities are continually found and fixed, so staying on the latest version helps protect against known exploits.

Securing the Django admin interface requires a multifaceted approach, including strong authentication and authorization practices, securing data transmission, and diligent monitoring and logging. By implementing the strategies discussed, developers can significantly enhance the security and integrity of their applications.

4.8   Implementing Custom Admin Views

Implementing custom admin views in Django serves as a powerful technique to extend the functionality of the Django admin beyond its out-of-the-box offerings. This approach enables developers to introduce new views tailored to specific requirements, thereby enhancing the overall productivity and efficiency of admin users. The basis of custom admin views lies in the understanding of how the Django admin URLs are structured and how they can be extended or overridden to introduce new functionalities.

To begin with, custom admin views require a well-defined URL pattern that directs to the custom view. This necessitates modifications in the urls.py file of the Django project. It's crucial to ensure that the custom URL is placed above the default admin URLs to avoid conflicts. The custom view is then defined in the views.py file, where the actual logic of the view is implemented.

Here is a basic example of adding a custom view to the Django admin:

```
1   # In your app's urls.py
2
3   from django.urls import path
4   from . import views
5
6   urlpatterns = [
7       path('admin/my_custom_view/', views.my_custom_view, name='my_custom_view'),
8   ]
```

Then, the corresponding view function might look like this:

```
1   # In your app's views.py
2
3   from django.shortcuts import render
4   from django.contrib.admin.views.decorators import staff_member_required
5
6   @staff_member_required
7   def my_custom_view(request):
8       # Implement your view logic here
9       return render(request, 'my_custom_template.html', {})
```

In this example, the @staff_member_required decorator is used to ensure that only users who are staff members can access this view, mirroring the access control typically found in Django admin interfaces.

To further integrate this custom view into the Django admin, one might want to add a link to it from within the admin. This can be achieved by overriding the admin template that generates the admin site's index page. This involves creating a custom template that extends the existing admin/index.html template and then inserting a link to the custom view:

```
1   {% extends "admin/index.html" %}
2
3   {% block content %}
4       {{ block.super }}
```

```
5       <a href="{% url 'my_custom_view' %}">My Custom View</a>
6   {% endblock %}
```

By extending the `admin/index.html` template and adding a custom block, you can seamlessly integrate links to custom views without disrupting the overall layout of the Django admin.

Moreover, custom admin views do not have to be restricted to simple page renders. They can be designed to handle forms, perform database operations, or even trigger background tasks. This versatility allows the Django admin to serve not just as a content management interface but also as a central hub for executing various administrative tasks.

For more complex interactions, Ajax can be employed within custom admin views to create dynamic user interfaces without requiring page reloads. This is particularly useful for actions that require immediate feedback, such as updating model values or generating reports.

Lastly, security considerations should never be overlooked when implementing custom admin views. Apart from the `@staff_member_required` decorator, other security practices such as validating form inputs and implementing proper error handling mechanisms are vital to safeguarding the admin interface against unintended actions or vulnerabilities.

Implementing custom admin views in Django offers a pathway to significantly amplify the capabilities of the Django admin. Through careful design and integration, these custom views can render the Django admin a more powerful and flexible tool, tailor-made to suit the unique needs of any project.

4.9   Extending Admin Templates

Extending admin templates in Django allows developers to modify the look and functionality of the Django admin interface, enabling a more tailored administrative experience. This customization process uses Django's template inheritance mechanism, which is powerful and flexible. Extending admin templates can range from simple changes, like altering the base color scheme, to more complex modifications, such as adding new blocks of content or functionality.

To begin with extending admin templates, it is crucial to understand Django's template loading mechanism. Django admin templates are loaded from the `django/contrib/admin/templates` directory by default. However, Django searches for templates in the order specified in the `TEMPLATES` setting's `DIRS` and `APP_DIRS` configurations. By creating an admin template with the same path and name in your project or application's template directory, you can override the default admin template. This technique is fundamental for customizing the admin interface.

For instance, to customize the index page of the admin site, you could create a template named `admin/index.html` in your project or application's template directory. The following code shows a simple extension of the base admin index template, adding a custom message at the top of the page:

```
1   {% extends "admin/index.html" %}
2
3   {% block content %}
4     <div class="custom-message">
5       Welcome to the Custom Admin Dashboard!
6     </div>
7     {{ block.super }}
8   {% endblock %}
```

This code snippet demonstrates extending the `admin/index.html` template by overriding the `content` block. The `{ block.super }` template tag is used to insert the content of the overridden block, ensuring that the original admin content is preserved and displayed after the custom message.

Beyond simple changes, extending admin templates can include modifying form layouts, adding custom JavaScript or CSS, and inserting additional blocks of content. For more complex modifications, understanding the structure and inheritance hierarchy of admin templates is necessary. The Django admin uses a consistent block naming convention, making it easier to identify the blocks you may want to override or extend, such as `extrahead` for additional head elements like CSS or JavaScript links, and `content` for the main page content.

To further customize the appearance and functionality of the admin forms, you can extend templates such as `admin/change_form.html` for the model change form. Here is an example that adds a custom JavaScript file to the model change form template:

```
1   {% extends "admin/change_form.html" %}
2
3   {% block extrahead %}
4     {{ block.super }}
5     <script type="text/javascript" src="{{ STATIC_URL }}js/my_custom_script.js"></
          script>
```

```
6  {% endblock %}
```

This approach allows developers to enhance the user interface and user experience of the Django admin without modifying the default admin files, ensuring that customizations are preserved across updates to the Django framework.

Extending admin templates provides a streamlined method for tailoring the Django admin interface. By leveraging Django's template inheritance and understanding the default template structure, developers can effectively customize and enhance the Django admin to meet specific project needs. Whether through minor aesthetic adjustments or significant functional extensions, the flexibility of Django's templating system supports a wide range of customization possibilities.

4.10 Django Admin Interface for Related Objects

Handling related objects in the Django admin interface is a critical aspect of leveraging Django's powerful ORM (Object-Relational Mapping) capabilities for efficient data management and representation. Django admin provides robust tools to display and interact with related objects, such as foreign keys and many-to-many relationships, directly within the admin interface. This section will discuss strategies for managing these relationships effectively, including inline model admin representations, custom formsets, and leveraging the 'select_related' and 'prefetch_related' methods for performance optimizations.

To begin with, Django admin allows the inclusion of related objects directly on the parent model's admin page using inlines. Inlines are a form of ModelAdmin which are nested inside a parent ModelAdmin and are extremely useful for editing models on the same page as a model that is related to them. For example, if one has a model 'Book' with a ForeignKey to 'Author', it's possible to edit the book information directly from the Author admin page. Here is a simple implementation using 'TabularInline':

```
1  from django.contrib import admin
2  from .models import Author, Book
3
4  class BookInline(admin.TabularInline):
5      model = Book
6      extra = 1
7
```

```
8   class AuthorAdmin(admin.ModelAdmin):
9       inlines = [BookInline,]
10
11  admin.site.register(Author, AuthorAdmin)
```

In the above example, 'BookInline' is a subclass of 'admin.TabularInline' which indicates that 'Book' objects should be displayed in a tabular form. The 'extra' field specifies how many empty new forms for related objects should be displayed.

For more complex scenarios involving multiple levels of nested inlines or custom form requirements, Django admin forms can be customized further by overriding the formset of the inline. However, one should exercise caution as deeply nested inlines can lead to significant performance degradation and a less user-friendly interface.

Optimizing queries for related objects is another crucial aspect of managing related objects in the Django admin. By default, Django generates a separate database query for each related object access, which can quickly become inefficient with numerous related objects. To mitigate this, Django offers the 'select_related' and 'prefetch_related' methods for forward foreign key and many-to-many fields respectively.

```
1   class AuthorAdmin(admin.ModelAdmin):
2       inlines = [BookInline,]
3       list_select_related = ['book',] # Assuming 'book' is a forward ForeignKey
4
5   class BookAdmin(admin.ModelAdmin):
6       list_filter = ['author',]
7       list_select_related = ['author',] # Optimizes ForeignKey access
```

However, it's important to use these methods judiciously as they increase the initial query size by including related objects, which can also impact performance negatively if not used correctly.

In addition to inline editing and query optimizations, Django admin supports customizing the display of related objects through specifying fields, fieldsets, list display, and list filters in the ModelAdmin. Custom actions and templates can also be employed to enhance the interface for related objects, providing a seamless and integrated experience for end-users.

For instance, custom admin actions can be defined to operate on selected related objects directly from the list display page. This is particularly useful for performing bulk updates or processing on related models without having to navigate away from the parent model's admin interface.

```
1   class BookAdmin(admin.ModelAdmin):
```

```
2    actions = ['mark_as_published']
3
4    def mark_as_published(self, request, queryset):
5        queryset.update(status='published')
6    mark_as_published.short_description = "Mark selected books as published"
```

In summary, managing related objects effectively in the Django admin interface significantly enhances the ease of data management and provides a more cohesive user experience. By utilizing inlines for direct editing, optimizing queries, and customizing the admin interface to fit the needs of related objects, developers can harness the full power of Django's admin capabilities for efficient and intuitive data administration. Mastery of these techniques is essential for developers looking to build sophisticated and performant web applications using Django.

4.11 Integrating Third-Party Tools with Django Admin

Integrating third-party tools with the Django admin interface can significantly enhance the functionality, usability, and appearance of an admin panel. These tools can range from visual enhancements, like advanced charting libraries, to functional utilities, such as import-export capabilities and rich text editors. This section will discuss how to incorporate such tools into the Django admin, focusing on the selection process, installation, configuration, and potential customizations.

Before integrating a third-party tool, it's crucial to assess its compatibility with your Django version, its maintenance status, and community support. A well-supported tool with active development is preferable, as it ensures long-term viability and access to updates and security fixes.

Selection Criteria: Choose tools that have comprehensive documentation and are widely used in the Django community. This eases the integration process and troubleshooting. Also, consider the tool's performance impact on the admin interface and its ability to scale with your application.

Upon selecting a third-party tool, the next step is installation, often done via pip, Python's package installer. For example, to integrate a popular Django-compatible charting library, you might execute:

```
pip install django-charting-library
```

Following installation, configuring the tool to work with your Django admin site typically involves adjustments to `settings.py` and `admin.py` files within your Django project. For instance, to enable a charting tool, you might add configuration settings in your `settings.py` file like so:

```
1  INSTALLED_APPS = [
2      ...
3      'django_charting_library',
4      ...
5  ]
```

And then customize your `admin.py` to utilize the library's features within the admin class definitions. For example, to display a chart based on a model's data, you might modify an admin class like this:

```
1   from django.contrib import admin
2   from .models import YourModel
3   from django_charting_library import Chart
4
5   @admin.register(YourModel)
6   class YourModelAdmin(admin.ModelAdmin):
7       def get_chart_data(self):
8           # Logic to fetch and aggregate data for the chart
9           return data
10
11      def changelist_view(self, request, extra_context=None):
12          extra_context = extra_context or {}
13          extra_context['chart'] = self.get_chart_data()
14          return super(YourModelAdmin, self).changelist_view(request, extra_context=
                 extra_context)
```

This example demonstrates altering the `changelist_view` to pass custom chart data to the admin template, illustrating the potential to expand the admin interface's capabilities significantly.

To ensure seamless integration, it might be necessary to extend or override admin templates. Django admin uses a templating system similar to Django's, where you can extend base templates and insert your custom content blocks. For a third-party tool that provides visual elements, you might need to override a template file to include necessary JavaScript and CSS files.

```
1   {% extends "admin/base_site.html" %}
2   {% block extrastyle %}
3   {{ block.super }}
4   <link rel="stylesheet" href="path_to_charting_library_css.css">
5   {% endblock %}
6
7   {% block extrahead %}
8   {{ block.super }}
9   <script src="path_to_charting_library_js.js"></script>
10  {% endblock %}
```

This approach allows integrating third-party JavaScript libraries and CSS frameworks into the Django admin, enhancing both functionality and aesthetics.

Finally, while integrating third-party tools can offer significant advantages, it's essential to consider security implications. Ensure that any added library does not introduce vulnerabilities into your application. Regularly review and update integrated tools to mitigate potential security risks.

In summary, the integration of third-party tools into the Django admin requires careful selection, installation, configuration, and potentially template customization. By following these steps, developers can significantly enhance the capabilities and user experience of the Django admin interface, making it a more powerful tool for managing application content.

4.12 Performance Optimization for the Django Admin Interface

Performance optimization for the Django Admin interface is crucial for ensuring that the admin site remains responsive and efficient, especially when handling large datasets. This section will discuss practical strategies to enhance performance by minimizing database queries, customizing list displays, implementing caching, and optimizing querysets.

To begin with, minimizing database queries is fundamental. The Django ORM is powerful but can inadvertently lead to inefficient database access patterns. One common scenario is the "N+1" queries problem, which occurs when fetching objects along with their related objects. To mitigate this, one should leverage the 'select_related' and 'prefetch_related' queryset methods. For instance:

```
1  from django.contrib import admin
2  from .models import Book
3
4  class BookAdmin(admin.ModelAdmin):
5      list_display = ['title', 'author_name']
6
7      def get_queryset(self, request):
8          return super().get_queryset(request).select_related('author')
9
10     def author_name(self, obj):
11         return obj.author.name
12  admin.site.register(Book, BookAdmin)
```

In the example above, 'select_related' is used to join the related 'Author' object to each 'Book', thus fetching all necessary data in a single database query, which significantly reduces the number of queries executed.

Customizing list displays is another critical area for performance tuning. By default, the Django admin loads all model fields in the list view. This behavior can lead to slow page loads if the model includes fields with large amounts of data or complex computations. To optimize this, carefully select the fields to display in the 'list_display' option, omitting heavy fields or those requiring complex calculations.

Further, implementing caching can substantially improve the performance of the Django admin interface. Django's cache framework can be used to cache entire views or parts of views as well as to cache the results of expensive queries. For admin pages that do not need real-time data, page caching can be applied:

```
from django.views.decorators.cache import cache_page

class MyModelAdmin(admin.ModelAdmin):

    def changelist_view(self, request, extra_context=None):
        @cache_page(60 * 15) # Cache for 15 minutes
        def view(request, *args, **kwargs):
            return super(MyModelAdmin, self).changelist_view(request, *args, **kwargs
                )
        return view(request)
```

Optimizing querysets directly impacts the performance of the Django admin. For models with a significant number of records, consider overriding the 'get_queryset' method in your ModelAdmin class to return a more optimized queryset. This approach can involve excluding fields that are not necessary for the admin view, using 'defer' to delay loading of certain fields until they are accessed, or even annotating querysets to add aggregated data that can be computed directly by the database.

For instance, after applying optimization techniques, the number of queries made to render a list page in the admin can often be reduced significantly, which is directly observable through Django's debugging toolbar or via logging.

Finally, when dealing with related objects, it's vital to think through how they are displayed and queried. Using 'list_select_related' for ForeignKey fields and defining a 'list_prefetch_related' method for many-to-many and reverse ForeignKey relationships can lessen the query load and thus improve the admin interface's performance.

Optimizing the performance of the Django Admin interface requires a blend of strategies focused on efficient database access, selective feature usage, and caching. By applying these practices diligently, developers can maintain a fast and responsive admin interface capable of handling large datasets with ease.

4.13 Advanced Techniques: Custom Admin Widgets and Form Fields

In this section, we will discuss how to further tailor the Django admin interface by implementing custom widgets and form fields. This capability significantly enhances the admin interface's usability and interactivity, providing a more intuitive and efficient experience for administrators managing site content.

Django's form widgets are the most critical components that determine how a form field should be rendered in the HTML interface, as well as how user input is collected and processed. By default, Django uses a standard set of widgets for displaying forms in the admin. However, projects with unique requirements may necessitate the creation of custom widgets.

To create a custom widget, you must inherit from an existing Django form widget or the base `Widget` class itself, then override certain attributes or methods to achieve the desired behavior. The primary method to override is `render`, which returns the HTML code for the widget. Additionally, custom JavaScript and CSS can be introduced to enhance the widget's functionality and aesthetics.

Consider a scenario where you need a more advanced text editor than the default textarea for entering rich text content. This example demonstrates creating a custom widget integrating a third-party JavaScript rich text editor, such as TinyMCE or CKEditor.

```
1  from django import forms
2  from django.conf import settings
3  from django.forms.widgets import Textarea
4
5  class RichTextEditorWidget(Textarea):
6      def __init__(self, attrs=None):
7          default_attrs = {'class': 'richtext-editor'}
8          if attrs:
9              default_attrs.update(attrs)
10         super().__init__(attrs=default_attrs)
11
12     def render(self, name, value, attrs=None, renderer=None):
13         rendered = super().render(name, value, attrs, renderer)
14         return f'{rendered}<script src="{settings.STATIC_URL}js/richtext_editor_init.
                js"></script>'
```

127

This example extends Textarea, adding a <script> tag to the widget's HTML output to include a JavaScript file that initializes the rich text editor functionality. The render method's customization injects additional HTML, ensuring the rich text editor JavaScript runs when the widget is loaded.

Beyond custom widgets, Django also allows the creation of custom form fields. These are particularly useful for handling specific data types not covered by Django's built-in field classes. To define a custom form field, inherit from forms.Field and provide implementations for to_python() and validate() methods, which convert the input to a Python data type and validate it, respectively.

```
1  from django import forms
2
3  class CustomDateField(forms.Field):
4      def to_python(self, value):
5          if not value:
6              return None
7          return parse_custom_date_format(value)
8
9      def validate(self, value):
10         super().validate(value)
11         # Add custom validation logic here
```

This custom field example introduces a CustomDateField for handling dates in a non-standard format, demonstrating the process of custom input parsing and validation within a Django form field.

In summary, creating custom widgets and form fields is a powerful mechanism for enhancing the user experience and functionality of the Django admin interface. By leveraging Django's form framework extensibility, developers can craft bespoke solutions that tightly align with the project's needs, vastly improving the management capabilities provided by the Django admin.

4.14 Deploying and Monitoring the Django Admin Interface

Deploying the Django admin interface involves a series of steps designed to ensure that the application is available and performs optimally in a production environment. Monitoring is an ongoing process that ensures the application continues to meet performance benchmarks and security standards after deployment. This section discusses the key aspects of deploying and monitoring the Django admin interface, focusing on ensuring security, performance, and reliability.

Deployment Considerations

When deploying the Django admin interface, security is paramount. The admin interface provides access to the entirety of the application's data, making it a critical part of the application to secure.

- **Use HTTPS:** Ensure that the admin interface is served over HTTPS to encrypt data in transit. This can be facilitated through Django settings by setting SECURE_SSL_REDIRECT to True and configuring SECURE_HSTS_SECONDS appropriately for enforcing HTTP Strict Transport Security (HSTS).

- **Limit Access:** Restrict access to the admin interface by IP addresses or through Virtual Private Networks (VPNs) to reduce the attack surface.

- **Two-Factor Authentication (2FA):** Implementing 2FA adds an additional layer of security, ensuring that users are authenticated through two different means.

Performance Optimization

The performance of the Django admin interface in a production environment can significantly impact user experience. Some strategies for optimization include:

- **Database Indexing:** Ensure that all fields used in list filters, searches, and ordering in the admin are indexed appropriately in the database, which will speed up query times.

- **Query Optimization:** The Django ORM makes it easy to accidentally produce queries that can slow down the admin interface. Use Django's select_related and prefetch_related query optimizations for foreign key or many-to-many relationships to reduce the number of database queries.

- **Caching:** Implement caching strategies for data that do not change often. Django's cache framework can be used to cache entire pages or parts of the admin interface, reducing database query load.

Monitoring Strategies

Effective monitoring of the Django admin interface post-deployment can provide insights into its performance, security, and usage patterns. Key components to monitor include:

- **Error Tracking and Logs:** Use tools like Sentry or Logstash to monitor and analyze errors and warnings. Django's logging framework can be configured to capture a wide range of events within the admin interface.

- **Performance Monitoring:** Tools such as New Relic or Datadog can provide real-time analysis of application performance, helping in identifying bottlenecks or potential areas of improvement.

- **Access and Activity Auditing:** Keeping a log of user activities and access patterns in the admin interface can help in detecting unauthorized access attempts or malicious activity early. Django packages such as django-simple-history or django-admin-logs can assist in implementing activity logging.

Continuous Integration and Deployment (CI/CD)

Implementing CI/CD pipelines can streamline the process of deploying updates to the Django admin interface. Automating testing and deployment ensures that changes are rigorously tested and deployed consistently. Key considerations include:

- Automated testing should cover security, functionality, and performance aspects of the admin interface.

- Deployment scripts should include steps for applying migrations, collecting static files, and conducting post-deployment checks to ensure the admin interface is operational.

Deploying and monitoring the Django admin interface require careful planning and execution to ensure security, performance, and reliability. By following the strategies outlined in this section, developers can create a robust environment for managing application data through the Django admin interface, ensuring that it remains a powerful and efficient tool for application administration in a production setting.

4.15 Best Practices for Django Admin Customization

In dealing with Django Admin customization, adopting best practices is crucial for developing a reliable, maintainable, and efficient admin interface. This section will discuss the strategies and guidelines that enhance the Django admin's functionality and user experience while ensuring the security and performance of the application.

Stick to Simplicity: While the Django admin is highly customizable, it's important to resist the temptation to over-customize. Begin with the built-in features that Django admin offers and only add customizations that are truly necessary for your project. This approach ensures that the admin interface remains user-friendly and maintainable.

Use Groups and Permissions Wisely: Django admin supports a robust permission and group system that helps in managing user access effectively. Always assign permissions and group memberships thoughtfully to ensure that users have access only to the sections of the admin they need. This not only enhances security but also prevents the admin interface from becoming cluttered for users.

Optimize Models for Admin: When registering models with the admin site, optimize them by specifying `list_display`, `list_filter`, and `search_fields`. This optimization improves the usability of managing entries in the admin by providing filters, search capabilities, and customized column displays.

```
1  from django.contrib import admin
2  from .models import MyModel
3
4  @admin.register(MyModel)
5  class MyModelAdmin(admin.ModelAdmin):
6      list_display = ['field1', 'field2']
7      list_filter = ['field1']
8      search_fields = ['field1', 'field2']
```

Form Customization for Data Integrity: Utilizing Django's form customization capabilities in the admin can help in maintaining data integrity. Creating custom forms for your models ensures that data validation is in place before data is saved, thus reducing the chances of corrupt or invalid data.

Leverage Django Admin Documentations: The Django documentation is an extensive resource that provides in-depth information on every aspect of admin customization. Regularly consulting the Django documentation can provide you with insights into more efficient ways of customization and help you stay updated on any changes to admin functionality.

Secure Your Admin Interface: Always change the default URL of the admin interface to obscure it from automated attacks. Implement SSL to secure the data transmission between the client and the server. Use Django's built-in features for securing the admin interface, such as enforcing strong passwords and using two-factor authentication for admin users.

Benchmark and Optimize Performance: For projects with a large volume of data or a high number of admin users, performance optimization becomes vital. Use Django's database profiling tools to identify slow queries and optimize them. Implement caching for static content and consider using a dedicated database for the admin interface if the load is significant.

Implement Custom Actions with Caution: Adding custom actions to the admin site can greatly enhance productivity. However, ensure that these actions are well tested and do not inadvertently affect the integrity of your data. Always provide confirmation prompts for actions that cannot be easily undone.

```
1   from django.contrib import admin
2
3   def make_published(modeladmin, request, queryset):
4       queryset.update(status='p')
5   make_published.short_description = "Mark selected stories as published"
6
7   class ArticleAdmin(admin.ModelAdmin):
8       actions = [make_published]
```

Testing Admin Customization: Regularly test your admin customizations to ensure they work as expected across different user roles and permissions. Automated tests can be very helpful in ensuring that your customizations do not break existing functionality.

Keep Your Customizations Maintainable: Organize your customization code into separate modules or applications. This modular approach makes your customizations easier to understand, maintain, and update. Additionally, document your customizations thoroughly to assist future development efforts.

Effectively customizing the Django admin interface entails a balanced approach that considers user convenience, security, and performance. By adhering to these best practices, developers can leverage the power of Django admin to create robust, efficient, and user-friendly interfaces for content management.

Chapter 5

Views and URL routing in Django

Django's views and URL routing system is foundational in defining how web applications respond to user requests. Simplifying the connection between URLs and Python callback functions, this framework offers a logical structure for web page creation and manipulation. The chapter will cover the implementation of both function-based and class-based views, effective URL design, and advanced techniques for rendering dynamic content. It aims to provide a thorough understanding of Django's request-response cycle, enabling the development of clean, maintainable, and efficient web applications.

5.1   An Overview of Views in Django

Let's start with the fundamental concept of views in Django. At its core, a view in Django is a Python function or class that takes a web request and returns a web response. This response could be the HTML contents of a webpage, a redirect, a 404 error, JSON, XML, or any other format. Views serve as a bridge between the models and templates in a Django application, fetching data from the database through models, processing it, and passing it to templates to be displayed to the user.

In the design of Django, views are placed under the application's views.py file, although they can also be organized in different modules if needed. Django's convenience allows for two distinct types of views: function-based views (FBVs) and class-based views (CBVs). Each has its advantages, use cases, and syntax.

```
from django.http import HttpResponse

def my_view(request):
    # View logic here
    return HttpResponse('Hello, World!')
```

The above code snippet demonstrates a basic example of a function-based view, where my_view is a simple view that returns a response containing "Hello, World!". This illustrates the simplicity with which views can be defined and returned in Django.

Class-based views, on the other hand, leverage Python's class system to encapsulate view functionality. They allow for reuse of common patterns and facilitate extending and customizing view behavior through inheritance.

```
from django.views import View
from django.http import HttpResponse

class MyView(View):
    def get(self, request):
        # View logic here
        return HttpResponse('Hello, World!')
```

This code snippet is an example of a class-based view, specifically demonstrating how to handle GET requests. CBVs offer a structured approach to view design, employing different methods for different HTTP methods (GET, POST, etc.), which promotes cleaner design and separation of concerns.

URL routing in Django is designed to map incoming requests to views based on a set of patterns. This mapping is defined in the application's urls.py file (or files) using Django's urlpatterns list. Entry in this list is a call to django.urls.path() function, which ties a URL pattern to a view, and optionally can name the route for easy reference throughout your project.

```
from django.urls import path
from .views import my_view

urlpatterns = [
    path('hello/', my_view, name='hello-world-view'),
]
```

This mapping directs any request to `yourhost/hello/` URL to the `my_view` view, demonstrating the linkage between a URL and a view function in Django. Through the URL configurations, Django facilitates the creation of SEO-friendly and readable URLs, which is a step towards creating user-friendly web applications.

The flexibility of Django's view architecture lies in its ability to support a wide range of response types and to handle complex data processing. From rendering templates filled with context data to processing forms and performing database operations, views can cater to various needs. Moreover, Django provides a set of generic class-based views for common patterns, such as displaying a list of objects or a detail page for a single object, further abstracting common web development patterns to expedite the development process.

Views are also the right place to enforce permissions and view-level access control, ensuring users can only perform actions they're authorized to. Django offers utilities and decorators like `@login_required` and permissions in class-based views to simplify this process.

Views in Django are a powerful and flexible mechanism for responding to user requests. Whether employing function-based views for simpler cases or leveraging the advanced features of class-based views, Django developers have a robust toolkit for web application development at their disposal.

5.2 Understanding URL Configuration and Routing

Django's URL configuration and routing system is a core component that maps URLs to the corresponding view functions responsible for returning the HttpResponse. This essential feature allows Django to serve different content to the user based on the URL path accessed. The concept is simple: a URL pattern is defined, and when a request matches this pattern, Django invokes the associated view function, passing an HttpRequest object as the first parameter and any values captured in the pattern as additional arguments.

The URL configuration is primarily defined in a module named `urls.py`, which is conventionally located at the project or application level. This module contains a list of URL patterns represented by instances of django.urls.path() or django.urls.re_path(), the latter providing regex pattern support. It is important to appreciate the hierarchical nature of Django's URL configuration. The root URLconf file is designated in the project's settings via the ROOT_URLCONF setting, typically pointing to the project's urls.py file. From there, URLs can delegate to other URLconfs in a tree-like structure, allowing for modular and scalable URL systems.

A critical part of defining URL patterns is the use of view functions. These functions take in a request object and return an HttpResponse object. The association between a URL pattern and a view is established in the urls.py file using the path() function, which takes at least two arguments: a route string and a view function. Optionally, one can also name the route, facilitating reverse URL matching throughout the project, enhancing maintainability and reducing hard-coding of URLs.

For example, to link a URL path to a view, one might use the following code snippet:

```
from django.urls import path
from . import views

urlpatterns = [
    path('articles/', views.article_list, name='article_list'),
]
```

In this example, a request to /articles/ will be routed to the article_list view in the application's views module. This pattern matching is case-sensitive and, by default, does not consider GET and POST parameters, focusing solely on the URL path.

Advanced URL routing is feasible with re_path(), which allows for regular expression patterns, offering finer control over URL pattern matching. This is particularly useful when the simplicity of path() is insufficient. For instance:

```
from django.urls import re_path
from . import views

urlpatterns = [
    re_path(r'^articles/(?P<year>[0-9]{4})/$', views.year_archive),
]
```

Here, the year_archive view will be invoked for URLs matching the pattern, capturing a four-digit year in the URL and passing it as a keyword argument to the view function.

Django's URL routing system also provides mechanisms for namespace partitioning of URLs, enabling the reuse of application names in different instances, thereby avoiding URL name collisions in larger projects. This is achieved using the include() function, allowing the inclusion of other URLconf modules into the root URL configurations. When utilizing namespaces, it's possible to refer to URLs unambiguously, which is crucial for projects comprising multiple apps.

```
1  from django.urls import include, path
2
3  urlpatterns = [
4      path('blog/', include('blog.urls', namespace='blog')),
5  ]
```

In this pattern, all URL patterns defined in the blog.urls module will be prefixed with /blog/, and they can be uniquely identified using the specified namespace.

Django's URL dispatcher is designed with performance in mind, lazily evaluating URL patterns to minimize startup time and memory consumption. This means that URL patterns are not compiled until the first request that necessitates their resolution is received.

Understanding and effectively leveraging Django's URL configuration and routing system is fundamental for developers aiming to build maintainable, scalable web applications. Proper URL design not only aids in creating a logically structured application but also enhances user experience by enabling clean, descriptive URLs that are search engine friendly. As we proceed to discuss the implementation of views in the next sections, a solid grasp of URL routing will be indispensable for connecting these views to the web application's interface.

5.3 Writing Function-Based Views

Function-based views in Django provide a straightforward way to write web application views by using simple Python functions. Each view function accepts an HttpRequest object as its first parameter, typically named request, and returns an HttpResponse object.

To begin creating a function-based view, import the HttpResponse class from the django.http module. Then, define a function that takes at least one parameter, the request object. The simplest form of a function-based view sends a basic HTTP response containing a string, as illustrated in the following example:

```
1  from django.http import HttpResponse
2
3  def welcome(request):
```

```
4      return HttpResponse("Welcome to Django!")
```

This code defines a view called welcome that returns a simple greeting message embedded within an HttpResponse object.

Next, it is essential to connect this view to a URL to make it accessible via a web browser. This connection is done in the URL configuration file, typically named urls.py. The Django URL dispatcher matches incoming requests against various URL patterns and directs them to the associated view functions. To link the welcome view function to a URL pattern, modify the urls.py file as follows:

```
1  from django.urls import path
2  from .views import welcome # Import the view function
3
4  urlpatterns = [
5      path('', welcome, name='welcome'),
6  ]
```

The path function creates a URL pattern. In this case, an empty string ('') specifies the root URL, and the second argument is the view function welcome, which gets called when the root URL is visited.

To render templates instead of returning plain text, import the render function from django.shortcuts. The render function combines a given template with a given context dictionary and returns an HttpResponse object with that rendered text. Below is a modified version of the welcome view that renders a template:

```
1  from django.shortcuts import render
2
3  def welcome(request):
4      return render(request, 'welcome.html', {'message': 'Welcome to Django!'})
```

In this example, render takes three arguments: the request object, the path to the template file (welcome.html), and a context dictionary that contains data to populate the template. The context dictionary here passes a message to the template, which can dynamically insert this message into the HTML content.

Handling GET and POST requests within function-based views helps in managing forms and user input. A common practice is to check the request object's method to differentiate between GET and POST requests as follows:

```
1  def form_view(request):
2      if request.method == 'POST':
3          # Process the form submission
4          pass
5      else:
```

140

```
6        # Display the form
7        pass
```

This form_view function checks if the method of the request is 'POST' to determine if the form has been submitted. If it is, the function processes the form data. If the request method is not 'POST' (typically 'GET'), it displays the form to the user.

Function-based views offer a simple and flexible method to define how web applications process requests and generate responses. By following the patterns outlined in this section—importing HttpResponse, defining a function that takes a request and returns an HttpResponse, and connecting the view function to a URL—developers can implement a wide range of application functionalities in Django. Additionally, utilizing template rendering and handling GET and POST requests within these views enables the creation of dynamic web pages and the management of user interactions efficiently.

5.4 Class-Based Views: An Introduction

Class-based views in Django offer a structured approach to handle HTTP requests and responses. Unlike function-based views which map views to URLs through functions, class-based views encapsulate view behavior within classes. This approach enhances code reusability and maintainability, making it easier to extend and customize web applications.

The Django framework provides a variety of generic class-based views that cover common web development tasks, such as displaying a list of objects or handling a form submission. By subclassing these generic views and overriding certain methods or attributes, developers can implement custom behavior without writing boilerplate code.

Creating a Simple Class-Based View

Let's start with an example of a simple class-based view that displays a page:

```
1   from django.http import HttpResponse
2   from django.views import View
3
4   class MyView(View):
5       def get(self, request):
```

141

```
6    # Return an HttpResponse with the rendered text
7    return HttpResponse('Hello, this is a class-based view')
```

To connect this view to a URL, Django uses a slightly different syntax compared to function-based views. Here is how to map the view to a URL in your urls.py:

```
1    from django.urls import path
2    from .views import MyView
3
4    urlpatterns = [
5        path('class-based-view/', MyView.as_view(), name='myview'),
6    ]
```

The as_view() class method converts the class into an actual view function that Django can use in the URLconf.

Understanding View Methods and Attributes

In class-based views, HTTP methods are handled by class methods named after the lowercase HTTP methods, such as get, post, put, delete, etc.

When a request is made, Django looks for a method within the view class that corresponds to the HTTP method of the request. For instance, if a request is a GET request, Django will search for a get() method within the class.

You can also define class attributes to customize the behavior of the view. For example, the template_name attribute allows you to specify a template to render for the view.

```
1    from django.shortcuts import render
2    from django.views.generic import TemplateView
3
4    class HomePageView(TemplateView):
5        template_name = 'home.html'
6
7        def get_context_data(self, **kwargs):
8            context = super().get_context_data(**kwargs)
9            context['latest_articles'] = Article.objects.all()[:5]
10           return context
```

In this example, HomePageView inherits from TemplateView, a generic view provided by Django for rendering templates. The get_context_data method is overridden to add extra context to the template, making it easy to pass variables to the template.

142

Mixins and Multiple Inheritance

One of the powerful features of class-based views is the ability to compose functionality through mixins. A mixin is a class that provides method implementations to be shared among multiple classes. Django includes a variety of mixins for common tasks, such as form handling and list rendering.

Class-based views in Django can inherit from multiple classes, allowing them to combine functionalities from different mixins. This feature follows the principle of "composition over inheritance," facilitating more flexible and maintainable code.

```
1  from django.contrib.auth.mixins import LoginRequiredMixin
2  from django.views.generic import ListView
3  from .models import ProtectedResource
4
5  class ProtectedResourceListView(LoginRequiredMixin, ListView):
6      model = ProtectedResource
7      context_object_name = 'protected_resources'
```

In the above example, ProtectedResourceListView combines LoginRequiredMixin and ListView. This results in a view that lists items of ProtectedResource, but only if the user is authenticated.

Class-based views provide a structured and modular approach to developing web applications in Django. Through inheritance and mixins, they allow for easy extension and customization, significantly reducing the amount of code required to implement common web patterns. Properly leveraging class-based views not only makes your Django projects more maintainable but also enables cleaner, more efficient development workflows.

5.5 Advanced Class-Based Views: Customizing and Extending

Class-based views in Django offer a highly reusable and extendable approach for handling web page requests. Once familiar with the basic class-based views, you can leverage Django's flexibility to tailor these views to your specific needs. This section delves into customizing and extending class-based views to manage complex web application requirements effectively.

Customizing existing views involves overriding certain methods or attributes to alter the default behavior. Django's class-based views are designed with this flexibility in mind, allowing developers to implement custom functionality with minimal code changes. For instance, the ListView and DetailView are two commonly used views that can be easily customized to suit different scenarios.

To begin customization, consider specifying attributes such as template_name or context_object_name in your view. The template_name attribute allows you to define a custom template for rendering the view, while context_object_name lets you specify a custom name for the context variable in the template. These adjustments can improve the readability and maintainability of your templates.

```
1  from django.views.generic import ListView
2  from .models import Book
3
4  class BookListView(ListView):
5      model = Book
6      template_name = 'books/book_list.html'
7      context_object_name = 'book_list'
```

Further customization can be achieved by overriding view methods. The get_queryset method, for instance, can be overridden to modify the default queryset. This is particularly useful for filtering results based on certain criteria, such as user preferences or permissions.

```
1  class BookListView(ListView):
2      model = Book
3
4      def get_queryset(self):
5          return Book.objects.filter(author=self.request.user)
```

Extending class-based views involves creating new views by inheriting from Django's generic views or other custom views. This technique allows for the reuse of common view logic, reducing code duplication. In practice, you might create a base view with shared functionality and then extend this base view for different models or purposes.

For example, suppose you have several models where you need to implement CRUD (Create, Read, Update, Delete) functionality. You can create a generic base view for handling common CRUD operations and then extend this base view for each specific model.

```
1  from django.views.generic import TemplateView
2
3  class CRUDBaseView(TemplateView):
4      model = None
5
```

```
6    def get_object(self, queryset=None):
7        obj = self.model.objects.get(pk=self.kwargs.get('pk'))
8        return obj
```

This base view could then be extended for different models by specifying the model attribute.

```
1    class BookCRUDView(CRUDBaseView):
2        model = Book
```

Customizing and extending class-based views in Django offers a powerful mechanism for handling a wide array of web application requirements. By understanding how to effectively utilize these techniques, developers can write less code, improve code readability, and enhance the maintainability of their Django applications. However, it is essential to be mindful of the inherent complexity that can arise from extensively customized or deeply nested inheritance hierarchies. Proper documentation and adherence to Django's best practices are crucial for avoiding future codebase complications.

5.6   Using Generic Views for Common Patterns

Django's generic views were developed to solve common problems and patterns in web development by providing ready-to-use solutions. These abstract views aim to reduce the amount of code developers need to write for performing routine tasks such as displaying a list of objects or handling forms. This section discusses the use of generic views in Django, particularly focusing on ListView, DetailView, CreateView, UpdateView, and DeleteView. The implementation of these views simplifies the execution of common web development patterns, enhancing the efficiency and maintainability of your code.

ListView and DetailView are used for displaying objects. ListView displays a collection of objects, while DetailView displays a detailed page for a type of object.

```
1    from django.views.generic import ListView, DetailView
2    from .models import MyModel
3
4    class MyModelListView(ListView):
5        model = MyModel
6        context_object_name = 'my_model_list'
7        template_name = 'myapp/my_model_list.html'
8
9    class MyModelDetailView(DetailView):
```

```
10      model = MyModel
11      context_object_name = 'my_model'
12      template_name = 'myapp/my_model_detail.html'
```

These snippets demonstrate the simplicity of creating views to display all instances of 'MyModel' and a detailed view for a specific instance. By subclassing 'ListView' and 'DetailView', the majority of the boilerplate code is abstracted away, adhering to the DRY (Don't Repeat Yourself) principle.

For handling forms, Django offers CreateView and UpdateView for creating and updating objects, respectively, along with DeleteView for deleting objects.

```
1   from django.views.generic.edit import CreateView, UpdateView, DeleteView
2   from django.urls import reverse_lazy
3   from .models import MyModel
4
5   class MyModelCreateView(CreateView):
6       model = MyModel
7       fields = ['field1', 'field2']
8       template_name = 'myapp/my_model_form.html'
9       success_url = reverse_lazy('my_model_list')
10
11  class MyModelUpdateView(UpdateView):
12      model = MyModel
13      fields = ['field1', 'field2']
14      template_name = 'myapp/my_model_form.html'
15      success_url = reverse_lazy('my_model_list')
16
17  class MyModelDeleteView(DeleteView):
18      model = MyModel
19      context_object_name = 'my_model'
20      template_name = 'myapp/my_model_confirm_delete.html'
21      success_url = reverse_lazy('my_model_list')
```

The generic views for creating, updating, and deleting are particularly powerful as they encapsulate the form handling logic, including displaying a form for input, validating submitted data, and redirecting upon successful form submission. This eliminates a significant amount of repetitive code.

Implementing AJAX calls in Django views enhances the user experience by allowing for asynchronous operations. AJAX calls in Django can be handled using both function-based views and class-based views. However, special attention must be paid to CSRF (Cross-Site Request Forgery) tokens to ensure security.

When it comes to managing permissions and user authentication in views, Django offers a robust system of decorators and mixins. For instance, the 'LoginRequiredMixin' can be used in class-based views to ensure that only authenticated users can access certain views.

```
1   from django.contrib.auth.mixins import LoginRequiredMixin
2
3   class MyProtectedView(LoginRequiredMixin, ListView):
4       model = MyModel
5       template_name = 'myapp/protected_list.html'
```

This example illustrates how the 'LoginRequiredMixin' mixin can be easily added to a view to protect it from unauthorized access.

In addition to these generic views, Django provides mechanisms for handling HTTP methods and status codes efficiently. The 'require_http_methods' decorator in function-based views and the 'http_method_names' attribute in class-based views facilitate this management. Custom error views for handling 404 and 500 errors can also be implemented to provide a better user experience during website navigation errors.

To optimize the performance of Django views, developers can leverage techniques such as query optimization, caching, and asynchronously executing long-running tasks. Properly optimized views contribute significantly to the responsiveness and scalability of web applications.

Integrating third-party applications into Django views can extend the functionality of your web applications. This integration often involves using API calls within your views or leveraging Django apps developed by the community.

Testing views is crucial for ensuring that your web application behaves as expected. Django's testing framework provides tools for unit testing and integration testing your views. Through the creation of test cases, developers can simulate requests to views and assert responses, effectively validating the application's behavior in various scenarios.

Debugging common issues with Django views involves understanding the error messages, using logging strategically, and employing Django's debugging tools such as the Django Debug Toolbar. Familiarity with these tools and techniques enables developers to quickly identify and resolve issues in their Django applications.

Django's generic views offer a powerful means to abstract common web development patterns, significantly reducing development time and boosting code maintainability. By understanding and effectively implementing these views, developers can create robust and efficient web applications with minimal boilerplate code.

5.7   Managing Forms with Class-Based Views

Class-based views in Django provide an object-oriented mechanism for handling not just HTTP requests, but also for managing forms. They encapsulate the form handling logic within classes, allowing for cleaner and more reusable code. This section will discuss how to use Django's class-based views to handle forms, both simple and complex.

Firstly, to manage a form using a class-based view, one typically leverages Django's `FormView` class. `FormView` extends the basic `View` class and is specifically designed to handle web forms. A basic implementation involves subclassing `FormView` and specifying the form class and a success URL.

```
from django.views.generic.edit import FormView
from django.urls import reverse_lazy
from .forms import ExampleForm

class ExampleFormView(FormView):
    template_name = 'example_form.html'
    form_class = ExampleForm
    success_url = reverse_lazy('success_view')

    def form_valid(self, form):
        # Process form data
        return super().form_valid(form)
```

In the above example, `template_name` specifies the template to render the form, `form_class` is the form to be managed, and `success_url` defines where to redirect the user upon successful form submission. The `form_valid` method is overridden to provide custom processing of form data.

For more complex forms, especially those involving relationships between models, Django's `CreateView` and `UpdateView` can be used. These views automatically handle form instantiation, saving, and redirection upon success. They are particularly useful for forms associated with creating or updating database records.

```
from django.views.generic.edit import CreateView
from .models import ExampleModel

class ExampleCreateView(CreateView):
    model = ExampleModel
    fields = ['field1', 'field2']
    success_url = reverse_lazy('success_view')
```

Here, the `CreateView` is used to create an instance of `ExampleModel`. The `fields` attribute specifies which model fields should be included

148

in the form. Upon form submission, Django automatically saves the model instance.

To manage formsets or more complex form interactions, overriding the get_context_data method becomes useful. This allows adding additional forms or context to the template.

```
1  def get_context_data(self, **kwargs):
2      context = super().get_context_data(**kwargs)
3      if 'formset' not in context:
4          context['formset'] = ExampleFormset()
5      return context
```

In handling user authentication and permissions with forms, Django's LoginRequiredMixin and PermissionRequiredMixin can be mixed into the class-based views. This ensures that only authenticated users or users with specific permissions can access the form view.

```
1  from django.contrib.auth.mixins import LoginRequiredMixin
2
3  class SecureExampleFormView(LoginRequiredMixin, FormView):
4      # View implementation
```

Managing forms with class-based views in Django not only standardizes form handling across different views but also significantly reduces the amount of boilerplate code. By leveraging FormView, CreateView, and UpdateView, along with Django's authentication and permission mixins, developers can create robust, secure, and maintainable form handling mechanisms within their web applications.

5.8 Implementing Ajax Calls with Django Views

Asynchronous JavaScript and XML (Ajax) has revolutionized the way web applications interact with servers. By using Ajax, web pages can asynchronously request data from the server and update themselves without the need to reload the entire page. This section will discuss the implementation of Ajax calls within Django views, which is critical for developing responsive web applications that provide a seamless user experience.

The first step in incorporating Ajax into Django is to define a view that will handle the asynchronous request. In Django, both function-based and class-based views can be used for this purpose. However, for the sake of simplicity, we will focus on function-based views.

149

Consider a scenario where we need to fetch user details asynchronously. We will start by creating a simple function-based view that returns user details in JSON format:

```
1   from django.http import JsonResponse
2   from django.views.decorators.http import require_http_methods
3   from .models import User
4
5   @require_http_methods(["GET"])
6   def fetch_user_details(request, user_id):
7       user_details = {}
8
9       try:
10          user = User.objects.get(pk=user_id)
11          user_details = {'name': user.name, 'email': user.email}
12      except User.DoesNotExist:
13          user_details = {'error': 'User not found'}
14
15      return JsonResponse(user_details)
```

In the code above, the `@require_http_methods` decorator is used to ensure that the view only handles GET requests. The `JsonResponse` object is then used to return user details in JSON format, which is easily interpretable by JavaScript on the client side.

Next, the URL routing needs to be configured to point to the newly created view. In the application's `urls.py` file, an entry is added as follows:

```
1   from django.urls import path
2   from .views import fetch_user_details
3
4   urlpatterns = [
5       path('ajax/user/<int:user_id>/', fetch_user_details, name='fetch_user_details'),
6   ]
```

With the server-side setup complete, the next step involves implementing the Ajax call on the client side using JavaScript. jQuery, a widely used JavaScript library, simplifies the process of making Ajax calls. Below is an example of how to fetch user details using jQuery:

```
1   <script>
2   $(document).ready(function(){
3       $("#fetchDetailsButton").click(function(){
4           var userId = $("#userId").val(); // Assuming an input field for user ID
5           $.ajax({
6               url: `/ajax/user/${userId}/`,
7               type: "GET",
8               dataType: "json",
9               success: function(data) {
10                  if(data.error){
11                      alert('User not found');
12                  }else{
13                      $("#userName").text(data.name); // Displaying the user name
14                      $("#userEmail").text(data.email); // Displaying the email
```

```
15        }
16      },
17      error: function(xhr, status, error) {
18          console.error("An error occurred: " + error);
19      }
20    });
21  });
22 });
23 </script>
```

In this JavaScript snippet, an Ajax GET request is sent to the /ajax/user/<user_id>/ URL upon clicking a button with the id #fetchDetailsButton. The returned JSON is then used to update HTML elements with the ids #userName and #userEmail to display the user's name and email, respectively.

However, when implementing Ajax in Django, one must also consider security implications, especially Cross-Site Request Forgery (CSRF) attacks. Django provides a CSRF token for protection against such attacks, which must be included in Ajax POST requests:

```
1 $.ajax({
2    url: `/ajax/user/${userId}/`,
3    type: "POST",
4    data: {
5        csrfmiddlewaretoken: $('input[name=csrfmiddlewaretoken]').val(),
6        // other data
7    },
8    // Additional AJAX setup
9 });
```

Furthermore, it is recommended to handle exceptions and return appropriate HTTP status codes from the server-side view. This enhances the robustness of the Ajax implementation and facilitates better error handling on the client side.

```
{"status": "error", "code": 404, "message": "User not found"}
```

By adhering to the above guidelines and examples, one can effectively implement Ajax calls within Django views. This not only improves the responsiveness and interactivity of web applications but also leverages Django's powerful backend capabilities to handle and serve asynchronous requests efficiently.

151

5.9   Securing Views: Permissions and User Authentication

Securing views within a Django application involves implementing mechanisms that ensure only authorized users can access certain parts of an application. This encompasses both permissions, which determine what an authenticated user is allowed to do, and authentication, which verifies the identity of a user. Django provides a robust system for managing these aspects, offering both simplicity and flexibility for developers.

Authentication in Django is handled by the framework's `django.contrib.auth` module, which is designed to authenticate users and attach their identities to requests. This module enables the straightforward creation of login and logout functionalities. For instance, the following code snippet shows how to use Django's built-in `LoginView` and `LogoutView` within an application's URL configuration:

```
1  from django.urls import path
2  from django.contrib.auth.views import LoginView, LogoutView
3
4  urlpatterns = [
5      path('login/', LoginView.as_view(), name='login'),
6      path('logout/', LogoutView.as_view(), name='logout'),
7  ]
```

The authentication system is also closely linked with Django's session framework, which keeps track of session data through cookies and the database, providing a seamless experience for users across requests.

Permission management in Django is achieved through the use of decorators and mixins that can be applied to views. These tools offer a granular level of control, allowing permissions to be set at the level of individual views or globally across a site. For function-based views, the `@login_required` decorator is a straightforward means to restrict access:

```
1  from django.contrib.auth.decorators import login_required
2
3  @login_required
4  def my_view(request):
5      # View code here
```

For class-based views, Django provides the `LoginRequiredMixin`, which can be used as a superclass to enforce that the user must be authenticated to access the view:

```
1   from django.contrib.auth.mixins import LoginRequiredMixin
2   from django.views.generic import View
3
4   class MyView(LoginRequiredMixin, View):
5       # View code here
```

Beyond simple authentication checks, Django supports more sophisticated permission schemes, such as assigning permissions to groups or individual users and creating custom permissions for models. Incorporating these permissions into views can be accomplished with the @permission_required decorator for function-based views and the PermissionRequiredMixin for class-based views.

For situations requiring fine-tuned control or handling of permissions not directly related to model instances, Django allows for the development of custom decorators and mixins. This custom logic can be integrated into the authentication and permissions system, offering a highly adaptable solution for complex requirements.

Django's user authentication and permissions system is thus a powerful tool for securing views. Its components integrate seamlessly to control access and protect sensitive parts of an application. By leveraging these built-in functionalities, developers can create secure, robust, and user-friendly web applications.

One critical aspect often overlooked is the role of secure handling of passwords and user sessions. Django's authentication system uses industry-standard practices for password handling, including hashing and salting of passwords. It's essential for developers to adhere to Django's guidelines when managing user authentication data to prevent security vulnerabilities.

Implementing AJAX calls within secured views adds another layer of complexity. Care must be taken to ensure that AJAX requests are also subject to authentication and permissions checks. This often involves passing the necessary CSRF tokens and managing session data in AJAX requests to maintain security.

Securing views within Django is a multifaceted endeavor, encompassing user authentication, permissions management, secure data handling, and more. By using Django's built-in functionalities and adhering to best practices, developers can effectively protect their applications from unauthorized access and ensure a safe experience for users.

5.10 Handling HTTP Methods and Status Codes

In this section, we will discuss how Django views handle HTTP methods and the significance of HTTP status codes. A deep understanding of these components is vital for developing robust and interactive web applications. Django, being a high-level Python web framework, provides a comprehensive system for managing HTTP requests and responses, which are the backbone of web communication.

When developing web applications, it is fundamental to differentiate between the different types of HTTP requests. The most common methods are GET and POST. However, HTTP supports several other methods, such as PUT, DELETE, PATCH, HEAD, and OPTIONS, each serving a distinct purpose in web communication. Django views facilitate the handling of these HTTP methods, enabling developers to define specific behaviors for each.

GET requests are used to request data from a specified resource, whereas POST requests are used to submit data to be processed to a specified resource. To handle these methods in Django views, one can use the `request.method` attribute, which contains a string representing the HTTP method used in the request.

Consider the following example of a function-based view that differentiates between GET and POST requests:

```
from django.http import HttpResponse

def my_view(request):
    if request.method == 'GET':
        # handle GET request
        return HttpResponse('This is a GET request')
    elif request.method == 'POST':
        # handle POST request
        return HttpResponse('This is a POST request')
```

For class-based views, Django provides the `http_method_names` attribute and the `as_view()` method for greater control over which HTTP methods a view should handle. The framework also offers the `View` class from which one can inherit to override methods like `get()` and `post()` to handle GET and POST requests, respectively.

Regarding HTTP status codes, they are essential for indicating the result of the request's processing. Status codes are grouped into five

154

classes: Informational responses (100–199), Successful responses (200–299), Redirection messages (300–399), Client error responses (400–499), and Server error responses (500–599).

Django simplifies the use of HTTP status codes through its HttpResponse class and subclasses like JsonResponse and HttpResponseRedirect. For instance, to return a 404 Not Found status code, Django provides the Http404 exception which can be raised in a view to indicate that a resource is not found.

```
from django.http import Http404

def my_view(request, id):
    try:
        # Attempt to fetch the resource
    except Resource.DoesNotExist:
        raise Http404("Resource not found")
```

Moreover, Django encourages the use of its generic views and mixins, such as the TemplateView and CreateView, which handle common patterns including those involving HTTP methods and status codes, enhancing development efficiency.

Understanding how to properly handle HTTP methods and status codes in Django views is paramount for creating interactive and user-friendly web applications. By leveraging Django's built-in mechanisms for dealing with these aspects of web communication, developers can construct more reliable, scalable, and maintainable web applications.

5.11 Custom Error Views: Handling 404 and 500 Errors

Handling errors effectively is crucial for maintaining the reliability and user-friendliness of web applications. Django provides a robust framework for managing HTTP errors, such as 404 (Not Found) and 500 (Internal Server Error), through custom views. This section outlines the process of customizing error views to improve the user experience and facilitate easier debugging during the development process.

A 404 error occurs when a user requests a webpage that does not exist on the server, either because it has been deleted or the user mistyped the URL. On the other hand, a 500 error indicates a server-side problem, such as a programming error, which prevents the server from fulfilling the request.

155

Customizing the 404 Error View

To customize the 404 error view in Django, you can create a template named 404.html and place it in the top-level `templates` directory of your project. Django will automatically use this template for 404 errors if it exists.

```
<!DOCTYPE html>
<html>
<head>
    <title>Page Not Found</title>
</head>
<body>
    <h1>404: Page Not Found</h1>
    <p>We're sorry, but the page you requested could not be found. Please check the
        URL and try again.</p>
</body>
</html>
```

This simple HTML template provides a user-friendly message to visitors encountering a 404 error. It is essential that the message guide users back to a working part of the site, such as including a link to the home page.

Customizing the 500 Error View

Customizing the 500 error view is similar to the 404 view, but with a focus on minimizing the risk of further errors. The template should be named 500.html and also placed in the `templates` directory.

Since a 500 error indicates a server-side issue, the template should be as simple as possible to avoid triggering additional errors. It is advisable not to include database queries or complex logic in this template.

```
<!DOCTYPE html>
<html>
<head>
    <title>Internal Server Error</title>
</head>
<body>
    <h1>500: Internal Server Error</h1>
    <p>We're experiencing some technical issues. Please try again later.</p>
</body>
</html>
```

Testing Custom Error Pages

To ensure that the custom error pages work as expected, you can test them by intentionally triggering errors in your local development environment.

For a 404 error, you can visit a URL that does not correspond to any patterns in your URL configuration. Django's development server should display your custom 404 template.

Testing a 500 error requires temporarily introducing an error in your code, such as dividing by zero in a view function. Remember to set DEBUG to False in your settings.py file, as Django does not use custom 500 templates when DEBUG is True.

```
1  # views.py
2
3  from django.http import HttpResponse
4
5  def test_error(request):
6      # Intentionally trigger a division by zero error
7      division_by_zero = 1 / 0
8      return HttpResponse("This should never be displayed.")
```

After verifying that your custom templates work correctly, ensure to remove any intentional errors and set DEBUG back to True if you're still in development.

Custom error pages offer a more graceful way to handle inevitable errors in web applications, improving user experience and potentially providing better information to the development team when errors occur. By utilizing Django's support for custom error views, developers can maintain the aesthetic consistency of their applications and provide helpful guidance to users when something goes wrong.

5.12 Optimizing Django Views Performance

Optimizing the performance of Django views is pivotal for enhancing the responsiveness and scalability of web applications. Performance optimizations can significantly improve the user experience and resource utilization, ensuring that applications can handle higher loads with lower latency. In this section, we will discuss various strategies for optimizing Django views, including database query optimization, caching strategies, and code efficiency improvements.

One of the most effective ways to improve the performance of Django views is to optimize database queries. Django's Object-Relational Mapping (ORM) makes it easy to interact with the database using Python code, but inefficient queries can lead to significant performance bottlenecks. To address this, it is crucial to use Django's query optimization tools effectively. For example, the `select_related` and `prefetch_related` methods can be used to reduce the number of database queries by preloading related objects in a single query. Additionally, the `only` and `defer` methods allow for loading only the necessary fields of a model, which can reduce memory usage and improve query execution time.

```
# Example of optimizing queries with select_related
posts = Post.objects.select_related('author').all()

# Example of reducing fields loaded with only
posts = Post.objects.only('title', 'summary')
```

Caching is another powerful technique for optimizing Django views. By storing the results of expensive operations, such as database queries or complex calculations, in a cache, subsequent requests can be served much faster since the computation or query does not need to be performed again. Django provides a robust caching framework that supports various backends, such as Memcached and Redis. Careful use of caching can dramatically improve the performance of Django views, especially for data that does not change frequently.

```
from django.views.decorators.cache import cache_page

@cache_page(60 * 15) # Cache this view for 15 minutes
def my_view(request):
    # View code here
```

Code efficiency is also critical for optimizing Django views. This involves writing clean, well-structured code that avoids unnecessary computations and utilizes Python's efficient data structures and algorithms. Profiling tools, such as Django's built-in 'silk' and 'django-debug-toolbar', can be invaluable for identifying slow code paths and inefficiently executed queries. Refactoring views to eliminate redundant operations, using list comprehensions instead of looping constructs where appropriate, and minimizing the use of heavy libraries in views can all contribute to improved performance.

```
django-debug-toolbar output showing slow queries and execution time
```

Managing HTTP methods and status codes efficiently is an often-overlooked aspect of optimizing Django views. Properly handling

GET, POST, PUT, and DELETE requests and returning appropriate status codes not only aligns with RESTful principles but also enables efficient client-side caching and error handling. For example, ensuring that GET requests are idempotent and leveraging HTTP caching directives can reduce server load and improve response times.

Finally, as an application grows, it becomes important to consider the structure and organization of views. Splitting views into smaller, reusable components, using Django's class-based views for common patterns, and abstracting business logic away from view functions can make the application more maintainable and easier to optimize.

```
1  from django.views.generic import ListView
2  from .models import Post
3
4  class PostListView(ListView):
5      model = Post
6      template_name = 'posts/list.html'
```

Optimizing Django views involves a multi-faceted approach focusing on efficient database queries, effective caching, code efficiency, proper HTTP method handling, and the strategic organization of views. By applying these strategies judiciously, developers can build Django applications that are faster, more scalable, and deliver a better user experience. Continuous performance monitoring and testing should accompany these efforts to ensure that optimizations are effective and do not introduce regressions or new bottlenecks.

5.13   Integrating Third-Party Applications into Django Views

Integrating third-party applications into Django views is a common requirement for extending the functionality of Django projects without reinventing the wheel. This process involves leveraging existing Django apps or external libraries, which can provide pre-built solutions for complex functionalities such as user authentication, social media integration, or payment processing. The successful integration of these applications requires an understanding of Django's settings, the third-party library's configuration, and Django's view and URL routing system.

To integrate a third-party application into your Django project, start by installing the required package using a package manager like pip.

For example, to integrate a social authentication application, you might execute a command similar to:

```
pip install django-allauth
```

After installation, add the application to the INSTALLED_APPS setting in your Django project's settings.py file. This step is essential for Django to include the application's configurations, models, and templates:

```
INSTALLED_APPS = [
    ...
    'django.contrib.sites',
    'allauth',
    'allauth.account',
    'allauth.socialaccount',
    ...
]
```

Following this, configure the application-specific settings as required. Many third-party Django applications will have a list of settings to be added or modified in your settings.py file. For example, you might need to specify callback URLs, API keys, or other preferences:

```
SITE_ID = 1
SOCIALACCOUNT_PROVIDERS = {
    'google': {
        'SCOPE': [
            'profile',
            'email',
        ],
        'AUTH_PARAMS': {
            'access_type': 'online',
        }
    }
}
```

Next, include the third-party application's URLs in your project's URL configuration. This step typically requires updating the urls.py file of your project or application to include the third-party application's URL patterns. You can do this using Django's include function:

```
1  from django.urls import path, include
2
3  urlpatterns = [
4      ...
5      path('accounts/', include('allauth.urls')),
6      ...
7  ]
```

This step integrates the third-party application's views into your Django project, making them accessible via the specified path.

160

Finally, integrate functionality into your views or templates as needed. Depending on the application, you might need to modify your views to use functionalities provided by the third-party app, or adjust your templates to include specific template tags or filters. For instance, integrating social media login buttons might require adding the following in your template:

```
1  {% load socialaccount %}
2  {% providers_media_js %}
```

This line loads the necessary JavaScript for rendering social login buttons, leveraging the template tags provided by the `django-allauth` application.

Integrating third-party applications into Django views allows for the extension of functionality in an efficient manner. By understanding the process of installation, configuration, URL inclusion, and the modification of views or templates, developers can seamlessly enhance their Django projects. This approach not only saves development time but also ensures that projects can leverage well-tested and community-supported solutions.

5.14 Testing Views: Unit Tests and Integration Tests

Testing views in Django is essential for ensuring that web applications behave as expected. This process typically involves both unit tests and integration tests, each serving distinct purposes. Unit tests focus on individual components in isolation, allowing developers to pinpoint specific areas of failure. Meanwhile, integration tests evaluate the cooperation between multiple components, providing insight into the system's overall functionality. In this section, we will discuss methods for effectively testing both function-based and class-based views, using Django's built-in testing tools alongside third-party libraries where applicable.

Unit tests for Django views concentrate on verifying the logic inside views, including the context data passed to templates and the HTTP responses returned. To accomplish this, Django offers a `TestCase` class from its `django.test` module. A simple unit test for a function-based view might look as follows:

```
1  from django.test import TestCase
```

```
2    from django.urls import reverse
3
4    class TestMyView(TestCase):
5        def test_view_response(self):
6            response = self.client.get(reverse('my_view_name'))
7            self.assertEqual(response.status_code, 200)
8            self.assertContains(response, 'Expected content in response')
```

This test checks that the view responds with a 200 HTTP status code and contains expected content. The reverse function is used to dynamically fetch the URL of the view by its name, reducing the need for hard-coded URLs in tests.

For class-based views, the testing approach remains similar, though you might need to test additional elements specific to class-based features, such as mixins or overridden methods. It is beneficial to verify the proper functioning of get, post, and other HTTP methods if they are implemented in the view.

Integration tests in Django aim to evaluate how well different parts of the application work together, such as views interacting with models, middleware, and templates. A more complex integration test could simulate user actions, like submitting a form through a view and verifying the correct redirect or database update:

```
1    from django.urls import reverse
2    from django.test import TestCase
3    from .models import MyModel
4
5    class TestMyModelView(TestCase):
6        def test_form_submission(self):
7            response = self.client.post(reverse('my_model_create_view'), {'field': '
                 value'})
8            self.assertEqual(response.status_code, 302)
9            self.assertTrue(MyModel.objects.exists())
```

This integration test posts data to a view responsible for creating MyModel instances and verifies whether the model instance was successfully created and if the response correctly indicates a redirect action by checking the status code 302.

While Django's testing framework is robust, integrating with third-party libraries like Factory Boy for generating model instances or selenium for browser-based tests can further enhance testing effectiveness. These tools facilitate more complex test scenarios that closely mimic user interactions with the application.

Regardless of the testing approach, the objective remains to cover as much of the codebase as possible with tests that validate both expected outcomes and handle exceptional cases gracefully. This includes testing for adequate security measures in views, such as permissions checks and data validation, to ensure that the application is resilient against unauthorized access and malicious input.

Comprehensive testing of Django views is paramount for the stability and security of web applications. By employing a mix of unit and integration tests, developers can achieve high confidence in their code's functionality and maintainability. Effective testing strategies lead to an accelerated development process, reduced debugging time, and improved application quality, which together contribute significantly to the project's success.

5.15 Debugging Common Issues with Django Views

Debugging common issues within Django views involves not just understanding the error messages but also the context in which these errors occur. This section will provide an in-depth analysis of frequent problems encountered when working with Django views and offer solutions to effectively resolve them.

One prevalent issue developers face is the 'NoReverseMatch' error. This error occurs when Django cannot find a view name or a URL pattern that matches a given argument. Typically, this error arises from misconfigured URL patterns in the urls.py file. To resolve this, ensure that the name passed to the reverse() function or the { % url %} template tag matches the name of a URL pattern in your URL configuration.

```
1  # Example of a URL pattern in urls.py
2  path('articles/<int:year>/', views.year_archive, name='article-year-archive')
```

Another common problem is the 'TemplateDoesNotExist' error. This error indicates that Django is unable to locate a template file specified in a view. This problem can often be resolved by ensuring that the template's name and path correctly correspond to the location within your templates directory. Also, verify that your settings file is properly configured to include the directories of your templates using the TEMPLATES configuration.

When dealing with class-based views, a typical issue is inadvertently omitting the as_view() method when defining URL patterns. Class-based views must be converted into actual view functions by calling as_view():

```
1  # Correct way to use a class-based view in urls.py
2  path('about/', views.AboutView.as_view(), name='about')
```

Developers might also encounter difficulties with form submission and handling within class-based views. Common manifestations of this issue include forms not validating or not saving correctly. It is crucial to properly implement the form_valid() and form_invalid() methods in your view classes. Additionally, ensuring the view's post method correctly processes the form data is essential for resolving these issues.

```
1  # Example of form handling in a class-based view
2  def form_valid(self, form):
3      form.save()
4      return super().form_valid(form)
```

Implementing Ajax calls in Django views presents its own set of challenges, often related to CSRF token management or correctly responding with JSON data. Ensure that your Ajax request passes the CSRF token and that the view returns a JsonResponse with the appropriate content type.

```
1  # Example of a view handling an Ajax request
2  from django.http import JsonResponse
3
4  def my_view(request):
5      data = {'success': True}
6      return JsonResponse(data)
```

Another aspect that necessitates attention is managing permissions and user authentication within views. Incorrect handling can lead to unauthorized access or broken user experiences. Utilize Django's built-in decorators and mixins, such as login_required and PermissionRequiredMixin, to streamline permission checks and secure your views against unauthorized access.

Handling HTTP methods and status codes effectively is essential for RESTful design and user feedback. Make use of Django's HttpRequest.method attribute to distinguish between GET, POST, and other HTTP methods within your views, and return appropriate HttpResponse status codes to inform the client of the outcome of their request.

Additionally, optimizing performance of Django views is crucial for a responsive user experience. Issues such as slow database queries or inefficient code can significantly impact performance. Use Django's query optimization techniques, like select_related() and prefetch_related(), and consider caching strategies to improve response times.

Finally, when errors occur, providing user-friendly error messages is imperative. Customize the `handler404` and `handler500` views in your URL configuration to display custom error templates instead of the default Django error pages.

Debugging views in Django effectively requires a methodical approach, attention to detail, and a deep understanding of the Django framework. By identifying the common issues outlined above and implementing the recommended solutions, developers can enhance the reliability, security, and performance of their Django applications.

Chapter 6

Templates and Static Files in Django

Django's template system offers a powerful yet straightforward way to custom-generate HTML dynamically, enabling the separation of presentation from business logic. Alongside handling static files, such as CSS, JavaScript, and images, it forms the cornerstone of Django's front-end capabilities. This chapter discusses setting up the template engine, template inheritance, custom tags and filters, and efficiently managing static files. By mastering these components, developers can create rich, interactive, and cohesive user interfaces that seamlessly integrate with Django's backend architecture.

6.1 Introduction to Django Templates

Django templates are a key component in the development of web applications using the Django framework. They provide a flexible mechanism for generating HTML dynamically, enabling the separation of presentation from business logic. This is crucial for maintaining clean code architecture and facilitating collaborative work between developers and designers. Templates are not only limited to HTML but can also be used for generating other text-based formats.

The Django template engine is both powerful and intuitive, designed to emphasize readability and ease of use. It operates by interpolating variables and evaluating expressions within a template, which is then rendered to produce the final HTML output. This process involves a few fundamental concepts which are essential for effective template design and utilization in Django projects.

First, templates in Django are composed of static parts and dynamic content. The static parts are the HTML (or other text formats) that do not change, while the dynamic content is generated from the context data passed to the template by a view. This separation allows for the dynamic generation of web pages based on the context provided, enabling personalized content delivery and interactive web experiences.

Regarding the syntax, Django templates use a simple language that includes variables, tags, and filters. Variables are enclosed in double curly braces {{}} and represent values passed into the template by the view. For instance, {{ variable_name }} in a template would be replaced by the value of variable_name from the context. Tags, on the other hand, are enclosed in {% % } and provide logic in templates. They can perform loops, conditionals, and other control structures within the template. Filters allow for the formatting of variable values and are used with a pipe symbol |. For example, {{ name|capitalize }} would capitalize the value of the name variable before rendering it in the template.

A significant advantage of Django templates is template inheritance, which promotes reuse and consistency across web pages. With this feature, templates can "inherit" from a base template, allowing developers to define a common structure for web pages and override or extend specific blocks of content as required. This simplifies the management of site-wide layouts and ensures a uniform user interface.

Moreover, Django's template system is pluggable, allowing for the use of custom template backends. This provides the flexibility to choose or build a template engine that best suits the project's needs if Django's built-in template engine does not meet specific requirements.

In summary, Django templates play a critical role in the development of dynamic web applications by offering a robust and user-friendly system for generating HTML. Understanding the template syntax, including variables, tags, filters, and inheritance, is fundamental for effectively building web interfaces in Django. Additionally, the pluggable nature of the template system offers flexibility in selecting or designing a template engine tailored to the project's demands. By mastering Django templates, developers can efficiently separate presentation from business logic, streamlining the web development process and facilitating collaboration.

6.2 Setting Up Django Template Engine

Let's start with the configuration of the Django template engine, which represents a crucial initial step in harnessing Django's capabilities for generating dynamic HTML content. The template engine is a fundamental part of Django's architecture, providing developers with a powerful tool for creating flexible web pages. To set up the template engine effectively, understanding the settings that govern its behavior is essential.

In the settings.py file of a Django project, the TEMPLATES setting plays a central role. This setting is a list of configurations, one for each template engine to be used. Django comes with a built-in engine, but additional engines can be specified if needed. The default configuration for the Django template engine usually looks something similar to the following code:

```
TEMPLATES = [
    {
        'BACKEND': 'django.template.backends.django.DjangoTemplates',
        'DIRS': [],
        'APP_DIRS': True,
        'OPTIONS': {
            'context_processors': [
                'django.template.context_processors.debug',
                'django.template.context_processors.request',
                'django.contrib.auth.context_processors.auth',
                'django.contrib.messages.context_processors.messages',
            ],
        },
    },
]
```

Each key within the dictionary specifies a different aspect of the template engine's behavior:

- 'BACKEND' denotes the template engine to be used. For the Django template engine, this is
  'django.template.backends.django.DjangoTemplates'.

- 'DIRS' is a list of filesystem directories to be searched for templates when they are not found in app directories. This is empty by default but can be configured to include paths to custom templates.

- `'APP_DIRS'` when set to True, enables the engine to look for templates within the `'templates'` subdirectories of installed applications. This convention is recommended for ease of template organization.

- `'OPTIONS'` contains a dictionary of options to be passed to the engine and its templates. One important set of options is `'context_processors'`, a list of dot-separated Python paths to functions that add variables to the context.

Context processors are a critical feature, as they dynamically add context variables available in all templates. For instance, the `'django.template.context_processors.debug'` context processor adds a boolean `'debug'` variable to the context, indicating whether the debug mode is on.

After configuring the TEMPLATES setting, ensuring that your project's INSTALLED_APPS include `'django.contrib.staticfiles'` is also necessary. This inclusion is critical for managing static files, which will be discussed in more detail in subsequent sections.

In addition to the TEMPLATES setting, modifying the STATIC_URL and STATIC_ROOT in the settings.py file helps manage static files such as CSS, JavaScript, and images. These settings define the URL to access static files and the filesystem path where they are collected, respectively.

With these configurations in place, the Django template engine is ready to be used. The next step involves creating templates, which are discussed in the following sections. By understanding and applying the settings described, developers can take full advantage of Django's powerful templating capabilities to create dynamic, efficient, and maintainable web applications.

6.3   Template Syntax: Variables, Tags, and Filters

Django's template language is designed with the principle of ease of use for front-end developers who may not have in-depth programming knowledge. The syntax is deliberately simplistic and mimics traditional HTML to a considerable extent, with some additions to cater to dynamic content generation. In this section, we will discuss the core components of Django's template syntax: variables, tags, and filters, which are instrumental for injecting dynamic data into static HTML pages.

A Django template receives a `context` dictionary from a view, in which keys are names accessible in the template and values are the corresponding data. This mechanism allows a separation of presentation from business logic, adhering to the Model-View-Template (MVT) architectural pattern on which Django is based.

Variables in Django templates are identified by double curly braces `{{ }}`. When the template engine encounters a variable, it evaluates that variable and replaces it with its value in the context. Consider the following example:

```
1  <p>Welcome, {{ user.name }}!</p>
```

In this case, `user.name` refers to the `name` attribute of a `user` object passed in the context. If `user.name` is "John Doe", the output will be:

```
<p>Welcome, John Doe!</p>
```

Tags serve as the programming logic within templates, controlling structures and behaviors, such as loops and conditionals, and are wrapped in `{% %}`. For instance, to iterate over a list of items:

```
1  \begin{itemize}
2  \{\% for item in item\_list \%}
3     \item {{ item }}
4  \{\% endfor \%}
5  \end{itemize}
```

This code snippet will generate a bulleted list of items present in `item_list`. Tags can also perform more complex logic, such as loading external template code with the `{% include %}` tag or extending base templates with the `{% extends %}` tag, facilitating reuse across templates.

Filters modify the appearance of variables and can be applied using the pipe symbol `|`. Filters can transform text, perform operations on dates, numbers, and lists, among other tasks. An example usage is the date filter, which formats Python `datetime` objects:

```
1  \{\{ publish_date|date:"D, d M Y" \}\}
```

This will format a `publish_date` variable to a string like "Wednesday, 4 Jul 2021". Filters can be chained, with the output of one filter being passed as input to the next.

171

Additionally, developers have the freedom to define custom filters and tags. Custom filters are particularly useful for tasks that are specific to the application's domain. They are defined in a Django app inside a module named `templatetags`, allowing them to be loaded and used in templates similar to built-in tags and filters.

Comprehending the interplay between variables, tags, and filters is crucial for dynamic content rendering in Django templates. By applying these components, developers can create highly interactive and dynamically generated web pages, enhancing the overall user experience. It is essential to adhere to best practices, such as escaping user-generated content to prevent injection attacks, which will be discussed further in the subsequent sections.

6.4   Working with Template Inheritance

Template inheritance is a foundational concept in Django's template system that promotes reusability and maintainability of code. This principle allows a base template to define a structure which other templates can inherit and override specific parts as needed. The mechanism is akin to class inheritance in object-oriented programming but applied to templates, facilitating a DRY (Don't Repeat Yourself) approach to writing HTML.

To implement template inheritance, Django uses a two-step process: defining a base template and creating child templates that extend the base template.

The base template, often referred to as the "parent" template, contains the overall HTML structure along with blocks that child templates can override. These blocks are placeholders indicating areas of the template that are dynamic or subject to change.

Begin by defining a base template, typically named `base.html`, with the following structure:

```
1   <!DOCTYPE html>
2   <html>
3   <head>
4       <title>{% block title %}My Website{% endblock %}</title>
5   </head>
6   <body>
7       <header>
8           {% block header %}Header content{% endblock %}
9       </header>
10      <main>
11          {% block content %}Main content goes here{% endblock %}
```

```
12    </main>
13    <footer>
14        {% block footer %}Footer content{% endblock %}
15    </footer>
16 </body>
17 </html>
```

In this base template, four blocks are defined: `title`, `header`, `content`, and `footer`. These blocks can be overridden by child templates to introduce specific content in these sections.

To extend this base template, a child template is created that begins with the `{% extends "base.html" %}` tag. This tells Django that the current template is a child template that inherits from `base.html`. Within the child template, the `{% block %}` tags are used to override the corresponding blocks in the parent template.

For instance, to customize the content area of the website, a child template named `home.html` might look like this:

```
1 {% extends "base.html" %}
2
3 {% block title %}Home Page{% endblock %}
4
5 {% block content %}
6     <h1>Welcome to My Website</h1>
7     <p>This is the home page.</p>
8 {% endblock %}
```

In this child template, the `title` and `content` blocks are overridden, replacing the default content specified in the base template. The `header` and `footer` blocks, not being overridden, will inherit the content from the base template when the child template is rendered.

Template inheritance dramatically simplifies the management of common structural elements across a website. By centralizing these elements in a base template, any changes to the layout or elements shared across multiple pages need only be made once, in the base template. This efficiency significantly reduces the potential for error and ensures consistency throughout the website.

In addition, Django's template inheritance allows for a flexible, hierarchical system of templates. Child templates can themselves be extended, allowing for a multi-level inheritance structure. This permits the creation of highly modular and reusable templates, catering to complex website architectures while maintaining clarity and simplicity in template design.

Leveraging template inheritance in Django applications streamlines the development process, ensuring a clean separation of content and presentation. It fosters the creation of maintainable and scalable websites, optimizing the developer's workflow and enhancing the end-user experience.

6.5 Creating Custom Template Tags and Filters

Django's template system supports a wide variety of built-in tags and filters, designed to address general functionalities required in template development. However, there are instances where the default set may not suffice for specific application needs. This gap can be filled by creating custom template tags and filters, allowing developers to extend the template system's capabilities tailored to their unique requirements.

Custom template tags and filters are implemented within a Django application by creating a Python module named `templatetags` within the application directory. This module is not created by default and must be manually added. It requires an __init__.py file to be recognized as a Python package, and the actual custom tags and filters are defined in one or more Python files within this module.

To begin, let's start by creating a simple custom filter. Custom filters are functions that take one or two arguments: the value the filter is applied to and an optional argument. They return a value that can be outputted to the template. Here is an example of a custom filter that multiplies an input value by a specified factor:

```
1   from django import template
2
3   register = template.Library()
4
5   @register.filter(name='multiply')
6   def multiply(value, arg):
7       try:
8           return value * arg
9       except (ValueError, TypeError):
10          return ''
```

In this example, the custom filter named `multiply` is implemented. It attempts to multiply the input `value` by the `arg` parameter. In case of an error, such as if the input values cannot be multiplied, it gracefully returns an empty string, thus avoiding template rendering errors.

174

Moving on to custom template tags, there are several types, including simple tags, inclusion tags, and assignment tags, each serving different purposes. A simple tag processes data and returns a string, an inclusion tag renders another template with context data, and assignment tags set a variable in the context.

To illustrate a simple tag, consider a tag that sets a current timestamp in the template:

```
1  from django import template
2  from django.utils.timezone import now
3
4  register = template.Library()
5
6  @register.simple_tag
7  def current_time(format_string):
8      return now().strftime(format_string)
```

This tag, `current_time`, takes a format string and returns the current timestamp as a string formatted according to the given format. It uses Django's timezone-aware now to ensure that the time is correctly handled according to the project's timezone settings.

Both custom tags and filters must be loaded into the template using the {% load %} tag before they can be used. Assuming the module containing these custom elements is named my_tags, they can be loaded as shown below:

```
1  {% load my_tags %}
```

After loading, the custom filter and tag can be utilized in the template as follows:

```
1  {{ 2|multiply:3 }} {# Outputs '6' #}
2
3  {% current_time "%Y-%m-%d %H:%M" %}
```

Note that the use of custom template tags and filters can significantly enhance the dynamic nature of Django templates. However, it's crucial to ensure they are designed with performance considerations in mind. Complex tags or filters that perform database queries or intensive computations may lead to performance bottlenecks if used extensively in templates. Therefore, it is advisable to use these tools judiciously and optimize their implementations.

Creating custom template tags and filters enriches the functionality of Django templates, enabling developers to perform specific operations that are not covered by the built-in tags and filters. By following the established patterns for creating and registering these custom extensions, developers can maintain a clear separation of concerns between presentation logic and business logic, adhering to Django's design principles.

6.6 Managing Static Files: Setup and Configuration

Managing static files, such as CSS, JavaScript, and images, is integral to developing web applications with Django. Static files are essential for styling, adding interactivity, and enhancing the user experience of web applications. This section covers setting up and configuring static files in Django, ensuring they are efficiently served in both development and production environments.

To begin, Django's handling of static files is governed by several settings in the settings.py file of your project. The most notable settings include STATIC_URL, STATIC_ROOT, and STATICFILES_DIRS.

- STATIC_URL specifies the URL to use when referring to static files located in STATIC_ROOT or using the static template tag.

- STATIC_ROOT is the directory where static files will be collected to when using the collectstatic command. It is mainly used in production to serve static files efficiently.

- STATICFILES_DIRS is a list of filesystem directories where Django will search for additional static files, in addition to the static directory of each application.

The configuration begins with defining the STATIC_URL in the settings.py file. This defines the URL pattern that will serve the static files. For example:

```
1  STATIC_URL = '/static/'
```

This setting tells Django that static files will be accessible from URLs that start with /static/.

Next, configuring the STATIC_ROOT setting is essential for deploying your application to a production environment. This setting defines the single directory on your filesystem where you will collect all static files. Here's an example configuration:

```
1  STATIC_ROOT = os.path.join(BASE_DIR, 'staticfiles')
```

This configuration indicates that all static files from all apps and extra directories specified in STATICFILES_DIRS will be collected into the staticfiles directory at the base of your project when you run the collectstatic command. Running this command is a necessary step before deploying your project to production, as it gathers all static files into STATIC_ROOT.

For local development, Django's development server automatically serves static files found in each application's static folder and any directories specified in STATICFILES_DIRS. However, in production, you will need to configure your web server (e.g., Nginx, Apache) to serve the static files from the STATIC_ROOT directory. This is not managed by Django and requires separate web server configuration.

The STATICFILES_DIRS setting enables the specification of additional directories to look for static files, beyond the default app/static/ directory. This is particularly useful when you have common static files that are used across different applications. Here's how to add a global static directory:

```
1  STATICFILES_DIRS = [
2      os.path.join(BASE_DIR, "global_static"),
3  ]
```

After configuring these settings, you can use the { % static % } template tag to include static files in your templates. This template tag generates the URL for static files based on the configured STATIC_URL:

```
1  <link rel="stylesheet" href="{% static 'css/style.css' %}">
```

Here, 'css/style.css' refers to a file located in one of the directories specified by STATICFILES_DIRS or inside an application's static directory. The { % static % } template tag generates the full URL based on the STATIC_URL setting.

Properly managing static files in Django involves configuring the STATIC_URL, STATIC_ROOT, and STATICFILES_DIRS settings in settings.py. By understanding and effectively utilizing these settings, developers can ensure their Django applications serve static files efficiently in both development and production environments.

6.7 Using Static and Media Files in Templates

Handling static files, like CSS, JavaScript, and images, and media files, which are typically uploaded by users, is a crucial part of web development that affects the performance, scalability, and user experience of a website. In Django, static and media files are managed differently due to their nature and usage. This section will focus on effectively using these files within Django templates to create responsive, engaging, and efficient web interfaces.

To begin with, Django distinguishes between 'static files' and 'media files'. Static files are those that do not change, such as CSS files, JavaScript files, and static images. Media files are content that users upload, like user profile pictures and documents. For handling these files, Django provides 'django.contrib.staticfiles' and configurations in 'settings.py' to manage file paths and storage.

The handling of static files in templates requires the '

```
1  {% load static %}
2  <link rel="stylesheet" type="text/css" href="{% static 'css/style.css' %}">
```

For media files, the approach is slightly different since these files come from the 'MEDIA_ROOT' directory defined in 'settings.py'. Django does not provide a template tag as it does for static files because media files are associated with models. Therefore, to include a media file in a template, one typically access it through the model instance. Assuming we have a 'UserProfile' model with an 'ImageField' named 'avatar', displaying the user's avatar in a template would look like this:

```
1  <img src="{{ user.profile.avatar.url }}" alt="User's avatar">
```

Here, 'user.profile.avatar.url' dynamically fetches the URL of the avatar image associated with a user profile instance. It is important to configure your URLs to serve media files during development by modifying the 'urlpatterns' in your 'urls.py' file. This typically involves importing 'settings' and 'static' from 'django.conf' and 'django.conf.urls' respectively, and then appending a call to 'static' with the appropriate arguments to 'urlpatterns' when 'DEBUG' is 'True':

```
1  from django.conf import settings
2  from django.conf.urls.static import static
3
4  # Your existing urlpatterns
5  urlpatterns = [
6      ...
7  ] + static(settings.MEDIA_URL, document_root=settings.MEDIA_ROOT)
```

Securing static and media files is also an aspect that should not be over-looked. For static files, permissions can largely be managed through the web server configuration. For media files, especially if they contain sensitive information or user-generated content, implementing proper access control in Django views is essential to prevent unauthorized access.

Optimizing the delivery of static and media files can significantly improve your web application's load time. Techniques such as using a Content Delivery Network (CDN), compressing files, and setting appropriate cache headers can be used to enhance the performance of your Django application.

In summary, Django provides a robust system for managing static and media files in templates. By understanding the proper techniques and best practices for their usage, developers can create more interactive, fast, and secure web applications. The integration of these files requires careful consideration, particularly when dealing with user-uploaded content, to ensure both functionality and security.

6.8 Template Context Processors

Context processors in Django are a versatile feature that allow developers to inject additional data into the context of every template without manually adding the data in each view function or class. Essentially, they enable global variables across all templates, which can be exceedingly useful for functionalities that need to be accessible site-wide, such as user authentication details, site settings, or common navigation elements.

A template context processor is a Python function that takes one argument, the HTTP request object, and returns a dictionary of items to be merged into the template context. It is important to emphasize that each entry in the returned dictionary becomes a template variable, available to every template rendered using Django's templating system.

Configuring Template Context Processors

To leverage template context processors in a Django project, it is imperative to configure them properly in the settings.py file of the Django project. Django provides several built-in context processors for tasks like handling static files, internationalization, and accessing the request's user. These can be found under the TEMPLATES setting, inside the OPTIONS dictionary's context_processors list. Adding a custom context processor involves defining its path in this list as a string.

```
TEMPLATES = [
    {
        ...
        'OPTIONS': {
            'context_processors': [
                ...
                'django.template.context_processors.static',
                'django.template.context_processors.request',
                'myapp.context_processors.custom_processor',
            ]
        },
    },
]
```

Here, 'myapp.context_processors.custom_processor' is a path to a custom context processor, which follows the "dot" notation from Python import syntax, pointing to a custom_processor function defined in the context_processors.py file of the application myapp.

Writing a Custom Template Context Processor

Creating a custom context processor entails defining a function that accepts the request object and returns a dictionary. The key aspect to ensure effectiveness is that this function does something useful with either the request object or other sources of data and adds this data to the context. For illustration, a simple context processor that adds a site-wide message could look like this:

```
def custom_processor(request):
    return {'site_wide_message': 'Welcome to our website!'}
```

This function can then be utilized by adding its path to the context_processors list in the settings.py, as previously described. Consequently, the variable site_wide_message will be accessible in all templates, allowing for the display of this welcome message without explicitly passing it through every view.

Security Considerations

While template context processors offer a powerful mechanism for efficiently passing common data to templates, they also introduce potential risks, especially related to security. It is critical to ensure that sensitive information is not inadvertently exposed to all templates, as any data added to the context is globally accessible. Always validate and sanitize the data being passed to the context to prevent cross-site scripting (XSS) and other injection attacks.

Performance Implications

Another consideration when using template context processors is their impact on performance. Since the function runs for every request that uses Django's template system, unnecessary complex operations can add significant overhead. It is advisable to keep the logic in context processors as lean as possible and utilize caching for data that does not change frequently.

In summary, template context processors in Django provide a highly efficient method to make data universally available across templates, which, when used judiciously, can significantly streamline the development of complex web applications. Through careful configuration, creation, and usage, they empower developers to maintain a clear separation of concerns between the presentation layer and the business logic, further enhancing the robustness and maintainability of Django projects.

6.9 Using Third-Party Template Tags and Filters

Third-party template tags and filters extend Django's native templating capabilities by integrating additional functionalities derived from external libraries or packages. These extensions can significantly enhance the flexibility and robustness of Django templates, enabling developers to implement complex logic and formatting without cluttering the template code with Python code or creating numerous custom tags and filters.

To begin utilizing third-party template tags and filters, one must first install the desired extension package via a package manager such as pip. Following the package installation, the module containing the template tags and filters must be added to the INSTALLED_APPS setting in the Django project's settings file. This is a crucial step as it makes Django aware of the newly added extensions and allows the template engine to locate and load them.

After ensuring the extension is recognized by Django, the next step involves loading the template tags or filters within the Django template. This is accomplished by using the {% load %} template tag at the beginning of the template file. It is essential to specify the exact name of the library the tags or filters belong to. For instance, to load a third-party library named *custom_tags*, the template directive would be {% load custom_tags %}.

Once the necessary tags and filters are loaded into the template, they can be utilized similarly to Django's built-in tags and filters. The syntax for using third-party tags follows the general pattern of {% tagname %} for tags and {{ value|filtername }} for filters. However, it is crucial to consult the documentation of the third-party library being used, as the syntax for tags and filters can vary based on the library's design and the functionality it provides.

To illustrate the application of third-party template tags, consider a scenario where a developer aims to implement a pagination feature with enhanced customization options that Django's built-in pagination tag does not offer. Assuming a library named *advanced_pagination* provides such functionality, the steps would include installing the library, adding it to INSTALLED_APPS, and loading its tags in the template:

```
1  {% load advanced_pagination %}
2  ...
3  {% advanced_pagination %}
```

This code snippet demonstrates how seamlessly third-party template tags can integrate into Django templates, expanding the possibilities beyond what is achievable with default tags and filters.

In using third-party filters, consider a situation where advanced formatting of dates is required, and a library named *date_extras* offers sophisticated date filters. After installation and configuration, using a filter from this library could be as simple as:

```
1  {{ post.publish_date|fancy_date }}
```

This would apply the *fancy_date* filter to the publish_date of a post, showcasing the simplicity and power of third-party filters in transforming template data.

While third-party tags and filters offer significant advantages, it is essential to exercise caution and perform due diligence before integrating them into a project. Considerations should include the library's license, its compatibility with the Django version being used, the frequency of updates and maintenance by the authors, and the community and documentation support available. Reliance on poorly maintained extensions can introduce bugs, security vulnerabilities, and compatibility issues.

Third-party template tags and filters are invaluable tools for Django developers seeking to enhance the functionality and maintainability of their templates. By carefully selecting and integrating these extensions, developers can achieve more with less code, adhere to the DRY (Don't Repeat Yourself) principle, and create more readable and expressive templates that better serve the needs of their applications.

6.10 Securing Templates Against Injection Attacks

Django's template system, while robust and feature-rich, is not inherently immune to security vulnerabilities such as injection attacks. An injection attack occurs when an attacker is able to send or inject malicious code into a system, where it is then executed or parsed as part of the system's operations. In the context of web development, this often manifests in the form of Cross-Site Scripting (XSS) or SQL injection attacks. This section will discuss strategies and best practices to secure Django templates against such vulnerabilities.

Django templates escape specific characters that are dangerous to HTML automatically. Characters such as '<', '>', and '&' are turned into their safe HTML entities equivalents, thus preventing the most common XSS attacks. For instance, if a template variable {{ user_input }} contains JavaScript code, it will be rendered in a way that the browser recognizes it as text rather than executable JavaScript. This behavior is Django's first line of defense against XSS attacks.

```
1  Example:
2  User input: <script>alert('Attack!')</script>
3  Rendered Output: &lt;script&gt;alert(&#x27;Attack!&#x27;)&lt;/script&gt;
```

However, certain scenarios require marking a string as safe manually when Django's auto-escaping is too restrictive. This can be achieved with the |safe filter. Be cautious when using this filter, as it tells Django to trust the string's content entirely and render it as raw HTML. This practice should be avoided unless absolutely necessary and only with content that has been thoroughly sanitized.

```
1  Correct use of the |safe filter:
2  Template code: \{\{ safe\_string|safe \}\}
```

Django provides several mechanisms to further secure templates against injection. The autoescape tag can explicitly enable or disable auto-escaping for blocks of a template. This tag is particularly useful for situations where the majority of a template should not escape its content, but certain parts should. However, the default should always be to escape content unless there's a compelling reason not to.

```
1  Example of using the autoescape tag:
2  \{\% autoescape off \%\}
3      \{\{ potentially\_unsafe\_content \}\}
4  \{\% autoescape on \%\}
```

Another critical aspect of securing Django templates involves handling URL parameters safely. The {% url %} template tag should be used for generating URLs, rather than manually concatenating strings within the template. This practice not only aids in maintaining the readability and maintainability of the code but also prevents injection attacks that might occur if unsanitized user input is used to construct URLs.

For securing forms in templates against Cross-Site Request Forgery (CSRF) attacks, Django provides the {% csrf_token %} template tag. When included in a form, this tag generates a hidden input field with a token that Django checks when the form is submitted. This mechanism ensures that the form is only submitted by the user who requested the page, thus preventing unauthorized actions.

```
1  Example of including a CSRF token in a form:
2  <form method="post">
3      \{\% csrf\_token \%\}
4      ...
5  </form>
```

Lastly, Django's Content Security Policy (CSP) middleware can be configured to add an additional layer of security. CSP allows web developers to define a policy for which sources the browser should allow to load resources. By controlling the sources from which scripts, images, and other resources can be loaded, developers can prevent attackers from injecting malicious content into their web pages.

Ensuring the security of Django templates against injection attacks involves leveraging Django's built-in escaping mechanisms judiciously, using template tags correctly, and employing additional protective measures such as CSRF tokens and CSP policies. While Django goes a long way in securing templates by default, a thorough understanding of these practices and vigilance in applying them is essential for developing secure web applications.

6.11 Optimizing Template Rendering Performance

Optimizing template rendering performance is essential for delivering an efficient and seamless user experience in web applications. Django's template engine, while powerful, can become a bottleneck if not used carefully. This section will discuss strategies to improve the rendering performance of Django templates, focusing on template structure, caching techniques, and the efficient use of tags and filters.

Firstly, it is crucial to understand the overhead that comes with complex template inheritance. While template inheritance is a powerful feature for avoiding code duplication and ensuring consistency across your site, excessive use can lead to a significant performance cost. Each level of inheritance introduces an additional file read operation and parsing step. To mitigate this, consider flattening the inheritance hierarchy where possible, combining templates or using include tags wisely to reduce the depth of template inheritance trees.

```
Example of a deep template inheritance hierarchy:

base.html -> layout.html -> page.html -> content.html
```

Reducing the levels of inheritance improves rendering speed by minimizing the number of templates that need to be parsed and combined into the final HTML output.

Next, the strategic use of caching can dramatically improve template performance. Django provides a robust caching framework that can be leveraged to cache entire templates or portions thereof. When properly applied, caching can reduce database queries and expensive computations to a minimum, serving pre-rendered content to users.

```
1  {% load cache %}
2  {% cache 500 template_name %}
3     ...expensive template rendering...
4  {% endcache %}
```

In the above example, the content enclosed within the cache tag will be cached with a timeout of 500 seconds. Django will serve the cached version of this content for subsequent requests, bypassing the need to re-render the template until the cache expires.

However, caching should be used judiciously. It's important to identify which parts of your templates are static and expensive to render and

185

which parts are dynamic and frequently changing. Overuse of caching can lead to stale content being served to users or increased memory usage on the server.

Another area of optimization is the efficient use of template tags and filters. Custom template tags and filters can introduce considerable overhead if they perform complex operations such as database queries or heavy computations. To optimize performance, ensure that:

- Custom tags and filters are used sparingly and only when necessary.

- Expensive operations within tags and filters are cached if possible.

- Database queries within custom tags or filters are optimized and minimized.

For example, a custom template filter that queries the database should be carefully optimized to use select_related or prefetch_related, if applicable, to reduce the number of database queries.

Furthermore, Django's template system allows for the pre-compilation of templates. This feature can be particularly beneficial in a production environment, where templates do not change frequently. Pre-compiling templates reduces the overhead of parsing templates on each request, leading to faster response times. To utilize this feature, Django's management command django-admin compiletemplatescan be executed as part of the deployment process.

Optimizing template rendering performance in Django involves a combination of strategies, including minimizing template inheritance complexity, judicious use of caching, efficient use of custom template tags and filters, and the pre-compilation of templates. By applying these techniques, developers can significantly enhance the speed and responsiveness of Django applications, providing a better experience for end-users.

6.12 Debugging Template Errors

Debugging template errors in Django requires an understanding of common issues encountered during template rendering and the tools

Django provides for diagnosing and resolving these problems. This section will discuss strategies for identifying and fixing errors in Django templates, including the use of Django's debugging tools, interpreting error messages, and common pitfalls to avoid.

Django templates are a crucial component of web development, bridging the gap between backend logic and the frontend presentation. However, errors in templates can lead to issues such as improperly displayed data, broken page layouts, or complete failure to render a page. Identifying the source of these errors is the first step toward resolution.

When a template error occurs, Django's built-in debugging mode can provide detailed information about the error, including the type of exception, a traceback of the call stack, and the specific template file and line number where the error occurred. To enable debugging information, ensure that the DEBUG setting in your Django project's settings file is set to True. It is essential to remember that this setting should be used only in development environments due to the sensitive information it can reveal.

```
DEBUG = True
```

Once debugging is enabled, encountering an error in a template will display an error page with comprehensive details. However, sifting through this information to locate the root cause requires understanding common template errors.

One prevalent source of errors is syntax mistakes within templates. Django's template language uses specific constructs such as variables, tags, and filters, which must follow precise syntax rules. For example, a missing closing tag or an incorrectly formatted filter can cause rendering issues. In the case of a syntax error, Django will raise a TemplateSyntaxError, pointing out the issue's location. Reviewing the indicated part of the template often reveals the syntax mistake.

Another common issue is problems with template variables. If a variable is not passed correctly to the template or is spelled incorrectly within the template, Django will not raise an error. Instead, the template system will replace the variable with an empty string, which can lead to missing or unexpected content on the web page. To debug this issue, verify the context dictionary passed to the template in the corresponding view function and ensure all variable names match between the view and the template.

Django also offers a template debugging tool through the `django.template.backends.django.Template.render` method, which can be used to programmatically render a template and inspect its contents within a view or a Django shell. This method is useful for testing templates in isolation from the rest of the project.

```
from django.template import engines

template_string = 'Hello {{ name }}!'
template = engines['django'].from_string(template_string)
context = {'name': 'World'}
rendered_string = template.render(context)
print(rendered_string)
```

```
Hello World!
```

When dealing with more complex errors, such as those involving custom template tags or filters, checking the implementation of these custom components is crucial. Ensure that the custom tags and filters are correctly registered with the template system and that their logic correctly handles all expected input scenarios.

Finally, it's vital to consider the possibility of errors stemming from misconfigured template settings or template loaders. Ensure that the TEMPLATES configuration in your Django settings is correctly set up, including the appropriate directories for finding templates and the correct order of template loaders, which can affect how templates are located and compiled.

In summary, debugging template errors in Django entails a thorough process of checking for syntax mistakes, verifying variable correctness and availability, inspecting custom template tags and filters, and ensuring proper configuration of template settings. Utilizing Django's debugging tools and being meticulous in reviewing the details of error messages can significantly aid in quickly identifying and resolving issues, leading to a smoother development process and a more stable web application.

6.13   Internationalization in Templates

Internationalization (i18n) in Django templates plays a pivotal role in making applications accessible to a global audience by displaying content in various languages based on user preference. Django's template engine supports internationalization through a set of tags and filters designed for handling language-specific content dynamically. This section will discuss the techniques for internationalizing static text and dynamic content in Django templates, along with considerations for template design to facilitate the process of internationalization.

To commence internationalization in templates, ensure that the Django project is configured to support i18n. This involves setting the USE_I18N and LANGUAGE_CODE in the project's settings file.

```
USE_I18N = True
LANGUAGE_CODE = 'en-us'
```

Once i18n is enabled, the primary mechanism for internationalization in Django templates involves wrapping text strings with the {% trans "your text here" %} template tag for static content and the {% blocktrans %} tag for dynamic content which might include placeholders.

```
1  {% load i18n %}
2
3  <h1>{% trans "Welcome to My Site" %}</h1>
4  <p>{% blocktrans with name=user.name %}Hello, {{ name }}!{% endblocktrans %}</p>
```

It is important to load the i18n template library at the beginning of the template file using {% load i18n %} to make i18n related tags and filters available within the template.

For dynamic content that includes variables, the {% blocktrans %} tag is used. It allows placeholders for variables to be translated in context, providing more accurate translations. The {% blocktrans %} tag can also include pluralization logic using the {% plural %} tag to correctly handle singular and plural forms based on the count of items.

```
1  {% blocktrans count counter=items|length %}
2  There is {{ counter }} item available.
3  {% plural %}
4  There are {{ counter }} items available.
5  {% endblocktrans %}
```

To support multiple languages, Django requires the creation of message files (.po) that map the original strings in the application to their corresponding translations. These files reside in a locale directory within the Django project. The django-admin makemessages command is used to generate these files, and the django-admin compilemessages command compiles them into .mo files, which Django then uses for rendering the translated strings in templates.

```
django-admin makemessages -l es
django-admin compilemessages
```

189

Designing templates with internationalization in mind requires mindful practices. Avoid concatenating strings or creating sentences by combining strings since this approach can lead to grammatical errors or nonsensical translations due to the varying syntax and structure of languages. Instead, use entire sentences within translation tags and employ placeholders for dynamic content to maintain linguistic integrity.

Moreover, when integrating internationalization in templates, consider the directionality of text. Use the `get_language_bidi` template tag provided by Django to determine whether the current language is written right-to-left and adjust the template's layout accordingly to ensure proper display for languages such as Arabic or Hebrew.

```
1  {% load i18n %}
2  <html {% if get_language_bidi %}dir="rtl"{% endif %}>
3  ...
4  </html>
```

Lastly, testing your templates with various languages is crucial to ensure that translations appear correctly and that the layout remains functional across languages. Django's `override` function can be useful for testing specific languages during development, allowing templates to be rendered with alternative language settings.

Internationalization in Django templates is facilitated through a comprehensive set of tags and filters that, combined with best practices in template design and message file management, enable developers to create multilingual applications. Adherence to these practices ensures that Django applications are globally accessible and provide a localized user experience that is coherent and culturally appropriate.

6.14 Best Practices for Templating and Static Files Management

In web development, the structure and organization of templates and static files significantly influence the efficiency, maintainability, and scalability of applications. Django, with its comprehensive template system and static files management, provides a robust framework for developers. However, leveraging these features to their fullest potential requires adherence to best practices that enhance the development workflow and the performance of the web application.

When working with Django's template system, it is imperative to utilize template inheritance effectively. This entails defining a base template that contains all the common elements of your site, such as headers, footers, and navigation bars. Child templates can inherit from this base template and override specific blocks of content. This strategy reduces code duplication and facilitates easier updates since changes made to the base template automatically propagate to all inheriting templates.

```
1  {% extends "base_generic.html" %}
2
3  {% block content %}
4  <!-- Unique page content goes here -->
5  {% endblock %}
```

For static files management, a methodical setup and organization are paramount. Static files should be categorized into directories based on their type (e.g., CSS, JavaScript, images) within each Django app's 'static' folder. Such structuring not only improves readability and maintenance but also optimizes static files' handling by Django's staticfiles app during development and deployment.

Leveraging Django's `staticfiles_tags` for referring to static files in templates is a recommended practice to ensure the correct resolution of static files' paths across different environments.

```
1  {% load static %}
2  <link rel="stylesheet" href="{% static 'css/style.css' %}">
```

Optimizing template rendering is crucial for improving the response time of Django applications. This can be achieved through:

- Minimizing the use of complex template tags and filters that can lead to increased processing time.

- Utilizing Django's `cachetemplates` loader to cache the compilation of templates, thus reducing the need to recompile on every request.

- Prefetching related database objects in views before passing them to templates to minimize database queries.

Furthermore, ensuring the security of templates is of utmost importance. Developers should:

- Escaping variables using Django's template auto-escaping feature to guard against Cross-Site Scripting (XSS) attacks.

191

- Exercise caution when using `safe` filter or `autoescape off` tag, as these can introduce security vulnerabilities if misused.

```
1   {{ variable|escape }}
```

Debugging template errors effectively necessitates familiarity with Django's template debugging tools like the `debug` template tag, which can provide insights into the template context and help identify issues swiftly.

For the management of static and media files in production, utilizing Django's `collectstatic` command to gather static files from various applications into a single directory is advised. Employing a Content Delivery Network (CDN) for serving static files can significantly enhance the performance and scalability of web applications by reducing the load on the application server.

Lastly, staying abreast of updates in Django's templating engine and static files management documentation is crucial, as new features, optimizations, and best practices are periodically introduced.

Adhering to these best practices in templating and static files management not only facilitates a smoother development process but also contributes to the overall performance, security, and maintainability of Django applications.

6.15 Combining Templates with Views and Forms

Combining templates with views and forms in Django is a fundamental concept for creating dynamic web applications. This integration allows the presentation layer (templates) to interact seamlessly with the business logic (views), facilitated through forms for data submission and modification.

When a Django application serves a webpage, it typically involves a view function or class-based view that processes business logic, fetching data from the database if necessary. This data is then passed to a template, which is rendered to HTML and returned to the client's browser. Forms come into play as a structured method for data submission from the frontend to the backend, often for creating or updating records in the database.

To illustrate this integration, consider an example of creating a blog post. A Django form class is defined to specify the fields required for creating a blog post. This form is then instantiated in a view, which handles the GET and POST requests of a webpage. On a GET request, the form is passed to a template, rendering it as HTML input fields. When the form is submitted, it's POSTed back to the same view, which then processes the form data, potentially saving a new blog post to the database.

```
from django.shortcuts import render, redirect
from .forms import BlogPostForm

def create_blog_post(request):
    if request.method == 'POST':
        form = BlogPostForm(request.POST)
        if form.is_valid():
            form.save()
            return redirect('blog-home')
    else:
        form = BlogPostForm()
    return render(request, 'app/create_blog_post.html', {'form': form})
```

In the above example, `BlogPostForm` is a Django form class that defines the structure of the blog post form. The view `create_blog_post` handles both GET and POST requests. On a GET request, a new instance of `BlogPostForm` is created and passed to the template. The template then renders the form:

```
{% extends "base.html" %}
{% block content %}
<form method="post">
    {% csrf_token %}
    {{ form.as_p }}
    <button type="submit">Post</button>
</form>
{% endblock %}
```

The template extends a base template and defines a form within the content block. The `{% csrf_token %}` template tag is essential for security against Cross-Site Request Forgery (CSRF) attacks. The `{{ form.as_p }}` renders the form fields as paragraph elements.

The data flow follows a cycle from request to response. A user requests to create a blog post (GET), the empty form is presented in the template, the user fills and submits the form (POST), the view processes the submitted form, potentially adding a new blog post to the database, and finally redirects the user, often back to the form or to another page indicating success.

This example demonstrates the cohesive interaction between templates, views, and forms. Templating provides the layout and structure for presenting and collecting data. Views manage the logic and flow of the application, deciding what to do with incoming requests and outgoing responses. Forms bridge the gap between user input and back-end processing, ensuring data integrity and simplification of data collection and processing.

Adopting this pattern of combining templates, views, and forms enhances the modularity, maintainability, and scalability of Django applications. It enables developers to independently work on the presentation layer without interfering with the business logic layer, ensuring a clear separation of concerns.

In summary, the effective combination of templates, views, and forms in Django applications facilitates robust and scalable web development by encapsulating presentation, business logic, and data collection into coherent, manageable components. Understanding and mastering this triad allows developers to build dynamic, data-driven web applications with efficiency and precision.

Chapter 7

Form Handling and File Uploads in Django

Django simplifies form creation, processing, and validation, along with handling file uploads, thereby streamlining user interactions within web applications. This chapter focuses on the mechanisms for defining forms, both from scratch and using Django's ModelForms, to encapsulate input and validation logic. It also examines how to manage file uploads efficiently, ensuring data integrity and security. Through practical examples and best practices, readers will learn to implement robust forms and handle file uploads, enhancing the interactivity and functionality of their Django projects.

7.1 Overview of Form Handling in Django

Django, a high-level Python web framework, eases the process of developing complex, data-driven web applications. One of the framework's core functionalities is its robust form handling system, designed to simplify the creation, processing, and validation of forms. This section will discuss the foundation of form handling in Django, covering the initial steps to build forms, manage submissions, and ensure data integrity through validation.

195

In Django, a form is a powerful tool for collecting user input. The framework provides a comprehensive system which includes ready-to-use classes and methods for creating forms, validating user input, and rendering HTML forms in templates. Django forms not only abstract the HTML form elements but also handle validation logic, significantly reducing development time and potential errors.

The essence of Django form handling can be broken down into several key components:

- **Form Class:** At the heart of Django's form handling are form classes. These are defined in a similar manner to Django models. A form class specifies the fields that are to be rendered in the HTML form, each represented by Django's form fields like `CharField`, `EmailField`, and `ChoiceField`. This abstraction allows developers to define the form logic and properties in a Pythonic way, decoupling it from the presentation layer.

- **Validation:** Django forms come with built-in validation for common data types and patterns. For instance, an `EmailField` will automatically check if the user input is a valid email address. Custom validation rules can also be added at both the field level and form level, allowing for complex data integrity checks before accepting the user input into the system.

- **Rendering:** Django provides mechanisms to render forms in templates easily. The framework offers several approaches, including rendering the whole form as-is, iterating over the form's fields to customize the presentation, or rendering individual fields manually. This flexibility allows for a wide variety of form designs without compromising the backend logic.

- **Handling Submissions:** When a form is submitted, Django simplifies the process of data retrieval and processing through form instances. By passing the request data to a form instance, the framework manages data parsing, validation, and cleaning. This streamlines the process of working with user input, ensuring that valid data can be processed or stored, and providing a straightforward way to return feedback on invalid submissions.

Let's start with a simple example to illustrate the creation of a basic Django form:

```
1  from django import forms
```

```
2
3   class ContactForm(forms.Form):
4       name = forms.CharField()
5       email = forms.EmailField()
6       message = forms.CharField(widget=forms.Textarea)
```

This code snippet defines a form class ContactForm with three fields: name, email, and message. The message field uses a special widget, Textarea, to allow multiline input. Implementing this form in a view and template could handle user submissions for a contact page.

Upon receiving a POST request, the form instance is created with request.POST data, and the form's is_valid() method is called to perform validation:

```
1   if request.method == 'POST':
2       form = ContactForm(request.POST)
3       if form.is_valid():
4           # Process the data in form.cleaned_data
5           ...
```

If the form data passes validation, the cleaned data is accessible via form.cleaned_data, allowing safe, validated data to be used in application logic.

This overview highlights the integral role of Django forms in web application development. By abstracting form creation, submission, and validation into a cohesive system, Django enables developers to focus on application logic rather than the intricacies of form management. Following sections will delve deeper into each component, providing a comprehensive guide to effective form handling and file uploads in Django.

7.2 Understanding Django Forms: A Primer

Django forms are a powerful abstraction layer that make it easy to work with user input by encapsulating common HTML form elements, validation logic, and input processing. This primer will delve into the essentials of Django forms, including their creation, rendering, and data handling processes. By understanding these concepts, developers can leverage Django's forms framework to simplify the task of gathering and validating data from users.

Let's start with the definition and creation of a simple Django form. A Django form is typically defined in a Python class that inherits from

197

django.forms.Form. Each form field is represented by a class variable, using classes that Django provides like forms.CharField for text inputs, or forms.EmailField for email inputs.

```
from django import forms

class ContactForm(forms.Form):
    name = forms.CharField(max_length=100)
    email = forms.EmailField()
    message = forms.CharField(widget=forms.Textarea)
```

In this code snippet, a contact form is defined with three fields: name, email, and message. The max_length parameter in the CharField constructor limits the input length, ensuring that the data fits defined constraints. The email field automatically validates that the input conforms to a valid email address. By specifying widget=forms.Textarea, the message field is rendered using a <textarea> element, which is more suitable for longer text input.

After defining a form, the next step involves rendering it in a template. Django provides template tags to streamline this process. The simplest way to render a form in a template is by using {{ form.as_p }}, which wraps each form field in a <p> tag.

```
<form method="post">
    {% csrf_token %}
    {{ form.as_p }}
    <button type="submit">Send</button>
</form>
```

Handling submitted form data is another critical aspect of working with forms in Django. Upon submission, it is essential to validate the form data to ensure it adheres to expected formats and constraints. This process is facilitated by Django's form validation mechanism, which is executed by calling the is_valid() method on an instantiated form object populated with request data.

```
def contact_view(request):
    if request.method == 'POST':
        form = ContactForm(request.POST)
        if form.is_valid():
            # Process the data in form.cleaned_data
            pass
    else:
        form = ContactForm()

    return render(request, 'contact.html', {'form': form})
```

In this example, a new instance of ContactForm is created and populated with data from request.POST when the form is submitted. The

198

is_valid() method checks the form's data against all validation rules defined for its fields. If the data is valid, it becomes accessible in the form.cleaned_data dictionary, ready for further processing. Otherwise, the form is re-rendered with errors shown, guiding the user to correct them.

To encapsulate validation logic within a form, Django allows for the definition of custom validation methods. These methods are prefixed with clean_ followed by the field name. Within this method, any custom validation logic can be implemented, and errors can be raised if the input doesn't meet the required criteria.

```
1  def clean_email(self):
2      email = self.cleaned_data.get('email')
3      if not "@example.com" in email:
4          raise forms.ValidationError("Please use an @example.com email address.")
5      return email
```

This custom validation ensures that the email address submitted with the form belongs to the "@example.com" domain, demonstrating a simple use case of custom field validation in Django forms.

The understanding of Django forms presented in this primer forms a foundation upon which more advanced topics can be explored, including model forms, file uploads, and formsets. Forms not only encapsulate a lot of the web form intricacies but also provide a rich set of tools to validate user input, making them a crucial component of any Django web application.

7.3 Creating and Using Django Forms

Creating and using Django forms involves several important steps, beginning with the definition of the form itself and extending through processing user input. This systematic approach leverages Django's powerful forms framework to handle user data with efficacy and security.

Defining a Form: The initial step is to define a form. In Django, a form is typically defined as a Python class that inherits from django.forms.Form for custom forms not tied directly to models, or django.forms.ModelForm for forms that are linked to a database model. Here's an example of a basic form definition that includes a text input field and a file upload field.

```
1  from django import forms
```

```
2
3  class ExampleForm(forms.Form):
4      title = forms.CharField(label='Title', max_length=100)
5      document = forms.FileField(label='Document')
```

Form Fields: Each field in a Django form class corresponds to a form field in the HTML output and a form widget controlling its appearance and attributes on the frontend. Django provides a wide variety of field types, such as `CharField` for text inputs, `EmailField` for email inputs, and `FileField` for file uploads. Each field type in Django is associated with default validation rules, which can be overridden or extended.

Rendering Forms in Templates: To display a form to the user, it must be rendered within a Django template. There are multiple approaches to rendering forms, ranging from manually rendering each field to using Django's templating shortcuts. A common practice is to pass the form instance to the template context and use Django's form handling syntax to render the form. Here's an example of rendering a form using Django's template language.

```
1  <form method="post" enctype="multipart/form-data">
2      {% csrf_token %}
3      {{ form.as_p }}
4      <button type="submit">Submit</button>
```

The `{% csrf_token %}` is essential for security, preventing Cross-Site Request Forgery attacks. The `enctype="multipart/form-data"` attribute is necessary when the form includes file uploads.

Processing Submitted Forms: Upon form submission, the Django view responsible for handling the request needs to differentiate between GET and POST requests, instantiate the form with submitted data in the case of a POST request, validate the form data, and act accordingly based on the validation results. Here is an example view function that implements the form handling logic.

```
1   from django.http import HttpResponseRedirect
2   from django.shortcuts import render
3   from .forms import ExampleForm
4
5   def example_view(request):
6       if request.method == 'POST':
7           form = ExampleForm(request.POST, request.FILES)
8           if form.is_valid():
9               # Process the data in form.cleaned_data
10              # Redirect to a new URL
11              return HttpResponseRedirect('/success/')
12      else:
13          form = ExampleForm()
14      return render(request, 'example_form.html', {'form': form})
```

If the form is not valid, the template will re-render the form with error messages displayed alongside the relevant fields.

Validation and Cleaning: Django automatically invokes validation for each field on the form upon calling is_valid(). This checks whether the data is in a correct and expected format. Custom validation rules can be implemented by overriding the clean_<fieldname>() method for a given field or the clean() method for cross-field validation within the form.

Django forms provide a robust mechanism for handling user input in a web application. By defining form classes, utilizing a wide range of field types, rendering forms in templates, and processing form data securely, Django developers can efficiently manage user data interactions. Through adhering to the Django form handling workflow, developers ensure data integrity, enhance user experience, and maintain the security of the application.

7.4 Advanced Form Features: Custom Validation and Cleaning

The process of form validation is pivotal in protecting a web application from erroneous or malicious data. Django's form system comes equipped with a multitude of built-in tools designed to automate much of this process, yet complex scenarios necessitate a deeper understanding and customization of validation and data cleaning techniques. This section will discuss how to implement custom validation logic and clean data within Django forms, ensuring both integrity and usability of the form data submitted by users.

Django's form validation works by checking that the data provided by a user fits into the expected format and meets predefined criteria. This involves a series of steps where data is cleaned and validated. Data cleaning refers to the process of transforming input data into a consistent format, while validation is the step where the cleaned data is compared against a set of rules.

To customize the cleaning and validation of form data, Django allows developers to override the clean() method on a form or form field level. The clean() method is where any general cleaning not specific to a particular field can take place, while clean_<fieldname>() methods enable field-specific cleaning.

```
1   from django import forms
2
3   class MyForm(forms.Form):
4       my_field = forms.CharField()
5
6       def clean_my_field(self):
7           data = self.cleaned_data['my_field']
8           if not data.startswith('Special'):
9               raise forms.ValidationError('Entry must start with "Special".')
10          return data
11
12      def clean(self):
13          cleaned_data = super(MyForm, self).clean()
14          # Additional cleaning logic can go here
```

The clean_<fieldname>() method is invoked during the form's validation process. It allows for field-specific validation rules to be implemented. If the validation fails, a forms.ValidationError should be raised, as shown in the example where the input for my_field is strictly required to start with the text "Special".

In contrast, overriding the clean() method facilitates broader validation that can involve multiple fields. This is particularly useful for enforcing cross-field constraints. For example, if a form contains fields for both start date and end date, one might use the clean() method to ensure that the start date precedes the end date.

```
1   def clean(self):
2       cleaned_data = super(MyForm, self).clean()
3       start_date = cleaned_data.get("start_date")
4       end_date = cleaned_data.get("end_date")
5
6       if start_date and end_date and start_date > end_date:
7           raise forms.ValidationError("End date should be after start date.")
```

It's critical to note that when the clean() method is overridden, it must end by returning the full dictionary of cleaned data, cleaned_data, for further processing by Django's form system.

Moreover, developers should be mindful of handling MultipleObjectsReturned exceptions within cleaning methods, particularly when the form is expected to validate the uniqueness of data against the database models. Proper error handling in these scenarios ensures a user-friendly experience by providing clear, actionable feedback.

Django also provides a hook for custom validators that can be reused across various forms or even directly within Django models. Defining a custom validator involves creating a function that takes a single value as an argument and raises a forms.ValidationError if the validation criteria are not met.

```
1  from django.core.exceptions import ValidationError
2
3  def validate_special_value(value):
4      if not value.startswith('Special'):
5          raise ValidationError('%(value)s does not start with "Special"',
6                                params={'value': value})
```

This validator can then be applied to any form field by including it in the field's validators list.

```
1  class MyForm(forms.Form):
2      my_field = forms.CharField(validators=[validate_special_value])
```

Using custom validators simplifies the code and promotes reuse, upholding the DRY (Don't Repeat Yourself) principle inherent in effective software development practices.

In summary, custom validation and data cleaning in Django forms allow for sophisticated data integrity checks and user input processing schemes. By overriding the `clean()` and `clean_<fieldname>()` methods, as well as employing custom validators, developers can enforce complex rules and ensure that the data being processed adheres to the application's requirements. These advanced form features significantly enhance the robustness and security of Django applications.

7.5 Working with Django ModelForms

Working with Django ModelForms significantly reduces the amount of boilerplate code required to create forms that are directly mapped from the application's models. This section will discuss the essentials of Django ModelForms, covering their creation, usage, and customization to accommodate the specific needs of web applications.

Django ModelForms are a subclass of forms.ModelForm. The primary advantage of using ModelForms is their ability to automatically generate a form field for each field in a model. This automatic generation adheres to the DRY (Don't Repeat Yourself) principle, ensuring that the data schema defined by the models is the single source of truth for form fields.

To begin with, creating a ModelForm involves defining a class that specifies which model it is associated with and optionally, the model fields to be included or excluded in the form. For instance, consider a simple model representing a book:

```
1   from django.db import models
2
3   class Book(models.Model):
4       title = models.CharField(max_length=100)
5       author = models.CharField(max_length=100)
6       summary = models.TextField()
7       genre = models.CharField(max_length=100)
8       publish_date = models.DateField()
```

To create a ModelForm for the Book model, one would define a form class as follows:

```
1   from django.forms import ModelForm
2   from myapp.models import Book
3
4   class BookForm(ModelForm):
5       class Meta:
6           model = Book
7           fields = '__all__'
```

In the above example, specifying `fields = '__all__'` indicates that all fields in the Book model should be included in the form. Alternatively, one could specify a tuple of field names to include or use the `exclude` attribute to list fields that should not be part of the form.

Django ModelForms also facilitate custom validation for model fields. This is achieved by defining method(s) prefixed with `clean_` followed by the field name. These methods are called when the form's `is_valid()` method is invoked, allowing for additional checks beyond those defined at the model level. For example, to ensure the title of a book is not merely "Untitled", one might add:

```
1   def clean_title(self):
2       title = self.cleaned_data.get('title')
3       if title == "Untitled":
4           raise forms.ValidationError("The title cannot be 'Untitled'.")
5       return title
```

Handling file uploads with ModelForms requires specifying a model field of type `models.FileField` or `models.ImageField`. When a form associated with such a model is submitted, Django handles the file upload automatically, provided the view handling the form submission properly manages uploaded files by passing `request.FILES` to the form instance.

For forms involving file uploads, the HTML form tag should include the attribute `enctype="multipart/form-data"`. Without this, the browser will not transmit the files, and Django will not receive them.

```
1   <form method="post" enctype="multipart/form-data">
2       {% csrf_token %}
```

```
3   {{ form.as_p }}
4     <button type="submit">Upload</button>
5   </form>
```

Advanced customization of ModelForms may involve overriding methods such as save(), to implement additional logic when saving form data to the database. While the default save() method creates or updates the associated model instance, overriding this method allows for manipulating data before saving or performing actions after saving.

Django ModelForms offer a streamlined approach for creating forms that are deeply integrated with the application's data models. By automatically generating form fields based on model definitions, facilitating custom validations, and simplifying file uploads, ModelForms enable developers to efficiently implement robust and dynamic forms within their Django applications.

7.6   Implementing File Uploads with Django

Implementing file uploads with Django requires understanding the framework's built-in features that support handling user-uploaded files. This encompasses modifying models, forms, and views to accommodate file inputs, validating and storing these files, and ensuring they are securely handled. This section will discuss the process of implementing file uploads, focusing on the necessary steps and best practices to follow.

To manage file uploads in Django, modifications in models are first necessary. Django provides a FileField and an ImageField for handling file and image uploads respectively. These fields need to be included in the model to store the uploaded files. For example, to add an image upload feature to a model representing a user profile, the model can be defined as follows:

```
1   from django.db import models
2
3   class UserProfile(models.Model):
4       user = models.OneToOneField(User, on_delete=models.CASCADE)
5       profile_picture = models.ImageField(upload_to='profile_pictures/')
```

The upload_to attribute specifies the directory where the files will be stored within the MEDIA_ROOT directory defined in the project's settings.

205

After defining the model, a form to handle the file upload is needed. Django forms can use a `FileField` or `ImageField` as well, corresponding to the model's fields. This ensures that file inputs are correctly rendered in the form and that Django will handle the file data upon submission. An example form for the user profile might look like this:

```
from django import forms
from .models import UserProfile

class UserProfileForm(forms.ModelForm):
    class Meta:
        model = UserProfile
        fields = ['user', 'profile_picture']
```

In the view that handles the form submission, it is important to handle the file data using the `request.FILES` object. This involves adjusting the view function to include this object when instantiating the form with POST data. An example view function for submitting a user profile form with a file upload can be presented as follows:

```
from django.shortcuts import render, redirect
from .forms import UserProfileForm

def upload_profile_picture(request):
    if request.method == 'POST':
        form = UserProfileForm(request.POST, request.FILES)
        if form.is_valid():
            form.save()
            return redirect('success_url')
    else:
        form = UserProfileForm()
    return render(request, 'upload.html', {'form': form})
```

For the file upload to work, it's essential to include the `enctype="multipart/form-data"` attribute in the form tag of the HTML template. This ensures that the file data is correctly encoded as part of the request.

```
<form method="post" enctype="multipart/form-data">
    {% csrf_token %}
    {{ form.as_p }}
    <button type="submit">Upload</button>
\end{form}
```

To serve the uploaded files in development, Django's `django.conf.urls.static.static` function can be used to add a URL pattern that serves the files from the `MEDIA_ROOT`. In production, a more robust setup involving a web server or a cloud storage service is necessary to serve static and media files securely and efficiently.

Regarding security considerations, it's crucial to validate the uploaded files to prevent malicious use. This involves checking the file size, file

206

type, and potentially scanning for viruses. Django's upload handlers and form field validation can be leveraged for implementing such checks.

In summary, implementing file uploads in Django requires careful consideration of the model, form, and view layers, along with appropriate handling of file data and security measures. By following the steps and best practices outlined, developers can effectively integrate file upload functionality into their Django applications, ensuring a robust and secure user experience.

7.7 Handling Multiple Files and Large Uploads

Handling multiple files and large uploads in Django necessitates a comprehensive understanding of file input from HTML forms, Django's file storage API, and techniques to ensure efficiency and security. This section will discuss the implementation strategies for managing multiple files and large uploads, focusing on Django's built-in capabilities and best practices.

When dealing with file uploads, the HTML form element should specify an encoding type of `multipart/form-data`, which allows files to be sent through POST method. In Django, the `FileField` or `ImageField` within a form or model takes care of handling upload file data.

```
1  from django import forms
2
3  class UploadFileForm(forms.Form):
4      title = forms.CharField(max_length=50)
5      file = forms.FileField()
```

This form can handle file uploads, but only one file per field. To allow multiple files to be uploaded at once, you can use the HTML input attribute `multiple` in your Django form by customizing its widget.

```
1  class MultipleUploadFileForm(forms.Form):
2      files = forms.FileField(widget=forms.ClearableFileInput(attrs={'multiple': True
          }))
```

For handling the files in views, it's crucial to iterate over `request.FILES` for each file submitted. Here is a simplified example:

```
1  def upload_multiple_files(request):
2      if request.method == "POST":
3          form = MultipleUploadFileForm(request.POST, request.FILES)
```

```
4        if form.is_valid():
5            files = request.FILES.getlist('files')
6            for f in files:
7                handle_uploaded_file(f)
8            return redirect('success_url') # Redirect as appropriate
9        else:
10           form = MultipleUploadFileForm()
11       return render(request, 'upload.html', {'form': form})
```

For large file uploads, the primary considerations are memory efficiency and upload time. By default, Django handles uploads using as little memory as possible. Files larger than 2.5 MB are routed to the server's temporary directory, avoiding loading the entire file into memory. This default behavior can be tailored further for optimization.

One practical approach for handling large uploads efficiently is to use Django's FileUploadHandler. This customization allows you to control the process of file uploads, such as chunking large files and storing them directly to their final storage location, bypassing the need for a temporary stored file.

The challenge with multiple and large file uploads doesn't merely lie in the upload itself but also in providing a responsive user experience. Employing Ajax for file uploads can significantly enhance this. With Ajax, files can be uploaded in the background, with progress indicators and error handling improving interactivity:

```
1   $("form#multiFileUpload").submit(function(e) {
2       e.preventDefault();
3       var formData = new FormData($(this)[0]);
4       $.ajax({
5           url: "/path/to/upload/",
6           type: "POST",
7           data: formData,
8           async: true,
9           success: function (response) {
10              console.log(response);
11          },
12          error: function (xhr, status, error) {
13              console.error(error);
14          },
15          contentType: false,
16          processData: false,
17          cache: false,
18      });
19  });
```

Handling multiple files and large uploads efficiently in Django involves leveraging Django's built-in features such as FileUploadHandler and file fields with the multiple attribute. Employing Ajax for the file upload process can further refine user experience, allowing for asynchronous uploads and real-time feedback.

Ensure to also consider security implications, like constraining file types and sizes, to safeguard against malicious uploads and potential security vulnerabilities.

7.8 Integrating Third-Party Form Fields and Widgets

Integrating third-party form fields and widgets into Django applications can significantly enhance the user interface and experience by providing more interactive and visually appealing elements. Django's flexible form handling mechanisms allow for the seamless integration of external form fields and widgets, extending the basic functionalities offered by Django's built-in components. This section will discuss the process of incorporating third-party form fields and widgets into a Django project, focusing on the selection criteria, installation, and implementation steps, followed by a detailed example.

Firstly, selecting the appropriate third-party form fields and widgets for integration involves careful consideration of several factors. These include compatibility with Django's version, maintenance and support by the developers, community usage and reviews, and, most importantly, the security aspects of the third-party components. It is advisable to choose well-documented and widely used libraries to ensure a smoother integration process and support for troubleshooting issues that may arise.

To integrate a third-party form field or widget into a Django project, the following general steps are usually followed:

- Identifying the third-party library that contains the desired form fields or widgets.

- Installing the library using a package manager like pip.

- Importing the necessary classes or functions from the library into your forms.py file.

- Replacing or augmenting Django's built-in form fields or widgets with the ones from the third-party library in your form definitions.

- Customizing the behavior or appearance of the third-party components as needed, following the library's documentation.

An example will clarify this process further. Consider a scenario where a project requires a more advanced date picker than what is provided by Django's default form widgets. A popular third-party library for this purpose is django-datetime-widget.

First, the library would be installed via pip:

```
1  $ pip install django-datetime-widget
```

Then, in the forms.py file, you would import the DateTimeWidget and use it in your form definition:

```
1  from django import forms
2  from datetimewidget.widgets import DateTimeWidget
3
4  class EventForm(forms.Form):
5      event_date = forms.DateTimeField(widget=DateTimeWidget(usel10n=True,
           bootstrap_version=3))
```

This code snippet demonstrates replacing Django's default DateTimeField widget with the third-party DateTimeWidget. The usel10n argument automatically localizes the date and time format based on the user's locale, and bootstrap_version ensures that the widget's styling is consistent with Bootstrap version 3.

For a real-world Django project, several additional considerations may need to be taken into account when integrating third-party form fields and widgets, including:

- Ensuring that any JavaScript or CSS dependencies required by the third-party widgets are included in your project's static files.

- Overriding or extending the base templates of your Django project to accommodate any custom behavior or styling required by the third-party widgets.

- Implementing any server-side handling that may be required for processing data submitted from third-party widgets, such as parsing non-standard date formats.

Integrating third-party form fields and widgets can greatly enhance the functionality and user experience of Django projects. By carefully selecting the appropriate third-party components, following the steps for installation and implementation, and addressing any additional considerations related to dependencies and data processing, developers can efficiently incorporate advanced UI elements into their Django forms.

7.9   Ajax Form Submission and Validation

Ajax, an acronym for Asynchronous JavaScript and XML, is a set of web development techniques that allows for the creation of dynamic and asynchronous web applications. In the context of Django forms, Ajax can be employed to submit forms and perform form validation without requiring a page reload. This section will discuss the integration of Ajax for form submission and validation in Django, detailing the necessary JavaScript and Django configurations to achieve a seamless user experience.

First, let's consider the typical flow of form submission and validation without Ajax. When a user submits a form, a full page request is made to the server. The server processes the request, performs validation, and then either returns error messages alongside the form if validation fails or processes the form data if validation passes. This traditional process works well but can be optimized using Ajax for a smoother user interaction by eliminating the need for full page reloads.

To implement Ajax form submission and validation, you will need to write some JavaScript code that intercepts the form submission event, sends the form data to the server using an XMLHttpRequest (XHR) or via the Fetch API, handles the server's response, and updates the UI accordingly without a page reload.

Here's a basic example of how you can achieve Ajax form submission with Django:

```
1  <form id="myForm" method="post" action="/submit-form/">
2      {% csrf_token %}
3      <!-- Your form fields here -->
4      <input type="submit" value="Submit" />
5  </form>
6  <div id="formResponse"></div>
```

```
1   document.addEventListener('DOMContentLoaded', function() {
2       var form = document.getElementById('myForm');
3       form.addEventListener('submit', function(e) {
4           e.preventDefault();
5           var formData = new FormData(form);
6           fetch(form.action, {
7               method: 'POST',
8               body: formData,
9               headers: {
10                  'X-Requested-With': 'XMLHttpRequest',
11                  'X-CSRFToken': form.querySelector('[name=
                        csrfmiddlewaretoken]').value,
12              },
```

```
13        })
14        .then(response => response.json())
15        .then(data => {
16            if (data.form_is_valid) {
17                // Update the UI to show success or redirect user
18            } else {
19                // Update the UI with form errors
20                document.getElementById('formResponse').innerHTML = data.
                    form_errors;
21            }
22        });
23    });
24 });
```

On the Django side, you would handle this in your view by returning a JsonResponse indicating whether the form is valid and any error messages to display:

```
1  from django.http import JsonResponse
2  from django.views.decorators.http import require_POST
3  from .forms import MyForm
4
5  @require_POST
6  def submit_form(request):
7      form = MyForm(request.POST)
8      if form.is_valid():
9          # Process the form data
10         return JsonResponse({'form_is_valid': True})
11     else:
12         # Return form errors as JSON
13         errors = form.errors.as_json()
14         return JsonResponse({'form_is_valid': False, 'form_errors': errors})
```

The JavaScript code listens for the form submission event, prevents the default form submission behavior, sends the form data to the server using the Fetch API, and then processes the JSON response from the server, updating the webpage as necessary based on whether the form is valid or not.

This approach to form submission and validation enhances user experience by providing immediate feedback and keeping the user on the same page. It also reduces server load by avoiding unnecessary page loads. However, it's crucial to design your Ajax interactions with fallback mechanisms for clients that do not support JavaScript or have it disabled, ensuring that the form can still be submitted and validated without Ajax.

In addition to XMLHttpRequest and Fetch API, developers can leverage modern JavaScript libraries and frameworks like jQuery, Axios, or React to streamline Ajax form submissions and handle complex UI updates.

Ajax form submission and validation bring a more interactive and user-friendly dimension to working with Django forms. Through the integration of client-side JavaScript and server-side Django configurations as demonstrated, developers can enhance form interactions, creating more responsive and dynamic user experiences without the delays associated with traditional full-page reloads.

7.10 Securing Django Forms: CSRF Protection and XSS Prevention

Ensuring the security of web forms is paramount in web application development to protect against common vulnerabilities such as Cross-Site Request Forgery (CSRF) and Cross-Site Scripting (XSS). Django offers built-in mechanisms to fortify forms against these types of attacks. This section will discuss the implementation of CSRF protection and methods to prevent XSS in Django forms.

CSRF Protection in Django

CSRF attacks involve tricking a user into submitting a request to a web application where they are authenticated without their knowledge or intention. Django mitigates this risk by including a CSRF token within forms. This token is a unique, random value that is checked by the server upon form submission to ensure the request originates from the correct user and site. Django's CSRF protection is enabled by default and is implemented through middleware and template tags.

To include a CSRF token in a Django form, use the {% csrf_token %} template tag within the form in your HTML template. For example:

```
<form method="post">
    {% csrf_token %}
    <!-- Form fields go here -->
</form>
```

When this form is processed, Django checks the CSRF token automatically. In case of a missing or incorrect CSRF token, Django will reject the request, returning a 403 Forbidden response, thus preventing CSRF attacks.

XSS Prevention in Django

XSS attacks involve injecting malicious scripts into web pages viewed by other users, exploiting the trust a user has for a particular site. Django forms mitigate XSS risks primarily through output encoding. By default, Django templates encode all variable outputs, effectively escaping characters that are significant in HTML and JavaScript, thus preventing injected script from being executed.

It is crucial when accepting user-generated content that could be rendered in templates, to ensure that this content is sanitized. Django provides a `mark_safe` function for marking strings as safe for HTML purposes, but it should be used sparingly and only when you are certain the string does not contain malicious code.

To further prevent XSS, it is recommended to:

- Avoid directly inserting user input into templates without proper sanitation.

- Use Django's template system to automatically escape variable outputs.

- Apply Django's built-in filters, such as `escape` and `striptags`, when rendering user input in templates.

By employing these practices, the risk of XSS in Django applications can be significantly reduced.

Security Best Practices for Django Forms

In addition to CSRF protection and XSS prevention, adopting the following security best practices is recommended to enhance the security posture of your Django forms:

- Always use Django's form classes to generate and process forms, taking advantage of Django's built-in security features.

- Validate all user input both on the client-side for usability and on the server-side for security.

- Implement rate limiting on form submission to prevent brute-force attacks.

214

- Use HTTPS to encrypt data in transit between the client and the server, protecting against man-in-the-middle attacks.

- Regularly update Django and its dependencies to the latest versions to ensure that known vulnerabilities are patched.

By integrating these security measures, developers can create Django forms that are not only functional but also resilient against common web vulnerabilities, providing a safer user experience.

Securing Django forms involves a comprehensive approach that includes CSRF protection, XSS prevention, and adherence to best security practices. Through the diligent application of Django's security features, developers can significantly reduce the vulnerability of their web applications to malicious attacks.

7.11 Formsets: Managing Multiple Forms on the Same Page

Formsets in Django provide a powerful mechanism for managing multiple forms on a single web page. This capability is particularly useful when the application requires the user to enter several instances of the same form data, such as during the submission of data for multiple objects of the same type. Understanding how to effectively utilize formsets can enhance the user experience and streamline data processing and validation in Django applications.

A formset is essentially a layer on top of Django forms that manages multiple instances of a form. While individual forms are designed to handle single records, formsets manage multiple records simultaneously, keeping track of each form's data and errors. Django supports formsets through its `django.forms.formsets` module, offering classes and functions to work with formsets efficiently.

To create a formset, Django provides a factory function called `formset_factory`. This function takes a form class as its primary argument and generates a formset class that can produce multiple, similar forms capable of being rendered, validated, and processed as a group. The basic usage of `formset_factory` is shown in the following example:

```
1  from django import forms
2  from django.forms import formset_factory
```

```
3
4    # Define a simple form
5    class ItemForm(forms.Form):
6        name = forms.CharField()
7        quantity = forms.IntegerField(min_value=1)
8
9    # Create a formset class for the ItemForm
10   ItemFormSet = formset_factory(ItemForm)
```

With the `ItemFormSet` class defined, it is now possible to manage multiple item forms within a single request. When rendering the formset in a template, Django provides a management form that includes the total form count, among other management-related fields necessary for Django to process the formset properly. This information allows Django to keep track of the number of forms submitted and handle them accordingly.

Handling the submission of a formset involves instantiating it with the POST data, similar to handling a single form. The formset can then be checked for validity, and each form in the set can be processed in turn. Here is an example of processing a formset in a view:

```
1    from django.shortcuts import render
2    from django.http import HttpResponseRedirect
3
4    def manage_items(request):
5        if request.method == 'POST':
6            formset = ItemFormSet(request.POST)
7            if formset.is_valid():
8                # Process each form in the formset
9                for form in formset:
10                   # Your processing code here
11                   pass
12               return HttpResponseRedirect('/success/')
13       else:
14           formset = ItemFormSet()
15       return render(request, 'manage_items.html', {'formset': formset})
```

For situations requiring the creation, update, or deletion of multiple database objects from a set of forms, Django introduces the concept of model formsets. A model formset is similar to a regular formset but is bound to a Django model. `modelformset_factory` is the factory function provided to create a model formset class, which requires both the model class and the model form class as arguments.

In addition to basic formsets, Django offers inline formsets through the `inlineformset_factory` function. Inline formsets are a subtype of model formsets designed to handle sets of objects that are related to a single instance of another model. This feature is useful in scenarios such as editing a set of related objects directly from the parent object's form.

216

Improperly managed formsets can lead to issues such as mass assignment vulnerabilities. Therefore, it is crucial to implement proper validation, cleaning methods, and safeguard techniques like limiting the maximum number of forms to prevent abuse or accidental misuse. Moreover, when dealing with large formsets or complex form logic, performance considerations become important. Efficient handling, such as using AJAX for form submission or selectively processing only changed forms, can significantly enhance the user experience.

In summary, formsets in Django offer a versatile and powerful tool for managing multiple forms on a single page. By carefully designing and handling formsets in your Django applications, you can provide users with robust and interactive interfaces for submitting and managing sets of data efficiently. Whether dealing with simple data entry tasks or complex data management scenarios, leveraging Django's formsets effectively can greatly simplify the development process and improve the functionality of your web applications.

7.12 Styling and Theming Django Forms with CSS and JavaScript

Django forms, by default, provide a fully functional but basic HTML representation. For most real-world applications, this default styling does not meet the desired aesthetic or usability requirements. Enhancing the appearance and interaction of forms improves user experience significantly. This section will discuss how to apply styles and themes to Django forms using CSS and JavaScript to create a more engaging and responsive user interface.

CSS (Cascading Style Sheets) is fundamental for customizing the look of Django forms. Applying CSS can change the form's layout, color, font, and even animate interactions, providing a rich user experience. JavaScript, on the other hand, can be used to add dynamic behaviors to forms, such as live validation, auto-completion, and responsive adjustments that react to user inputs in real-time.

Applying CSS to Django Forms:

To style Django forms with CSS, developers can either directly include style attributes within Django form definitions or, preferably, apply external stylesheets. The latter approach is more maintainable and scalable, separating the presentation layer from the logic of form handling.

The following are steps to apply external CSS to Django forms:

- Create a CSS file within the static directory of the Django project, for instance, `styles/form_styles.css`.

- Define CSS rules targeting HTML form elements or use Django-generated CSS classes. Django forms render form fields as HTML input elements and use the field name as the class name.

- In the HTML template that renders the form, include the stylesheet using the `<link>` tag within the `<head>` section.

For example, to increase the font size and change the border color of all text input fields, the CSS file could contain:

```
input[type="text"], input[type="email"] {
    font-size: 16px;
    border: 1px solid #007BFF;
}
```

And in the Django template:

```
{% load static %}
<head>
    <link href="{% static 'styles/form_styles.css' %}" rel="stylesheet">
</head>
```

Enhancing Forms with JavaScript:

JavaScript can be utilized to enhance form functionality, making forms more interactive and responsive to user actions. Common enhancements include real-time validation feedback, dynamically showing or hiding form fields, and auto-filling form fields based on previous inputs.

To integrate JavaScript with Django forms, follow these steps:

- Include a JavaScript file in the static directory, for example, `scripts/form_behaviors.js`.

- Write JavaScript functions to implement desired behaviors, such as validating input or toggling visibility of form fields based on specific conditions.

- In the Django template that renders the form, include the JavaScript file using the `<script>` tag, usually placed at the end of the `<body>` tag to ensure all HTML elements are loaded before the script executes.

218

A simple JavaScript function to validate an email field could look like:

```
1   document.addEventListener("DOMContentLoaded", function() {
2       const emailField = document.querySelector('input[type="email"]');
3       emailField.onchange = function() {
4           const pattern = /^[^\s@]+@[^\s@]+\.[^\s@]+$/;
5           if (!pattern.test(this.value)) {
6               alert("Please enter a valid email address.");
7               this.focus();
8           }
9       };
10  });
```

To include it in the template:

```
1   {% load static %}
2   <script src="{% static 'scripts/form_behaviors.js' %}"></script>
```

Styling and adding interactive behaviors to Django forms enhances the user interface and improves the user experience significantly. This is achieved through the application of CSS for designing the visual aspects and JavaScript for adding dynamic functionalities. It is recommended to keep the style and script files separate from the Django form logic and HTML to maintain a clear separation of concerns, facilitating easier maintenance and scalability of web applications.

7.13 Performance Optimizations for Django Forms

Performance optimization is crucial for maintaining responsive and scalable web applications. When it comes to optimizing Django forms, the focus is on reducing server load, minimizing response times, and ensuring efficient data processing. This section will discuss a series of techniques aimed at optimizing the performance of Django forms.

Firstly, the use of 'Form' and 'ModelForm' constructors can significantly impact the performance of your forms. When initializing a form, passing an 'instance' or 'queryset' directly to the form can lead to unnecessary database queries, especially in cases where the form is not rendered to the user. To mitigate this, consider lazily loading these objects or using conditionals to only instantiate forms with objects when necessary. Here's an example:

```
1   if request.method == "POST":
2       form = MyForm(request.POST)
3   else:
4       form = MyForm()
```

Secondly, when dealing with 'ModelChoiceField' or 'ModelMultiple-ChoiceField', Django queries the database for all objects to display in the select options. This can be inefficient for models with a large number of instances. To address this, override the 'queryset' attribute of these fields with a more targeted query, or use 'select_related()' and 'prefetch_related()' to optimise related object retrieval. Here's how you could optimize the queryset:

```
class MyForm(forms.ModelForm):
    my_choice_field = forms.ModelChoiceField(
        queryset=MyModel.objects.select_related('related_field').all()
    )
```

Thirdly, form validation plays a critical role in performance. Each field's clean method is called during form validation, which can lead to multiple database hits if not handled correctly. It's essential to optimize these operations, for instance, by caching results of expensive operations or batch fetching related objects outside of the clean methods.

Handling bulk data in forms, such as with 'Formsets', requires careful consideration. When processing large amounts of data, the overhead of validating and saving each form individually can become a bottleneck. Use 'bulk_create' or 'bulk_update' for efficiently processing these operations in fewer queries:

```
MyModel.objects.bulk_create([
    MyModel(**form.cleaned_data) for form in formset
])
```

In addition to server-side optimizations, client-side performance significantly affects user experience. Efficient use of JavaScript for client-side validation reduces unnecessary server requests. However, ensure server-side validation is always implemented as a fallback, since client-side validation can be bypassed.

Caching form outputs using Django's caching mechanisms can also lead to performance gains, particularly for forms that do not change frequently or are expensive to render. For instance, rendering form options that are static or rarely change can be cached for faster retrieval.

Finally, integrating AJAX for form submissions and validations can significantly improve user experience by providing immediate feedback and reducing page reloads. This approach demands careful architectural decisions to balance between client and server-side validations and efficiently handle AJAX requests on the server.

Optimizing Django forms involves a multifaceted approach, focusing on efficient data handling, minimizing database queries, leveraging client-side technologies, and using Django's built-in features judiciously. Following the mentioned strategies will help ensure that your Django forms contribute positively to the overall performance of your web applications.

7.14 Advanced Techniques: Dynamic Forms and Custom Widgets

In this section, we will discuss the implementation of dynamic forms and the creation of custom widgets in Django. This involves leveraging Django's built-in capabilities alongside JavaScript to enhance user interaction and form complexity without compromising performance or security.

Dynamic forms in Django are forms whose structure can change during runtime, depending on certain conditions or user interactions. This flexibility is essential for creating a responsive user experience, especially in cases where the form fields cannot be determined upfront. For example, a survey application might present different questions based on a user's previous answers.

The foundation of implementing dynamic forms is the Django form class. However, to modify a form's composition on the client side, JavaScript is employed to add, remove, or change form fields as required.

```
from django import forms

class DynamicSurveyForm(forms.Form):
    def __init__(self, *args, **kwargs):
        dynamic_fields = kwargs.pop('dynamic_fields', None)
        super(DynamicSurveyForm, self).__init__(*args, **kwargs)

        if dynamic_fields is not None:
            for field_name, field_widget in dynamic_fields.items():
                self.fields[field_name] = forms.CharField(widget=field_widget)
```

This Python code snippet introduces a DynamicSurveyForm that can dynamically add char fields based on a passed dictionary of field names and widgets. On the front end, JavaScript can be used to adjust the dynamic_fields argument, allowing the form to respond to user inputs in real-time.

Custom widgets in Django enhance this further by allowing developers to define how form fields should be rendered, including the use of custom HTML and JavaScript. This is particularly useful for integrating third-party JavaScript libraries or creating highly specialized form inputs.

```
1   from django.forms.widgets import Widget
2
3   class DatePickerWidget(Widget):
4       template_name = 'widgets/datepicker.html'
5
6       def __init__(self, attrs=None):
7           super().__init__(attrs)
8
9       def get_context(self, name, value, attrs):
10          context = super().get_context(name, value, attrs)
11          context['widget'].update({
12              'class': 'datepicker',
13              'type': 'date',
14          })
15          return context
```

This example defines a `DatePickerWidget`, a custom widget for selecting dates. It specifies a custom template and extends the widget's context to include HTML5 date picker functionality. When used in a form, this widget renders a date field that pops up a calendar for easy date selection, greatly enhancing the user experience.

For dynamic modification and customization, JavaScript plays a crucial role. It can manipulate the Document Object Model (DOM) to modify form elements based on user actions or application state changes. This, combined with Django's capability to handle dynamic forms and custom widgets on the backend, provides a powerful toolset for creating flexible and interactive web applications.

To ensure a seamless integration of dynamic forms and custom widgets, careful attention must be paid to the interaction between Django and JavaScript. This can involve using Django's template system to dynamically generate JavaScript code or employing AJAX to fetch form changes without reloading the page.

```
1   document.addEventListener('DOMContentLoaded', function() {
2       const fieldContainer = document.getElementById('dynamic-field-
            container');
3       const addButton = document.getElementById('add-field-button');
4
5       addButton.addEventListener('click', function() {
6           const newField = document.createElement('input');
7           newField.setAttribute('type', 'text');
8           newField.setAttribute('name', 'dynamicField');
9           fieldContainer.appendChild(newField);
```

```
10       });
11     });
```

This JavaScript snippet dynamically adds a text input field to the form whenever a button is clicked, showcasing a simple yet effective way to modify forms in real-time based on user interaction.

The use of dynamic forms and custom widgets in Django can significantly enhance the flexibility and user experience of web applications. Through careful integration of Django's form system with client-side technologies like JavaScript, developers can create interactive, responsive, and user-friendly forms that address the complex needs of modern web applications.

7.15   Testing and Debugging Django Forms

Testing and debugging form functionality in a Django application is essential for ensuring that user inputs are properly received, validated, and processed. This chapter will guide you through various strategies to test and debug forms effectively in Django, covering both unit and integration testing methodologies.

Unit Testing Django Forms

Unit testing involves testing the smallest parts of an application in isolation. When applied to Django forms, it focuses on verifying individual fields, validation rules, and form methods.

- **Testing Field Types**: Ascertain that each form field is of the correct type. For example, for a model with an EmailField, the corresponding form should use an EmailField as well.

- **Validation Testing**: Ensure that the form's custom validation logic works as expected. For instance, testing that a phone number field rejects invalid formats.

- **Default Values and Initial Data**: Check that forms populate with the correct initial data or defaults where applicable.

A test case for validating an email field might look like this:

```
1  from django.test import TestCase
2  from .forms import ContactForm
3
4  class ContactFormTest(TestCase):
5      def test_email_field_validation(self):
6          form = ContactForm(data={'email': 'invalid', 'message': 'Hello'})
7          self.assertFalse(form.is_valid())
8          self.assertIn('email', form.errors)
```

Integration Testing with Django Client

Integration testing involves testing the interactions between different parts of the application, such as the form and the view that processes it.

```
1   from django.test import Client, TestCase
2   from django.urls import reverse
3
4   class ContactFormIntegrationTest(TestCase):
5       def setUp(self):
6           self.client = Client()
7
8       def test_form_submission(self):
9           response = self.client.post(reverse('contact'), {'email': 'user@example.com'
                , 'message': 'Hello'})
10          self.assertEqual(response.status_code, 200)
```

In this example, the Django `Client` object simulates a POST request to the contact form's URL. The test checks that the form submission results in a successful response.

Testing File Uploads

Testing forms that handle file uploads requires simulating the upload process. The `SimpleUploadedFile` class can be used to create a mock file object.

```
1  from django.core.files.uploadedfile import SimpleUploadedFile
2  from django.test import TestCase
3  from .forms import PhotoUploadForm
4
5  class PhotoUploadFormTest(TestCase):
6      def test_file_upload(self):
7          file_mock = SimpleUploadedFile(name='test_image.jpg', content=b'',
               content_type='image/jpeg')
8          form = PhotoUploadForm(files={'image': file_mock})
9          self.assertTrue(form.is_valid())
```

Debugging Forms

Debugging Django forms involves inspecting form errors, examining POST data, and using logging strategically. The form's .errors attribute is particularly useful for unveiling issues with field data and validation logic.

```
>>> form = ContactForm(data={})
>>> form.is_valid()
False
>>> print(form.errors)
{'email': ['This field is required.'], 'message': ['This field is required.']}
```

Additionally, consider leveraging Django's logging framework to record form processing steps and capture issues, particularly for intricate validation scenarios or complex business logic.

```
1   import logging
2
3   logger = logging.getLogger(__name__)
4
5   def form_view(request):
6       if request.method == 'POST':
7           form = ContactForm(request.POST)
8           if form.is_valid():
9               # Process form
10              pass
11          else:
12              logger.error('Form invalid: %s', form.errors)
13      # Render form
```

Thorough testing and methodical debugging are crucial for developing robust form handling in Django projects. By applying unit and integration testing principles, leveraging Django's testing utilities, and employing strategic logging, developers can ensure their forms are reliable, secure, and user-friendly.

Chapter 8

Authentication and Authorization in Django

Django provides a comprehensive system for managing user authentication and authorization, enabling developers to secure their applications by controlling access to resources based on user credentials and permissions. This chapter delves into setting up the authentication framework, customizing user models, handling passwords securely, and implementing permission-based access controls. It also covers integrating third-party authentication providers for social logins. By the end of this chapter, readers will be equipped with the knowledge to create secure, user-centric applications, ensuring that users can only access the data and actions permitted to them.

8.1 Introduction to Authentication and Authorization

Authentication and authorization constitute the core mechanisms through which security in web applications, including those developed in Django, is maintained. Authentication refers to the process of verifying the identity of a user, typically through a username and password, although more sophisticated methods, such as biometrics or one-time passwords (OTPs), are increasingly common. Authorization, on the other hand, involves determining the resources and actions that an authenticated user is permitted to access or perform, based on predefined rules or permissions.

In Django, the framework provides an extensive infrastructure designed to manage both authentication and authorization in a seamless and efficient manner. This infrastructure is built around the Django User model, which serves as the foundation for storing user information, including credentials and permissions. Django's authentication system is configured to work out of the box, facilitating tasks such as user account creation, password management, and user authentication. The framework also supports the grouping of users and the assignment of permissions at both the group and individual user levels, enabling a granular level of access control.

The importance of implementing secure authentication and authorization mechanisms cannot be overstated. These processes not only protect sensitive user data from unauthorized access but also ensure that users can perform only those actions for which they have been granted permission. This is particularly crucial in applications that handle personal or financial data, where the consequences of a security breach could be severe.

One of the key strengths of Django's authentication and authorization system is its extensibility. While the default User model and associated permissions system meet the needs of many applications, Django allows developers to extend or completely replace these components to accommodate specific requirements. This includes defining custom user models, customizing the authentication process, and implementing fine-grained permissions.

To facilitate secure password management, Django employs hashing to store user passwords securely. Hashing converts the original password into a fixed-length string of characters that cannot be easily reversed. This means that even if the data store is compromised, the original passwords are not exposed. Django further enhances security by incorporating password validation tools and mechanisms for resetting and changing passwords, which are critical for maintaining the integrity of the user authentication process.

Another aspect of Django's authentication system is its support for session management. When a user successfully logs in, Django creates a session to track the user's activity throughout their interaction with the application. Sessions are integral to maintaining the state of authenticated users across requests, and Django provides robust mechanisms for creating, updating, and terminating sessions as needed.

Additionally, Django facilitates the integration of third-party authentication providers, enabling developers to offer users the option to log in using external services such as Google, Facebook, or Twitter. This not only enhances the user experience by simplifying the login process but also allows developers to leverage the security infrastructure of these established platforms.

In summary, Django's comprehensive approach to authentication and authorization enables developers to build secure, scalable web applications. By providing robust mechanisms for user identification and access control, Django helps ensure that applications remain secure and user data is protected, while also offering the flexibility to customize and extend the built-in functionalities to meet the unique needs of any project.

8.2 Setting Up Django's Built-in Authentication System

Django's built-in authentication system provides developers with the capability to manage user authentication and session tracking efficiently and securely. It encompasses a robust framework that includes mechanisms for user accounts, groups, permissions, and cookie-based user sessions. This section will discuss the setup process of Django's authentication system, focusing on configurations essential for activating and customizing its features to match the requirements of a secure web application.

To begin, it is vital to ensure that the necessary Django authentication system applications are included in the application's settings. This involves modifying the INSTALLED_APPS setting in your project's settings.py file to include 'django.contrib.auth' and 'django.contrib.contenttypes'. These are crucial for the functioning of the authentication system. The 'django.contrib.sessions' app is also required for enabling session management. Here is how these applications might be added:

```
INSTALLED_APPS = [
    ...
    'django.contrib.auth',
    'django.contrib.contenttypes',
    'django.contrib.sessions',
    ...
]
```

Following this, the next step involves configuring the middleware to utilize Django's authentication system fully. Middleware are hooks into Django's request/response processing. It is necessary to add `'django.contrib.sessions.middleware.SessionMiddleware'` and `'django.contrib.auth.middleware.AuthenticationMiddleware'` to the MIDDLEWARE setting of your settings.py file. These middleware are responsible for managing session data and attaching the user to the request respectively. This can be configured as follows:

```
1  MIDDLEWARE = [
2      ...
3      'django.contrib.sessions.middleware.SessionMiddleware',
4      'django.contrib.auth.middleware.AuthenticationMiddleware',
5      ...
6  ]
```

The session middleware should be positioned before the authentication middleware to ensure that request objects have session attributes added before attempting to attach a user to those requests.

With the middleware configured, the next step is to set up the URL patterns to include Django's authentication views. Django auth provides several views for handling operations like login, logout, and password change, among others. To use these views, include the `django.contrib.auth.urls` module in the urls.py of your project or application, as shown:

```
1  from django.urls import path, include
2
3  urlpatterns = [
4      ...
5      path('accounts/', include('django.contrib.auth.urls')),
6      ...
7  ]
```

This inclusion automatically configures URLs for authentication-related views following the pattern accounts/login/, accounts/logout/, etc.

The next crucial aspect of setting up the authentication system is ensuring secure password management. Django's auth system supports various password hashing algorithms that are strongly recommended for secure password storage. The default algorithm used is PBKDF2, but this can be customized through the PASSWORD_HASHERS setting in settings.py. While the default hasher offers a good balance between security and performance, developers may choose to specify an alternative hasher or a list of hashers, like so:

```
1  PASSWORD_HASHERS = [
```

```
2    'django.contrib.auth.hashers.PBKDF2PasswordHasher',
3    'django.contrib.auth.hashers.Argon2PasswordHasher',
4    ...
5  ]
```

Finally, activating Django's in-built authentication system necessitates running migrations to create the necessary database tables for users, groups, and permissions. This is achieved by executing the command:

```
1  python manage.py migrate
```

This command applies migrations for the 'auth', 'contenttypes', and 'sessions' apps, establishing the database schema required for Django's authentication system to function.

By following these steps—configuring installed apps, middleware, URL patterns, password hashers, and applying migrations—you will have successfully set up Django's built-in authentication system. This setup forms the foundation for building secure web applications, allowing for the implementation of more advanced features like custom user models, permission-based access controls, and integrating third-party authentication providers, which are covered in subsequent sections.

8.3 Custom User Models: Extending the Default User

Django's authentication framework comes with a built-in User model that is designed to meet the requirements of many web applications. However, it is common for applications to have unique user requirements that are not fulfilled by the default User model. This necessitates the extension or complete customization of the User model to accommodate such specific needs. Extending the default User model in Django can be accomplished in several ways, each with its own set of considerations and best practices.

The primary motivation for customizing the User model could be to add additional fields, such as a birthdate, profile picture, or a bio. It could also be for more complex functional requirements, such as supporting multiple types of users with distinct attributes. Regardless of the motivation, Django provides the flexibility to either extend the existing User model or substitute it with a completely custom model.

To extend the default User model while maintaining the benefit of Django's authentication system, one common approach is to create a one-to-one link to the User model. This is typically done through a UserProfile model, which can be defined as follows:

```
1   from django.db import models
2   from django.contrib.auth.models import User
3
4   class UserProfile(models.Model):
5       user = models.OneToOneField(User, on_delete=models.CASCADE)
6       bio = models.TextField()
7       profile_picture = models.ImageField(upload_to='profiles/')
8       birthdate = models.DateField()
9
10      def __str__(self):
11          return self.user.username
```

This approach allows developers to add additional information about the user without altering the existing structure of the User model. It is straightforward and leverages Django's built-in User model capabilities. However, it requires additional queries to access the extended fields, which may not be optimal for performance in all cases.

For scenarios where the application needs a completely customized user model that diverges significantly from the default User model, Django allows the User model to be substituted with a custom model by extending AbstractBaseUser and PermissionsMixin. This approach provides maximum flexibility but requires careful consideration of the implications, such as the need to redefine fields and methods that are provided by Django's default User model. A simple example of a custom user model might look like this:

```
1   from django.db import models
2   from django.contrib.auth.models import AbstractBaseUser, BaseUserManager,
        PermissionsMixin
3
4   class MyUserManager(BaseUserManager):
5       def create_user(self, email, date_of_birth, password=None):
6           if not email:
7               raise ValueError('Users must have an email address')
8           user = self.model(
9               email=self.normalize_email(email),
10              date_of_birth=date_of_birth,
11          )
12          user.set_password(password)
13          user.save(using=self._db)
14          return user
15
16      def create_superuser(self, email, date_of_birth, password=None):
17          user = self.create_user(
18              email,
19              password=password,
20              date_of_birth=date_of_birth,
21          )
22          user.is_admin = True
```

```
23        user.save(using=self._db)
24        return user
25
26 class MyUser(AbstractBaseUser, PermissionsMixin):
27     email = models.EmailField(max_length=255, unique=True)
28     date_of_birth = models.DateField()
29     is_active = models.BooleanField(default=True)
30     is_admin = models.BooleanField(default=False)
31
32     objects = MyUserManager()
33
34     USERNAME_FIELD = 'email'
35     REQUIRED_FIELDS = ['date_of_birth']
36
37     def __str__(self):
38         return self.email
```

When substituting the User model, it's critical to define the USERNAME_FIELD and optionally the REQUIRED_FIELDS, as shown in the example above. This informs Django which field is used for login and what additional fields should be prompted for when creating a user via the command line.

Upon deciding to extend or substitute the User model, it is imperative to make this decision early in the project before running the initial migrations. Changing the user model mid-project can be complex and requires careful migration to avoid data loss or corruption.

In summary, Django's flexibility in allowing the extension or substitution of the User model enables developers to tailor the authentication system to the unique requirements of their applications. Whether choosing to extend the existing User model with a UserProfile or substituting it with a completely custom model, careful consideration and implementation are vital to successfully leveraging Django's powerful authentication framework to build secure and user-centric applications.

8.4 Creating and Managing User Accounts

Managing user accounts is a critical component of any web application. In Django, this entails not only the creation of user accounts but also their subsequent management, including updates and deletions. This section will discuss the mechanisms provided by Django for these operations and how they can be used effectively to manage user data.

The Django framework comes with a built-in User model located in django.contrib.auth.models, which is designed to meet the common requirements of web applications. However, developers often need to extend or customize this model to fit their specific needs. Before diving into account management, it is important to understand how user accounts can be created both programmatically and through Django's admin interface.

Creating User Accounts Programmatically

Creating user accounts programmatically allows developers to integrate account creation logic within their application code. Django provides utility functions such as create_user and create_superuser for the UserManager, which simplify the process. Here is a basic example demonstrating how to create a user:

```
1  from django.contrib.auth.models import User
2
3  user = User.objects.create_user('username', 'email@example.com', 'password')
4  user.first_name = 'John'
5  user.last_name = 'Doe'
6  user.save()
```

In this example, a new user is created with a username, email, and password. Additional attributes like first_name and last_name are optional and can be added before calling save() to persist the user to the database.

Creating User Accounts via Django Admin

Django's admin site provides a graphical interface for creating and managing users. Admin users can create new user accounts by navigating to the Users section and filling out the web form provided by the interface. This method is particularly useful for administrators or non-technical staff who need the ability to manage users without direct access to the codebase.

Managing User Accounts

Once user accounts are created, Django offers several mechanisms for managing these accounts. Users can be updated or deleted programmatically or via the admin interface. To update a user programmatically, one must query the user object, make the necessary changes, and then save the object:

234

```
1  user = User.objects.get(username='username')
2  user.email = 'new_email@example.com'
3  user.save()
```

This code snippet fetches an existing user by their username and updates their email address. The save() method is called to write these changes to the database.

User deletion is similarly straightforward. The delete() method can be called on any user object to remove the user's account from the database:

```
1  user = User.objects.get(username='username')
2  user.delete()
```

It is important to handle user data management with care, especially concerning data retention policies and privacy laws. Deleting a user may have implications for related data and system integrity, so it is essential to consider these factors when implementing deletion logic.

Django provides powerful and flexible mechanisms for creating and managing user accounts, catering to a wide range of web application requirements. Whether through programmatically creating users or utilizing Django's admin interface for user management, developers and administrators can effectively control user access and maintain the security of the application. Understanding and leveraging these capabilities is crucial for building robust, user-centric web applications with Django.

8.5 Password Management: Hashing, Resetting, and Changing

Password management is a crucial aspect of securing user accounts in any web application. Django provides robust tools and techniques for handling passwords securely, emphasizing hashing, resetting, and changing passwords. This section will explore each of these elements in detail.

Passwords should never be stored in plaintext due to the severe security risks. Instead, Django uses password hashing to transform the password into a fixed-size string of characters, which is virtually impossible to reverse-engineer. Django employs the PBKDF2 algorithm with a SHA256 hash, offering a secure way to store passwords. When a user logs in, Django hashes the provided password and compares it with the stored hash. This method ensures that the actual passwords are never exposed, even if the data storage is compromised.

```
from django.contrib.auth.hashers import make_password

# Creating a hashed password from a plain password
hashed_password = make_password('plain_password')
```

```
pbkdf2_sha256$216000$B4Gk2334k7Vv$98vU...[TRUNCATED]
```

Changing a user's password is straightforward using Django's built-in functionality. It requires the current password for validation and a new password to replace it. This process is critical for maintaining account security and should be readily accessible within the application.

```
from django.contrib.auth.models import User
from django.contrib.auth import update_session_auth_hash

# Assuming you have a user instance and the new password
user.set_password('new_password')
user.save()

# To keep the user logged in after their password has been changed
update_session_auth_hash(request, user)
```

Password resetting is another important feature, allowing users who have forgotten their passwords to securely create new ones. Django simplifies this process via its authentication framework, primarily through the use of email. A token is generated and sent to the user's email address, which is then used to verify their identity and prompt them to enter a new password.

```
from django.contrib.auth.forms import PasswordResetForm

# Assuming you have the user's email
form = PasswordResetForm({'email': 'user@example.com'})

if form.is_valid():
    request = None # This would normally be the actual HTTP request
    form.save(
        request=request,
        use_https=True,
        email_template_name='registration/password_reset_email.html',
        subject_template_name='registration/password_reset_subject.txt'
    )
```

Managing passwords securely involves more than just the technical handling of password storage and retrieval; it includes educating users about creating strong passwords and enforcing password strength policies. Django can be extended with third-party packages such as django-stronghold to enforce password strength requirements, ensuring that users create passwords that are resistant to brute-force attacks.

Moreover, implementing CAPTCHA or similar mechanisms to thwart automated attempts to reset passwords can add an extra layer of security. It is worth noting that security is a continuously evolving field, and staying updated with the latest best practices is crucial.

To summarize, Django's authentication system provides a comprehensive suite of tools for managing passwords securely. By leveraging password hashing, facilitating easy password changes, and ensuring a secure reset process, developers can protect user accounts from unauthorized access. Additionally, adopting security measures such as enforcing password strength policies and protecting against automated attacks can further enhance the security of a Django application.

8.6 Implementing Login and Logout Functionality

Implementing robust login and logout functionality is a cornerstone in the development of web applications that require user authentication. Django, with its built-in authentication system, provides a straightforward way to add these features to applications, ensuring a secure and user-friendly mechanism for users to gain access to their accounts and safely exit when done.

To begin with the implementation of login functionality, it is essential to utilize Django's `authenticate` and `login` functions. These are part of Django's `django.contrib.auth` module, which provides the necessary mechanisms for verifying user credentials and initiating a user session upon successful authentication.

The login process can be initiated through a view that handles the login request. This typically involves creating a form where users can submit their username and password. Upon form submission, the credentials are passed to the `authenticate` function to verify if they match a user in the database. If the credentials are valid, the `login` function is called with the request and user objects, establishing a session for the user.

The following is an illustration of how a login view might be implemented in Django:

```
1   from django.contrib.auth import authenticate, login
2   from django.http import HttpResponse
3   from django.shortcuts import render, redirect
4
5   def user_login(request):
6       if request.method == "POST":
7           username = request.POST.get('username')
8           password = request.POST.get('password')
9           user = authenticate(request, username=username, password=password)
10          if user is not None:
11              login(request, user)
12              return redirect('dashboard')
13          else:
14              return HttpResponse("Invalid login details")
15      else:
16          return render(request, 'login.html')
```

This example assumes the existence of a 'login.html' template for the login page and a 'dashboard' view to redirect authenticated users. It is important to note that Django handles the session management aspects behind the scenes, providing a secure and efficient way to maintain user state across requests.

For logout functionality, Django provides the logout function, which also resides in the django.contrib.auth module. Invoking this function clears the session, effectively logging the user out. A logout view can be as simple as the following:

```
1   from django.contrib.auth import logout
2   from django.shortcuts import redirect
3
4   def user_logout(request):
5       logout(request)
6       return redirect('login')
```

This would redirect users to the login page after logging them out, ensuring they cannot access any views requiring authentication until they log in again.

To complement login and logout functionality, Django's authentication framework supports mechanisms for handling situations such as failed login attempts and session timeouts, enhancing security and usability. For example, developers can customize the authentication process to lock accounts temporarily after a certain number of unsuccessful login attempts or prompt users to re-authenticate after periods of inactivity.

Implementing effective login and logout functionality is vital for securing user sessions and ensuring that access to application resources is tightly controlled. By leveraging Django's built-in features and best practices, developers can create sophisticated authentication mechanisms with minimal effort, providing a seamless and secure user experience.

8.7 User Permissions and Groups for Authorization

In this section, we will discuss Django's framework for handling user permissions and groups which play a critical role in authorizing users to access specific parts of a web application. Django's permission and group management capabilities allow developers to specify exactly what actions a user can and cannot do, bridging an essential aspect of web security and user management.

Django associates permissions with models. By default, Django automatically creates three permissions for each model in your application: add, change, and delete. These permissions are stored in the auth_permission table in the database and can be assigned to users and groups to regulate CRUD (Create, Read, Update, Delete) operations on model instances.

The creation of custom permissions to extend the default ones for more granular access control is also supported. Custom permissions can be defined within a model's Meta class using the permissions attribute, which takes a list of tuples, each representing a permission with a machine-readable name and a human-readable description.

```
1  class Project(models.Model):
2      # Model fields go here
3      class Meta:
4          permissions = (
5              ("view_project", "Can view project"),
6              ("edit_project_notes", "Can edit the notes of a project"),
7          )
```

Once the custom permissions are defined, applying them to user and group objects involves using the .has_perm() and .has_perms() methods for users, and assigning permissions directly to groups or users via the Django admin interface or programmatically.

Groups are a logical collection of users that can be managed together. Permissions assigned to a group automatically apply to all users within that group, simplifying the management of permissions for multiple users. Django's auth.Group model is used for creating and managing groups.

The process of creating a group and assigning permissions programmatically can be illustrated as follows:

```
1   from django.contrib.auth.models import Group, Permission
2   from django.contrib.contenttypes.models import ContentType
3   from myapp.models import Project
4
5   # Create a new group
6   new_group, created = Group.objects.get_or_create(name='Project Managers')
7
8   # Fetch the model content type and specific permissions
9   ct = ContentType.objects.get_for_model(Project)
10  view_permission = Permission.objects.get(codename='view_project', content_type=ct)
11  edit_permission = Permission.objects.get(codename='edit_project_notes',
        content_type=ct)
12
13  # Assign permissions to the group
14  new_group.permissions.add(view_permission, edit_permission)
```

After setting up groups and permissions, Django also provides decorators such as @permission_required and @user_passes_test to secure views by checking if a user has a specific permission or meets a certain condition. For example, to ensure that only users with the view_project permission can access a view, one can use:

```
1   from django.contrib.auth.decorators import permission_required
2
3   @permission_required('myapp.view_project')
4   def project_view(request):
5       # View code here
```

Managing permissions in templates is straightforward with Django's perms template variable, allowing for granular display of content based on the user's permissions. For instance, displaying a link to edit project notes only if the user has the edit_project_notes permission can be achieved as follows:

```
{% if perms.myapp.edit_project_notes %}
    <a href="/projects/edit-notes/">Edit Project Notes</a>
{% endif %}
```

Django's system for managing permissions and groups provides a robust framework for implementing authorization in web applications. By efficiently utilizing permissions at the model level, extending those permissions, and applying them through users and groups, developers can secure their applications and ensure that users interact only with the data and actions they are authorized to. This system, combined

240

with Django's built-in decorators and template tags, empowers developers to create secure and user-centric web applications efficiently.

8.8   Customizing Authentication Forms

Let's discuss customizing authentication forms in Django. Django's authentication framework is robust and flexible, providing built-in forms for the most common use cases, such as logging in and out, and password changing. However, for applications requiring distinct functionality or styling, customization of these forms becomes essential. This may include adding extra fields, changing validation rules, or tailoring the appearance to match the application's design.

The process of customizing authentication forms involves subclassing the existing Django forms provided by the django.contrib.auth.forms module. Here, one has access to classes such as AuthenticationForm, UserCreationForm, and PasswordChangeForm, each serving different purposes in the authentication process.

To begin with, let's customize the user login form by subclassing AuthenticationForm. This involves overriding the form to add a new field or alter existing ones:

```
from django import forms
from django.contrib.auth.forms import AuthenticationForm

class CustomAuthenticationForm(AuthenticationForm):
    remember_me = forms.BooleanField(required=False)

    def __init__(self, *args, **kwargs):
        super(CustomAuthenticationForm, self).__init__(*args, **kwargs)
        self.fields['username'].widget.attrs.update({'class': 'form-control'})
        self.fields['password'].widget.attrs.update({'class': 'form-control'})
        self.fields['remember_me'].widget.attrs.update({'class': 'form-check'})
```

This customization adds a "remember me" checkbox to the form, a feature not present in the default AuthenticationForm. It further customizes the HTML attributes of the fields, such as adding form-control class for styling with Bootstrap.

After creating a custom form, the next step is to utilize it within the view. Django's class-based views offer a convenient way to specify a form class that a view should use. The LoginView, for example, can be instructed to use the CustomAuthenticationForm as follows:

```
from django.contrib.auth.views import LoginView
```

```
2
3   class CustomLoginView(LoginView):
4       authentication_form = CustomAuthenticationForm
```

Now, any route tied to `CustomLoginView` will render the customized form instead of the default authentication form.

Furthermore, it might be necessary to customize form validation logic. This involves overriding the `clean` method of the form to implement custom validation rules or behaviors:

```
1   def clean(self):
2       super().clean()
3       remember_me = self.cleaned_data.get('remember_me')
4       if remember_me:
5           self.request.session.set_expiry(1209600) # 2 weeks
```

Here, the form's `clean` method is overridden to extend validation logic, setting session expiry if the "remember me" option is checked. This serves as an essential customization for enhancing user experience by offering persistent logins.

To conclude, customization of authentication forms in Django allows developers to tailor the user experience and integrate custom functionality beyond the default offerings. By subclassing and modifying the built-in authentication forms, one can easily add new fields, alter styling, and modify validation logic. It is essential to ensure that these customizations do not compromise the security of the authentication process. Adequate testing should be performed to confirm that forms handle user input securely and behave as expected in all scenarios.

8.9   Integrating Social Authentication

Integrating Social Authentication in Django applications provides users with a convenient and familiar way to sign in using their existing social media accounts, such as Google, Facebook, or Twitter. This not only enhances the user experience by reducing the need for multiple passwords but also accelerates the registration process. This section will discuss configuring Django to support social authentication, selecting and setting up third-party packages, and handling user data securely.

To integrate social authentication, a third-party package like django-allauth or python-social-auth can be utilized. These packages support multiple authentication backends and simplify the process of authenticating users through various social media platforms. For the purpose of this section, let's focus on using django-allauth due to its comprehensive documentation and active community support.

First, django-allauth needs to be installed using pip:

```
1  pip install django-allauth
```

After installation, add "django.contrib.sites", "allauth", "allauth.account", and "allauth.socialaccount" to the 'IN-STALLED_APPS' in the Django settings. Moreover, you must declare a 'SITE_ID', typically set to '1', to associate social accounts with a specific domain.

```
1   INSTALLED_APPS = [
2       ...
3       'django.contrib.sites',
4       'allauth',
5       'allauth.account',
6       'allauth.socialaccount',
7       ...
8   ]
9
10  SITE_ID = 1
```

Django's urlpatterns need to be updated to include urls from allauth:

```
1   urlpatterns = [
2       ...
3       path('accounts/', include('allauth.urls')),
4       ...
5   ]
```

The next step involves choosing which social platforms to support and configuring them in the Django admin panel. Each platform requires creating an application in their respective developer platforms to obtain API keys or secrets. These keys are then entered into the 'Social applications' section of the Django admin, associating them with the site defined by 'SITE_ID'.

Handling user data securely is paramount when implementing social authentication. Ensure that the information retrieved from social platforms is limited to what is necessary for authentication and potentially profile creation. Settings in django-allauth allow developers to specify the scope of permissions when making requests to these platforms.

```
1   SOCIALACCOUNT_PROVIDERS = {
2       'google': {
3           'SCOPE': [
4               'profile',
5               'email',
```

243

```
 6      ],
 7      'AUTH_PARAMS': {
 8          'access_type': 'online',
 9      }
10    }
11  }
```

When a user authenticates via a social account for the first time, django-allauth can automatically create a corresponding user in the Django application. Developers have the option to customise the process, for example, by requiring users to provide additional information or to undergo an approval process before their account is fully activated.

In terms of the user experience, django-allauth integrates seamlessly with Django's authentication system, providing ready-to-use templates for login, logout, and signup processes. However, customization of these templates is often necessary to maintain the look and feel of the application. This can be achieved by overriding the default templates in the project's template directory.

Integrating social authentication certainly elevates the user experience, but it's important to underscore the significance of security considerations. Storing API keys securely, using environment variables for sensitive information, and regularly updating the authentication packages to their latest versions are necessary steps to mitigate potential vulnerabilities.

Integrating social authentication in Django applications with django-allauth is a streamlined process that enhances user experience by simplifying the sign-in and registration process. With cautious handling of user data and adherence to security best practices, developers can provide a secure and efficient way for users to access their applications.

8.10 Token-based Authentication for APIs

Token-based authentication is a method that allows users to access a website or application by providing a token instead of a username and password. This approach is particularly useful for APIs, as it enables secure access over the Internet. In Django, token-based authentication is implemented using the Django REST framework (DRF), which provides a powerful and flexible toolkit for building Web APIs.

Let's discuss the process of setting up token-based authentication in a Django REST framework-based application. The primary focus will be on using DRF's built-in token authentication mechanism, although we will also touch upon how to extend and customize this mechanism for more complex scenarios.

The first step in implementing token authentication is to add the Django REST framework and its token authentication module to your project. This involves modifying your project's settings.py file to include rest_framework and rest_framework.authtoken in the INSTALLED_APPS section:

```
1  INSTALLED_APPS = [
2      ...
3      'rest_framework',
4      'rest_framework.authtoken',
5      ...
6  ]
```

Next, you need to configure the authentication classes used by your application by adding a REST_FRAMEWORK dictionary to your settings.py file. Within this dictionary, specify TokenAuthentication as a default authentication class:

```
1  REST_FRAMEWORK = {
2      'DEFAULT_AUTHENTICATION_CLASSES': [
3          'rest_framework.authentication.TokenAuthentication',
4      ],
5  }
```

With the necessary settings configured, the next step involves creating or modifying your user model to handle token creation. DRF provides a management command to create tokens for all users in your database. However, to ensure that a new token is created whenever a user is created, you can override the save method of your user model or use signals to generate a token automatically:

```
1  from django.db.models.signals import post_save
2  from django.dispatch import receiver
3  from rest_framework.authtoken.models import Token
4  from django.contrib.auth.models import User
5
6  @receiver(post_save, sender=User)
7  def create_auth_token(sender, instance=None, created=False, **kwargs):
8      if created:
9          Token.objects.create(user=instance)
```

This signal ensures that every time a user is saved and the created parameter is True, a new token for that user is automatically created. Note, for this signal to work, it must be imported and connected in your application's apps.py or the __init__.py of your application.

245

After setting up your user model and the necessary configurations, you can create views that use token authentication. DRF provides a view that can be used for obtaining tokens given the username and password. You would typically add a URL pattern in your urls.py to enable this functionality:

```
from django.urls import path
from rest_framework.authtoken.views import obtain_auth_token

urlpatterns = [
    path('api-token-auth/', obtain_auth_token, name='api_token_auth'),
]
```

When a POST request is made to this URL with the correct username and password, the response will include the user's token, which can then be used for authenticated requests to your API.

Token authentication is stateless, meaning that the server does not need to keep a record of tokens. The token is included in the HTTP header of each request, allowing the server to authenticate the request without the need to maintain session information. Here is an example of how the token is used in an HTTP header:

```
Authorization: Token 9944b09199c62bcf9418ad846dd0e4bbdfc6ee4b
```

To secure your views, you use the @api_view decorator (for function-based views) or the APIView class (for class-based views), and specify the appropriate permissions. By default, without any permissions, all requests would require authentication. However, you can customize this behavior by setting the permission_classes attribute:

```
from rest_framework.permissions import IsAuthenticated
from rest_framework.decorators import api_view, permission_classes

@api_view(['GET'])
@permission_classes([IsAuthenticated])
def example_view(request, format=None):
    content = {
        'user': str(request.user),
        'auth': str(request.auth),
    }
    return Response(content)
```

This view will only be accessible to users who provide a valid token in the request's HTTP header, effectively restricting access based on the token-based authentication.

To summarize, token-based authentication in Django, using the Django REST framework, provides a secure and scalable method to manage authentication in APIs. It simplifies the process of handling user authentication, especially for web and mobile applications, by utilizing tokens rather than traditional session-based authentication mechanisms. With proper implementation and customized handling for specific requirements, token-based authentication can significantly enhance the security and efficiency of your Django applications.

8.11 Using Django Permissions in Views and Templates

Django's authentication framework includes a robust permission system that allows developers to specify what actions each user can perform on different objects within the application. In this section, we will discuss how to use Django's permissions in views and templates to control access to various resources and functionality based on the user's permissions.

Django defines permissions as a triplet of strings: (app_label, model, permission_name). By default, Django automatically creates three permissions for each model: add, change, and delete. It's also possible to define custom permissions for models by specifying a permissions attribute in the model's Meta class.

To check whether a user has a specific permission, you can use the user.has_perm() method, passing in the permission string as argument. For example, to check if a user has the permission to change a BlogPost object, one would use:

```
1  user.has_perm('app_label.change_blogpost')
```

In views, this mechanism can be used to restrict access to certain actions. For instance, before proceeding to update a blog post, you can check if the user has the required permission and handle the case accordingly:

```
1   from django.http import HttpResponseForbidden
2   from django.shortcuts import render, get_object_or_404
3   from .models import BlogPost
4
5   def edit_blog_post(request, post_id):
6       post = get_object_or_404(BlogPost, pk=post_id)
7       if not request.user.has_perm('app_label.change_blogpost'):
8           return HttpResponseForbidden("You do not have permission to edit this post."
                )
9
10      # Proceed with the view logic for editing the post
11      return render(request, 'edit_post.html', {'post': post})
```

247

Moreover, Django provides decorators such as @login_required and @permission_required to simplify permission checks in views. The @permission_required decorator takes a permission string and automatically denies access if the current user does not have the permission:

```
from django.contrib.auth.decorators import permission_required

@permission_required('app_label.change_blogpost', raise_exception=True)
def edit_blog_post(request, post_id):
    # View logic here
```

To utilize permissions in templates, Django injects the user variable into each template's context, which represents the current user. You can use this variable along with the perms template variable to check permissions. The perms variable is a template context processor that allows checking permissions directly in the templates:

```
{% if perms.app_label.change_blogpost %}
    <a href="{% url 'edit_blog_post' post.id %}">Edit Post</a>
{% endif %}
```

This allows for a dynamic display of links and actions based on the user's permissions, enhancing both security and user experience by ensuring that users only see options they are allowed to perform.

In summary, utilizing Django's permission system in views and templates is straightforward and highly effective in controlling access to resources based on user permissions. Through the use of methods like has_perm(), decorators such as permission_required, and template conditionals, developers can secure their applications and provide a customized user experience based on each user's permissions.

8.12 Securing Views with Decorators and Middleware

In this section we will discuss two powerful Django features for securing views: decorators and middleware. These tools enable developers to enforce authentication and authorization checks efficiently, ensuring that only authenticated and authorized users can access certain views or execute specific actions within a web application built with Django.

Decorators in Django are a key feature for securing views. A decorator is essentially a function that takes another function as an argument, wraps its behavior, and then returns a new function with enhanced capabilities. In the context of Django views, decorators are used to add access control capabilities by wrapping view functions. The most commonly used decorators for securing views in Django are @login_required, @permission_required, and @user_passes_test.

The @login_required decorator is used to restrict access to a view, so that only authenticated users can access it. If an unauthenticated user attempts to access a view protected by @login_required, Django redirects the user to the login URL defined in the project's settings, appending the originally requested URL as a query string parameter named next, for post-login redirection. Usage of the @login_required decorator is straightforward, as shown in the example below:

```
1  from django.contrib.auth.decorators import login_required
2
3  @login_required
4  def my_secure_view(request):
5      # View code here. Only authenticated users can access.
```

The @permission_required decorator takes it a step further by not only checking if a user is authenticated but also verifying if the user has specific permissions to access a view. This is particularly useful for scenarios where access control needs to be more granular, allowing only users with certain permissions assigned to perform an action or access a resource. For instance:

```
1  from django.contrib.auth.decorators import permission_required
2
3  @permission_required('app_label.permission_codename')
4  def my_permission_protected_view(request):
5      # View code accessible only to users with specific permission.
```

The @user_passes_test decorator offers the highest degree of flexibility, allowing developers to define custom test functions that must return True for a user to access the view. It is useful for implementing custom access control logic:

```
1  from django.contrib.auth.decorators import user_passes_test
2
3  def check_user_condition(user):
4      # Implement custom test logic.
5      return True
6
7  @user_passes_test(check_user_condition)
8  def my_custom_protected_view(request):
9      # View code here. Access controlled by custom test logic.
```

Middleware in Django is another mechanism to enforce global access control policies. Middleware components are hooks into Django's request/response processing. They are executed before and after a view

249

is called, providing a convenient way to apply security checks across multiple views or the entire application. For securing views, middleware can be used to inspect user credentials, perform redirection for unauthenticated or unauthorized access, and log access attempts, among other tasks.

Implementing custom middleware for access control consists of defining a class with specific methods that Django invokes during the request/response cycle. The process_view() method is particularly pertinent for view security, as it allows the inspection and modification of view call arguments before the view is executed. A simplified example of a middleware component enforcing custom access control logic is shown below:

```
from django.http import HttpResponseForbidden

class CustomAccessControlMiddleware:
    def __init__(self, get_response):
        self.get_response = get_response

    def __call__(self, request):
        return self.get_response(request)

    def process_view(self, request, view_func, view_args, view_kwargs):
        # Implement access control logic here.
        # Return HttpResponseForbidden if access is denied,
        # otherwise return None to continue normal processing.
        if not request.user.is_authenticated:
            return HttpResponseForbidden()
```

To activate a middleware, it must be added to the MIDDLEWARE list in Django's project settings. Ordering within this list is important, as it affects the request processing sequence.

The combination of decorators and middleware provides a powerful and flexible framework for enforcing access control in Django applications. Decorators offer fine-grained control over individual views, while middleware enables global policies to be applied transparently across multiple views or the entire application. By understanding and leveraging these features, developers can enhance the security of their Django applications, ensuring that users can only access the data and actions permitted to them.

8.13   Auditing and Logging User Actions

Auditing and logging are crucial components in building secure web applications. They provide a mechanism to record and monitor user actions, offering insights into usage patterns, identifying potential security breaches, and ensuring compliance with various regulatory standards. In the context of Django, there are multiple methods and tools available to facilitate the auditing and logging of user actions effectively.

Let's start with implementing logging in Django. Django utilizes Python's built-in logging module to log various system events. To log user actions specifically, developers can define custom logging configurations in the settings.py file of their Django project. Here is a basic setup for logging user actions:

```
LOGGING = {
    'version': 1,
    'disable_existing_loggers': False,
    'handlers': {
        'file': {
            'level': 'INFO',
            'class': 'logging.FileHandler',
            'filename': '/path/to/your/logs/django_user_actions.log',
        },
    },
    'loggers': {
        'django': {
            'handlers': ['file'],
            'level': 'INFO',
            'propagate': True,
        },
    },
}
```

This configuration snippet directs Django to log all INFO level messages to a specified log file. Developers can then use the logging module throughout their codebase to log specific user actions. For example, after a successful login, one might log the event as follows:

```
import logging

logger = logging.getLogger('django')

def login_success(request, user):
    logger.info('User %s logged in successfully.', user.username)
```

Beyond basic logging, auditing user actions requires more detailed tracking, often necessitating the storage of logs in a database for easier querying and analysis. The Django ecosystem provides several tools and libraries for this purpose, such as Django-Auditlog. Django-Auditlog is a pluggable app that automatically logs changes made to models and associates them with the user who made those changes.

Here is how to integrate Django-Auditlog with your project:

- First, install Django-Auditlog using pip:

```
1  pip install django-auditlog
```

- Next, add 'auditlog' to the INSTALLED_APPS list in your settings.py file:

```
1  INSTALLED_APPS = [
2      ...
3      'auditlog',
4      ...
5  ]
```

- Finally, add Auditlog's middleware to the MIDDLEWARE list to capture user information:

```
1  MIDDLEWARE = [
2      ...
3      'auditlog.middleware.AuditlogMiddleware',
4      ...
5  ]
```

Once integrated, Django-Auditlog will automatically track and log any changes to registered models. Models can be registered with Django-Auditlog by importing the Auditlog model and attaching it as an attribute:

```
1  from django.db import models
2  from auditlog.registry import auditlog
3
4  class MyModel(models.Model):
5      name = models.CharField(max_length=100)
6      description = models.TextField()
7
8  auditlog.register(MyModel)
```

The audit logs captured by Django-Auditlog can be accessed and an-alyzed through the Django admin interface, which provides an audit trail of who did what and when. This capability is indispensable for security auditing, investigating incidents, or simply understanding user behavior over time.

Auditing and logging user actions are vital practices for maintaining the security and integrity of web applications. By leveraging Django's logging capabilities and third-party libraries like Django-Auditlog, de-velopers can implement robust mechanisms for tracking user behavior and changes within their applications. These logs not only serve as a critical security tool but also aid in debugging, monitoring, and compliance efforts.

8.14 Testing Authentication and Authorization

Testing is a critical component of software development, ensuring that code behaves as expected and that modifications do not introduce regressions. Within the context of authentication and authorization in Django, testing verifies that only authenticated users can access restricted areas and that permissions are correctly enforced. This section will discuss strategies for effectively testing Django's authentication and authorization mechanisms, including user authentication, permission checks, and the security of password management functions.

To start, it is important to leverage Django's built-in test framework, which extends Python's unittest library, providing a set of tools designed to test Django web applications. Firstly, the `TestCase` class from `django.test` should be used to create test cases. This class includes a client instance (`self.client`) that can simulate requests to the application, allowing tests to interact with the application as if it were being accessed by a real user.

When testing user authentication, the process involves verifying that the login process works as expected and that unauthenticated users are redirected or denied access to protected views. An example test might look like the following:

```
1  from django.test import TestCase
2  from django.urls import reverse
3  from django.contrib.auth.models import User
4
5  class AuthenticationTest(TestCase):
6      def setUp(self):
7          self.user = User.objects.create_user(username='testuser', password='secret')
8
9      def test_login(self):
10         response = self.client.post(reverse('login'), {'username': 'testuser', '
               password': 'secret'})
11         self.assertRedirects(response, reverse('home'))
12
13     def test_access_restricted_page_without_login(self):
14         response = self.client.get(reverse('restricted_page'))
15         self.assertEqual(response.status_code, 302)
```

This example demonstrates testing the login functionality and ensuring that a user cannot access restricted pages without being logged in. The `setUp` method creates a dummy user which is then authenticated in the `test_login` method. `assertRedirects` and `assertEqual` are used to verify the expected outcomes.

Testing permissions involves creating scenarios where users with different permission levels attempt to access resources or perform actions. Django's `Permission` model and the `@permission_required` or `@user_passes_test` decorators can be used to manage access controls in views. Tests should be designed to cover all possible authorization scenarios:

```
from django.contrib.auth.models import Permission

class PermissionTest(TestCase):
    def setUp(self):
        self.user = User.objects.create_user(username='user', password='password')
        self.permission = Permission.objects.get(codename='can_view_resource')
        self.user.user_permissions.add(self.permission)

    def test_user_with_permission(self):
        self.client.login(username='user', password='password')
        response = self.client.get(reverse('protected_resource'))
        self.assertEqual(response.status_code, 200)

    def test_user_without_permission(self):
        self.client.login(username='user', password='password')
        self.user.user_permissions.remove(self.permission)
        response = self.client.get(reverse('protected_resource'))
        self.assertEqual(response.status_code, 403)
```

In addition to direct authentication and authorization tests, it's critical to test password management functionalities, including password hashing, resetting, and changing procedures, to verify their security and robustness.

Lastly, Django's test framework supports testing sessions and middleware, which are essential for authentication workflows. Testing these components involves verifying that user sessions are correctly initiated and terminated and that middleware correctly intercepts requests based on user authentication status and permissions.

Efficient testing of authentication and authorization mechanisms not only requires checking that the implemented security measures work as intended but also demands a thorough consideration of edge cases and potential security vulnerabilities. A well-structured suite of tests will help ensure that the application reliably manages user access, protecting both user data and system integrity.

8.15 Best Practices for Secure Authentication and Authorization

In web development, the security of user data and access control are paramount. This section will discuss the best practices for implementing secure authentication and authorization in Django applications. These strategies not only safeguard against common vulnerabilities but also ensure that user data is handled with the utmost privacy and integrity.

Firstly, it is crucial to utilize Django's built-in user authentication system effectively. This system, being robust and well-tested, provides a solid foundation for managing user accounts, sessions, and password hashing. When extending the default user model, ensure that custom user models inherit from `AbstractBaseUser` and `PermissionsMixin`. This approach preserves Django's built-in security features while allowing flexibility in user model customization.

Implementing strong password policies is another essential practice. Django's built-in validators under `AUTH_PASSWORD_VALIDATORS` should be leveraged to enforce password strength requirements, such as minimum length and complexity. Furthermore, Django's password management tools, including hashing algorithms like PBKDF2, bcrypt, and Argon2, should be utilized to ensure that stored passwords are resistant to cracking attempts.

Securely managing session data is equally important. Enabling Django's secure and HttpOnly session cookies flags prevents unwanted access or manipulation of session IDs. For applications deployed over HTTPS, setting the `CSRF_COOKIE_SECURE` and `SESSION_COOKIE_SECURE` settings to True ensures that cookies are only sent over secure connections, mitigating the risks of man-in-the-middle attacks.

In addition to authentication, implementing fine-grained authorization controls is vital. Django's permission system should be used to restrict user access to specific resources based on roles or permissions. Utilizing groups to manage user permissions can simplify the administration of authorization rules, especially in large-scale applications. For more complex scenarios, Django's content types framework can be employed to dynamically assign permissions to models, offering a granular level of control.

For views that require user authentication, decorators such as `@login_required` and permission-based decorators like `@permission_required` provide a convenient method to enforce access restrictions. Middleware can also be utilized for global authentication checks or to secure AJAX calls and API endpoints.

Integrating third-party authentication providers via Django's social auth or OAuth libraries introduces additional security considerations. Ensuring that third-party libraries are kept up-to-date and configuring OAuth callbacks securely are critical to preventing vulnerabilities inherent in these integrations.

Token-based authentication, particularly for RESTful APIs, requires careful management of access tokens. Implementing token expiration and rotation strategies can mitigate the risk of token theft or misuse. Libraries like Django OAuth Toolkit or djangorestframework-simplejwt can assist in managing tokens securely while providing compliance with standards like OAuth2.

Logging and auditing are indispensable for tracking user activities and identifying security incidents. Django's logging framework should be configured to record login attempts, password changes, and permission violations. These logs can be invaluable for forensic analysis in the event of a security breach.

Finally, routine testing and security audits should not be neglected. Automated testing tools such as Django's test framework and third-party security scanners can uncover vulnerabilities before they are exploited. Regular code reviews and updating Django and its dependencies to their latest secure versions are also recommended practices.

In summary, securing authentication and authorization in Django applications encompasses a comprehensive approach, from leveraging Django's built-in features to implementing secure password practices, access control mechanisms, and vigilant monitoring. By adhering to these best practices, developers can significantly enhance the security posture of their applications, thereby protecting user data and maintaining trust.

Chapter 9

RESTful APIs with Django Rest Framework

Django Rest Framework (DRF) is a powerful and flexible toolkit for building Web APIs, offering developers a systematic approach to create RESTful interfaces efficiently. This chapter introduces the principles of REST and how DRF enables rapid API development by providing serialization for ORM and non-ORM data sources. Topics include setting up DRF, authentication, permissions, serialization, request and response handling, and viewsets for CRUD operations. By integrating best practices and advanced features, such as pagination and versioning, developers can build scalable, maintainable, and secure APIs that extend the functionality of Django applications to web, mobile, and other platforms.

9.1 Introduction to RESTful APIs and Django Rest Framework

Representational State Transfer (REST) is an architectural style that defines a set of constraints to be used for creating web services. These services provide interoperability between computer systems on the internet. RESTful APIs, which adhere to these constraints, allow for actions such as creating, retrieving, updating, and deleting (CRUD operations) data across different platforms using standard HTTP methods.

The principles of REST insist on stateless communication, cacheable responses, a uniform interface, and a client-server architecture, making APIs developed under this paradigm highly scalable, efficient, and easy to modify.

Django Rest Framework (DRF) is a powerful toolkit for building Web APIs in the Django framework. It leverages Django's capabilities to handle web requests and responses, offering a coherent layer above Django models and views to serialize data and handle complex web API logic. By abstracting away many of the lower-level details of HTTP interactions, DRF enables developers to focus on writing the business logic of their applications. It supports class-based views and offers a rich set of tools for authentication, permissions, and content negotiation, making it an ideal choice for building RESTful services.

To start building a RESTful API using Django Rest Framework, one first needs to understand serialization. Serialization is the process of converting complex data types, such as Django model instances, into native Python datatypes that can then be easily rendered into JSON, XML, or other content types. DRF provides serializers for this exact purpose, simplifying the task of converting model instances into JSON for HTTP responses, and vice versa, for consuming data sent by clients.

```
1  from rest_framework import serializers
2  from myapp.models import MyModel
3
4  class MyModelSerializer(serializers.ModelSerializer):
5      class Meta:
6          model = MyModel
7          fields = ['id', 'title', 'description']
```

In the example above, a serializer for a Django model 'MyModel' is defined, specifying which fields should be included in the serialized output. This serializer can now be used in views to handle the incoming and outgoing data for 'MyModel' instances.

HTTP methods play a crucial role in RESTful APIs, where each method - GET, POST, PUT, DELETE - corresponds to CRUD operations. Django Rest Framework supports these operations through its views and viewsets, making the development of APIs intuitive and structured. A viewset in DRF can provide the logic for all the CRUD operations for a model, reducing the amount of code needed to create these endpoints.

```
1  from myapp.models import MyModel
2  from myapp.serializers import MyModelSerializer
3  from rest_framework import viewsets
4
5  class MyModelViewSet(viewsets.ModelViewSet):
6      queryset = MyModel.objects.all()
```

```
7    serializer_class = MyModelSerializer
```

By declaring a 'ModelViewSet', DRF automatically provides implementations for CRUD operations over the model 'MyModel', using the 'MyModelSerializer' for data serialization. This dramatically reduces boilerplate code and streamlines the process of API development.

Developing RESTful APIs with Django Rest Framework not only improves productivity but also enhances the scalability and maintainability of web applications. Its compatibility with Django's ORM (Object-Relational Mapping) system enables developers to work with complex databases efficiently. Furthermore, DRF's support for authentication, permissions, and pagination ensures that APIs are secure, accessible only to authorized users, and capable of handling large datasets.

In summary, RESTful APIs facilitate seamless communication and data exchange across different systems over the web. By leveraging Django Rest Framework, developers can build these APIs more efficiently, taking advantage of the framework's robust architecture, comprehensive tooling, and ease of integration with Django projects. This introductory section has covered the foundational aspects of REST and DRF, setting the stage for a deeper exploration of more advanced features and best practices in the subsequent sections.

9.2 Setting Up Django Rest Framework in Your Django Project

Let's start with the initial setup required to integrate Django Rest Framework (DRF) into your Django project. This process involves several steps that are crucial for leveraging DRF's capabilities in creating RESTful APIs.

First, ensure that Django is already installed in your environment. If Django is not installed, you can do so by running pip install django in your terminal. Once Django is set up, the next step is to install Django Rest Framework. This can be achieved by executing the following command:

```
1   pip install djangorestframework
```

After installing DRF, you need to add it to the INSTALLED_APPS section of your Django project's settings.py file. This step is necessary for

259

Django to recognize the installed framework and its associated functionalities. Add `'rest_framework'` to the list:

```
1   INSTALLED_APPS = [
2       ...
3       'rest_framework',
4   ]
```

With DRF added to your Django project, you can now proceed to create your first API. However, before diving into the API development, it is worth discussing the concept of serialization in DRF. Serialization is the process of converting complex data types (such as Django models) into Python data types that can then be easily rendered into JSON, XML, or other content types. DRF provides powerful serialization that makes it straightforward to serialize queryset or model instances.

To demonstrate serialization, let's create a simple model and serialize it. Assuming you have an app named myapp, define a model in `myapp/models.py`:

```
1   from django.db import models
2
3   class MyModel(models.Model):
4       title = models.CharField(max_length=100)
5       description = models.TextField()
```

Next, create a serializer for MyModel in a new file `myapp/serializers.py`:

```
1   from rest_framework import serializers
2   from .models import MyModel
3
4   class MyModelSerializer(serializers.ModelSerializer):
5       class Meta:
6           model = MyModel
7           fields = ['id', 'title', 'description']
```

The serializer class `MyModelSerializer` created above specifies which model to serialize and the fields to include in the serialized data.

After defining the serializer, the next step is to create a view that will use the serializer to respond to web requests. DRF supports function-based views (FBV) and class-based views (CBV), but for simplicity and convention, we will use CBV. In `myapp/views.py`, define a view that returns all instances of MyModel:

```
1   from rest_framework.views import APIView
2   from rest_framework.response import Response
3   from .models import MyModel
4   from .serializers import MyModelSerializer
5
6   class MyModelList(APIView):
```

```
7     def get(self, request, format=None):
8         my_models = MyModel.objects.all()
9         serializer = MyModelSerializer(my_models, many=True)
10        return Response(serializer.data)
```

The MyModelList view handles GET requests by retrieving all MyModel instances, serializing them, and returning the serialized data in the response.

Finally, to make the MyModelList view accessible via HTTP, you need to map it to a URL in myapp/urls.py. If this file does not exist, create it and then define the URL pattern:

```
1   from django.urls import path
2   from .views import MyModelList
3
4   urlpatterns = [
5       path('mymodels/', MyModelList.as_view(), name='my_model_list'),
6   ]
```

Include myapp/urls.py in the project's main urls.py file to ensure the newly defined paths are served:

```
1   from django.urls import include, path
2
3   urlpatterns = [
4       ...
5       path('api/', include('myapp.urls')),
6   ]
```

With the view and URL configuration in place, your Django project is now equipped with a basic DRF-powered API endpoint. By navigating to /api/mymodels/, you should be able to see the serialized representation of all MyModel instances in your database.

This setup illustrates the foundational steps for integrating DRF into a Django project. It highlights the simplicity and power of DRF in facilitating the rapid development of RESTful APIs, from serialization to handling HTTP requests and routing.

9.3 Serializers: Converting Data for the Web

At the core of Django Rest Framework (DRF) lies the concept of serializers, which serve as a crucial bridge between complex data types and the web-friendly JSON format. Serializers not only play a pivotal role in converting data into JSON but are also responsible for deserialization, which involves parsing incoming JSON data into Python data types. This dual functionality enables developers to seamlessly convert complex querysets and model instances into JSON, and then back to complex types after the data has been manipulated client-side. In this section, we will discuss the implementation and customization of serializers within DRF for effective data conversion in web APIs.

To begin, let's define a simple model and subsequently illustrate how to serialize this model using DRF. Consider a Django model named Item, which represents items in an inventory system. The model may be defined as follows:

```
1  from django.db import models
2
3  class Item(models.Model):
4      name = models.CharField(max_length=100)
5      description = models.CharField(max_length=300)
6      price = models.DecimalField(max_digits=10, decimal_places=2)
7      in_stock = models.BooleanField(default=True)
```

Given this model, the next step is to serialize it. DRF provides a ModelSerializer class for this purpose, which automatically generates a serializer based on the model definition. Here is how the serializer for the Item model can be implemented:

```
1  from rest_framework import serializers
2  from .models import Item
3
4  class ItemSerializer(serializers.ModelSerializer):
5      class Meta:
6          model = Item
7          fields = ['id', 'name', 'description', 'price', 'in_stock']
```

The Meta class within the serializer definition specifies the model it serializes and the fields that should be included in the serialized output. DRF then takes care of translating querysets and model instances into JSON format. For instance, to serialize a single item, one would perform the following:

```
1  from .models import Item
2  from .serializers import ItemSerializer
3
4  item = Item.objects.get(id=1)
5  serializer = ItemSerializer(item)
6  print(serializer.data)
```

The serializer's data property contains the serialized data ready to be rendered into JSON. For multiple items, the serializer is instantiated with a queryset, and the many=True argument is passed to indicate serialization of multiple objects:

```
1  items = Item.objects.all()
```

```
2  serializer = ItemSerializer(items, many=True)
3  print(serializer.data)
```

The serialization process can also be reversed for deserialization purposes. Given JSON data, DRF serializers parse this input and validate
it against the model constraints, converting it into Python data types.
This feature is invaluable for creating or updating model instances
based on JSON input from clients. Below is an example demonstrating
deserialization and object creation:

```
1  serializer = ItemSerializer(data={'name': 'New Item', 'description': 'Brand new
       item', 'price': 10.99, 'in_stock': True})
2  if serializer.is_valid():
3      serializer.save()
4  else:
5      print(serializer.errors)
```

The serializer's is_valid() method validates the incoming data, and if
it is valid, the save() method creates a new instance of the Item model
with the provided data.

While DRF's model serializers dramatically simplify the task of serializing and deserializing data, customization may be necessary for more
complex scenarios, such as adding additional fields that do not exist
on the model, implementing field-level validation, or customizing the
way particular fields are serialized. This can be achieved by declaring
custom fields, validators, or create and update methods within the
serializer class.

In summary, serializers are a foundational concept in DRF, enabling
efficient and effective data conversion between complex Python types
and JSON for web APIs. Through the use of ModelSerializer, developers can quickly generate serializers for their models and customize
them as needed to meet the requirements of their API endpoints. By
mastering serializers, developers are equipped to build robust, efficient, and scalable web APIs with Django.

9.4 Handling HTTP Methods: GET, POST, PUT, DELETE

In this section we will discuss how to handle the primary HTTP methods: GET, POST, PUT, and DELETE within the context of Django Rest
Framework (DRF). The correct handling of these methods is central to
developing a RESTful API that adheres to the standard principles of

REST. Each HTTP method corresponds to one of the CRUD operations: Create, Read, Update, and Delete, which are foundational to web APIs. With DRF, the handling of these methods is abstracted in a way that allows for clean, maintainable code.

GET Method: This method is used to retrieve information from the server. In DRF, the GET method can be handled using a Serializer class for converting Python objects into a format that can be understood over the web, typically JSON or XML. ViewSets and generic views in DRF automatically handle GET requests by querying the database for the requested resources.

```
1   from rest_framework.views import APIView
2   from rest_framework.response import Response
3   from .models import MyModel
4   from .serializers import MyModelSerializer
5
6   class MyModelList(APIView):
7       def get(self, request, format=None):
8           queryset = MyModel.objects.all()
9           serializer = MyModelSerializer(queryset, many=True)
10          return Response(serializer.data)
```

POST Method: This method is used to create a new resource on the server. When implementing POST in DRF, data sent by the client is typically serialized and then saved to the database. Validations are performed during serialization to ensure the data's integrity and conformance to the server's requirements.

```
1   def post(self, request, format=None):
2       serializer = MyModelSerializer(data=request.data)
3       if serializer.is_valid():
4           serializer.save()
5           return Response(serializer.data, status=201)
6       else:
7           return Response(serializer.errors, status=400)
```

PUT Method: This method is used for updating an existing resource completely. DRF handles PUT requests similarly to POST requests but involves retrieving the existing resource, updating it with the request data, and saving it back to the database.

```
1   def put(self, request, pk, format=None):
2       obj = MyModel.objects.get(pk=pk)
3       serializer = MyModelSerializer(obj, data=request.data)
4       if serializer.is_valid():
5           serializer.save()
6           return Response(serializer.data)
7       return Response(serializer.errors, status=400)
```

DELETE Method: This method removes the specified resource from the server. In DRF, implementing DELETE involves querying for the resource in the database and then calling the `delete` method on that instance.

```
def delete(self, request, pk, format=None):
    obj = MyModel.objects.get(pk=pk)
    obj.delete()
    return Response(status=204)
```

While DRF provides views and viewsets that abstract much of the manual handling of these methods, understanding how each HTTP method maps to database operations is crucial for customizing and extending DRF. This knowledge ensures that APIs developed with Django and DRF not only follow RESTful principles but are also efficient, secure, and maintainable.

9.5 Class-Based Views and ViewSets for Efficient API Development

In this section we will discuss how Django Rest Framework (DRF) leverages the power of class-based views and ViewSets to facilitate efficient and rapid API development. This approach contrasts with the function-based views in Django, offering a structured method for handling HTTP requests with less code, enhanced reusability, and improved maintainability.

Class-based views in DRF abstract common patterns to class methods, allowing for modular, reusable API endpoints. A single class can define methods for different HTTP requests, such as `get` for retrieving data or `post` for creating it. This method significantly reduces code duplication and promotes a clear separation of concerns, where each method in the class corresponds to a specific HTTP action.

The following is an example of a simple class-based view in DRF that handles GET and POST requests:

```
from rest_framework.views import APIView
from rest_framework.response import Response
from rest_framework import status
from .serializers import MyModelSerializer
from .models import MyModel

class MyModelList(APIView):
    def get(self, request, format=None):
        models = MyModel.objects.all()
        serializer = MyModelSerializer(models, many=True)
        return Response(serializer.data)

```

```
13    def post(self, request, format=None):
14        serializer = MyModelSerializer(data=request.data)
15        if serializer.is_valid():
16            serializer.save()
17            return Response(serializer.data, status=status.HTTP_201_CREATED)
18        return Response(serializer.errors, status=status.HTTP_400_BAD_REQUEST)
```

This code snippet demonstrates the simplicity and elegance of class-based views. The get method retrieves all objects from the database, serializes them, and returns the serialized data. Conversely, the post method deserializes the request data to create a new instance of MyModel.

Moving a step further, DRF introduces ViewSets, which abstract the logic of handling the common set of actions performed on a resource, such as creating, listing, retrieving, updating, and deleting items. A ViewSet in DRF can automatically provide implementations for these actions without explicitly writing methods for each.

The advantage is profound: developers can concentrate on what their APIs do (the business logic) rather than how they're implemented, leading to cleaner, more concise codebases.

Here is how a ModelViewSet could be implemented for the same functionality:

```
1  from rest_framework import viewsets
2  from .serializers import MyModelSerializer
3  from .models import MyModel
4
5  class MyModelViewSet(viewsets.ModelViewSet):
6      queryset = MyModel.objects.all()
7      serializer_class = MyModelSerializer
```

The ModelViewSet class takes care of every common operation needed for MyModel. It utilizes the queryset and serializer_class attributes to handle CRUD operations on the MyModel items, significantly reducing the amount of code needed to create fully functional API endpoints.

To bind these ViewSets to URLs, DRF employs routers that automatically generate URL patterns for the ViewSet actions. This further enhances the development velocity by reducing boilerplate code for URL configuration:

```
1  from rest_framework.routers import DefaultRouter
2  from django.urls import path, include
3  from .views import MyModelViewSet
4
5  router = DefaultRouter()
6  router.register(r'mymodel', MyModelViewSet)
```

```
7
8   urlpatterns = [
9       path('', include(router.urls)),
10  ]
```

Class-based views and ViewSets embody the principle of DRY (Don't
Repeat Yourself) in API development. They encapsulate common patterns into reusable classes and methods, drastically reducing boilerplate and making the code cleaner, more maintainable, and easier to
understand. By leveraging these features of Django Rest Framework,
developers can efficiently produce robust, scalable APIs.

9.6 Authentication and Permission in REST-ful APIs

Authentication and permission play crucial roles in the security and integrity of RESTful APIs developed with Django Rest Framework (DRF).
They ensure that only authorized users can access specific resources
and perform actions on those resources. This section will discuss
the mechanisms DRF provides for handling authentication, managing
permissions, and how they can be effectively implemented in a Django
project to secure an API.

Authentication in DRF is the process of verifying the identity of a user
or an application. This is typically achieved through various means
such as token authentication, session authentication, or third-party
authentication (e.g., OAuth, JWT). Each of these methods has its own
set of advantages and use cases.

- **Token Authentication:** This method involves sending a token
  along with each request, which proves the client's identity. A
  token is generated when a user signs in and is validated with each
  request.

```
1   from rest_framework.authentication import TokenAuthentication
2   from rest_framework.permissions import IsAuthenticated
3   from rest_framework.views import APIView
4
5   class ExampleView(APIView):
6       authentication_classes = [TokenAuthentication]
7       permission_classes = [IsAuthenticated]
8
9       def get(self, request, format=None):
10          content = {'message': 'Hello, World!'}
11          return Response(content)
```

- **Session Authentication:** Utilizes Django's session framework to authenticate users. This is more common in traditional web applications where Django's frontend interacts with its backend.

- **Third-party Authentication:** Allows integration with external authentication providers like Google, Facebook, or authentication protocols like OAuth2, leveraging libraries such as `django-oauth-toolkit` or `djangorestframework-jwt` for JWT handling.

Following successful authentication, permissions determine the actions an authenticated user can perform. DRF provides a flexible permission system, which can be globally applied or customized for each view.

Permissions are evaluated as boolean expressions. If any permission check fails, DRF will deny access to the resource. Developers can use built-in permissions, such as `IsAuthenticated`, `IsAdminUser`, or `IsAuthenticatedOrReadOnly`, or define custom permission classes by extending `BasePermission`.

```
from rest_framework.permissions import BasePermission, SAFE_METHODS

class IsOwnerOrReadOnly(BasePermission):
    """
    Custom permission to only allow owners of an object to edit it.
    """

    def has_object_permission(self, request, view, obj):
        # Read permissions are allowed to any request,
        # so we'll always allow GET, HEAD or OPTIONS requests.
        if request.method in SAFE_METHODS:
            return True
        # Write permissions are only allowed to the owner of the object.
        return obj.owner == request.user
```

This flexibility in defining permissions allows for the implementation of complex security policies suitable for modern web applications' needs.

To ensure the secure operation of an API, DRF encourages the combined use of authentication and permissions. Comprehensive authentication identifies the user associated with each request, while granular permissions control the user's access to API resources. This dual-layer security model is essential for developing secure RESTful APIs that protect sensitive data and functionality from unauthorized access.

By leveraging DRF's support for sophisticated authentication and permission systems, developers can build robust security models tailored to their application's requirements. These systems not only secure API access but also provide a way to manage user roles and access levels within an application, making DRF a powerful tool for API development in Django projects.

9.7 Working with Nested Resources and Relationships

In the context of RESTful APIs developed with Django Rest Framework (DRF), managing nested resources and the relationships between different entities in your data model is a crucial aspect that requires careful consideration. Entities in a web application often have relationships defined by foreign keys in a relational database, such as one-to-many or many-to-many relationships. For instance, a blog post may have many comments, or a course might have many students enrolled. In this section, we will discuss how to effectively handle these relationships within DRF to create a coherent and intuitive API design.

The DRF provides several tools and techniques to handle nested resources and relationships, including nested serializers, 'Hyperlinked-ModelSerializer', and the use of related fields. Understanding how to leverage these tools is essential for exposing related objects in your API responses or for accepting nested data in your API requests.

Nested Serializers

Nested serializers enable you to represent relationships between entities in your JSON responses. To create a nested serializer, you simply define a serializer for the child entity and include it as a field in the parent entity's serializer.

Consider the following example where we have two models, 'BlogPost' and 'Comment'. A 'BlogPost' can have multiple 'Comment's:

```
1  from rest_framework import serializers
2  from .models import BlogPost, Comment
3
4  class CommentSerializer(serializers.ModelSerializer):
5      class Meta:
6          model = Comment
7          fields = ['id', 'author', 'content', 'created_at']
8
9  class BlogPostSerializer(serializers.ModelSerializer):
10     comments = CommentSerializer(many=True, read_only=True)
```

```
11
12    class Meta:
13        model = BlogPost
14        fields = ['id', 'title', 'content', 'author', 'comments']
```

In the 'BlogPostSerializer', we specify the 'comments' field to use 'CommentSerializer', and set 'many=True' to indicate that there may be multiple comments associated with a single blog post. This setup enables the API to return nested comment data within a blog post response, providing a rich, hierarchical data structure to the client consuming the API.

HyperlinkedModelSerializer and Related Fields

Using 'HyperlinkedModelSerializer' is another approach to handling relationships between entities. This serializer replaces primary keys with hyperlinks to the related entities, offering a more HATEOAS (Hypermedia as the Engine of Application State) compliant API.

To illustrate, modifying the 'CommentSerializer' to use 'HyperlinkedModelSerializer' involves:

```
1    from rest_framework.serializers import HyperlinkedModelSerializer
2
3    class CommentSerializer(HyperlinkedModelSerializer):
4        class Meta:
5            model = Comment
6            fields = ['url', 'id', 'content', 'author', 'created_at']
```

With 'HyperlinkedModelSerializer', each comment object in the API response now includes a URL to the detailed view of that comment, making it easier for clients to navigate related resources.

Furthermore, DRF's 'related fields' such as 'HyperlinkedRelatedField' or 'PrimaryKeyRelatedField' allow for customization of how relationships are represented. You can specify how related objects should be included in serialized representations, either by their primary key, their URL, or any other representation you define.

Handling Nested Data for Write Operations

While nested serializers are excellent for read operations, they require additional consideration for create and update operations. DRF does not support writable nested representations by default, owing to the

270

complex validation and potential data integrity issues involved. However, you can override the 'create' and 'update' methods of a serializer to explicitly define how nested data should be handled.

For example, to support creating a blog post along with new comments in one request, you might write:

```
class BlogPostSerializer(serializers.ModelSerializer):
    comments = CommentSerializer(many=True)

    class Meta:
        model = BlogPost
        fields = ['title', 'content', 'comments']

    def create(self, validated_data):
        comments_data = validated_data.pop('comments')
        blog_post = BlogPost.objects.create(**validated_data)
        for comment_data in comments_data:
            Comment.objects.create(blog_post=blog_post, **comment_data)
        return blog_post
```

This example demonstrates overriding the 'create' method to manually handle the creation of related comment objects when a new blog post is created. A similar approach can be used for the 'update' method.

Effectively working with nested resources and relationships in DRF requires a thorough understanding of serializers and the relationships between models in your Django application. By using nested serializers and overriding the 'create' and 'update' methods when necessary, you can build an API that thoughtfully exposes and manipulates related entities. Always consider the implications of nesting on the performance and complexity of your API, as excessive nesting can lead to slower responses and a harder-to-follow API structure. With careful design and consideration for frontend requirements, nested resources can greatly enhance the richness and usability of your API.

9.8 Implementing Pagination, Filtering, and Sorting

Implementing pagination, filtering, and sorting in Django Rest Framework (DRF) considerably enhances the usability, performance, and scalability of web APIs. These features allow clients to interact with the API by retrieving subsets of resources, searching based on specific criteria, and ordering results according to relevant attributes. This section will discuss the steps involved in adding these capabilities to a DRF-based project.

Pagination mitigates the performance issues caused by loading large datasets at once by dividing the data into smaller, manageable chunks or pages. DRF provides several pagination styles out of the box, including limit/offset pagination, cursor-based pagination, and page number pagination. To enable pagination, you need to define the pagination style in your project's settings or directly within your view.

For example, to use page number pagination globally, you can add the following configuration to your settings.py file:

```
1  REST_FRAMEWORK = {
2      'DEFAULT_PAGINATION_CLASS': 'rest_framework.pagination.PageNumberPagination',
3      'PAGE_SIZE': 10
4  }
```

This setup specifies that the API should use page number pagination with 10 items per page. When a client accesses a paginated endpoint, DRF will include pagination information in the response, such as the total number of pages and links to the next and previous pages.

Filtering allows clients to narrow down the query results by specifying criteria. DRF supports several filtering backends, including DjangoFilterBackend for complex queries. To enable filtering, you must specify the desired filtering backend in your view and then define the fields that should be filterable.

To demonstrate, consider configuring a simple filter for a model named 'Book' with fields 'title' and 'author'. First, add the DjangoFilterBackend to your view:

```
1   from rest_framework import generics
2   from django_filters.rest_framework import DjangoFilterBackend
3   from .models import Book
4   from .serializers import BookSerializer
5
6   class BookListView(generics.ListAPIView):
7       queryset = Book.objects.all()
8       serializer_class = BookSerializer
9       filter_backends = [DjangoFilterBackend]
10      filterset_fields = ['title', 'author']
```

This setup enables clients to filter books by 'title' and 'author' using query parameters in the URL.

Sorting, or ordering, allows clients to specify the order in which records should be presented. DRF supports ordering of querysets out of the box, requiring minimal setup. To enable sorting, you can specify the 'OrderingFilter' in your view and define a list of fields on which clients can sort.

272

For instance, to allow sorting by 'title' and 'publish_date' in the 'Book' model, you would update the view as follows:

```
from rest_framework import generics
from rest_framework.filters import OrderingFilter
from .models import Book
from .serializers import BookSerializer

class BookListView(generics.ListAPIView):
    queryset = Book.objects.all()
    serializer_class = BookSerializer
    filter_backends = [OrderingFilter]
    ordering_fields = ['title', 'publish_date']
```

Clients can then use query parameters to request a sorted list of books, such as appending '?ordering=publish_date' to the request URL to sort the books by their publication date.

Implementing these features in DRF requires careful consideration of the API's design and the needs of its consumers. Pagination ensures that the API can scale by delivering content in manageable chunks. Filtering allows clients to find specific resources efficiently, while sorting improves the usability of the API by presenting data in a logical order. Together, these features make DRF a powerful tool for building flexible, user-friendly web APIs.

9.9 Versioning Your API for Future Compatibility

Versioning an API is a critical aspect of its design that ensures backward compatibility and facilitates the smooth evolution of the API over time. As the needs of consumers evolve and as the software itself changes, being able to introduce new features, modify existing ones, or even deprecate parts of the API without disrupting dependent applications is essential. In this section, we will discuss various strategies for versioning APIs built with Django Rest Framework (DRF) and how to implement them effectively.

The first step in versioning is to choose a versioning scheme. Common schemes include URL path versioning, query parameter versioning, and header versioning. Each of these methods has its advantages and trade-offs, and the choice among them should be guided by the API's specific requirements and the preferences of its consumer base.

- URL path versioning involves adding the version of the API directly in the URL path. For example, calling \api\v1\items to access version 1 of the items endpoint. This method is straightforward and makes the version explicit in the API call.

- Query parameter versioning uses a query parameter to specify the version, such as \api\items?version=1. This approach keeps URLs cleaner but can lead to more complex handling logic on the server side.

- Header versioning relies on HTTP headers to convey version information. The consumer specifies the desired version through a custom header, like `Accept: application/myapi.v1+json`. This method keeps URLs invariant across versions but can obscure the versioning from users not familiar with HTTP header manipulation.

DRF provides built-in support for these versioning schemes through its `VERSIONING_CLASS` setting. To deploy a specific versioning strategy, one needs to update the Django settings file with the desired versioning class provided by DRF. For instance, to enable URL path versioning, one would add the following configuration:

```
REST_FRAMEWORK = {
    'DEFAULT_VERSIONING_CLASS': 'rest_framework.versioning.URLPathVersioning'
}
```

After choosing a versioning scheme and configuring DRF accordingly, the next step is to implement version-aware behavior in the API. This might involve creating different serializers for different versions, employing conditional logic within views to handle version-specific requests, or even maintaining distinct sets of URLs for different versions of the API.

As an example, consider a scenario where version 1 of an API returns a basic set of fields for a resource, while version 2 adds additional fields. Implementing this with URL path versioning could involve the following:

```
# views.py
from rest_framework import views
from .serializers import ItemSerializerV1, ItemSerializerV2

class ItemView(views.APIView):
    def get(self, request, version, *args, **kwargs):
        if version == 'v1':
            serializer_class = ItemSerializerV1
        elif version == 'v2':
```

```
10          serializer_class = ItemSerializerV2
11          # Logic to fetch and serialize items
12
13  # urls.py
14  from django.urls import path
15  from .views import ItemView
16
17  urlpatterns = [
18      path('api/<version>/items', ItemView.as_view()),
19  ]
```

This approach uses conditional logic within the view to choose the correct serializer based on the version specified in the URL.

Ensuring that an API can evolve while maintaining compatibility for existing clients is crucial for its longevity and usability. The versioning of an API, properly implemented and communicated, reduces the risk of breaking changes and enables the provision of new functionalities without disruption. It's important to document versioning choices and their implementation details clearly in the API documentation to guide consumers in navigating and utilizing the different API versions effectively.

Adopting a strategic approach to versioning from the start of API development with Django Rest Framework not only future-proofs the API but also underscores a commitment to a reliable and professional development ethos.

9.10 Documenting Your API with Tools like Swagger

In this section, we will discuss the significance of documenting RESTful APIs and how Swagger, an open-source tool, facilitates the creation, maintenance, and dissemination of API documentation. Proper documentation is crucial for the development lifecycle of APIs, as it ensures that the functionality is accessible and understandable to both the API creators and its consumers.

Swagger, which is now part of the OpenAPI Specification, provides a powerful yet straightforward way to describe your API's endpoints, request/response cycles, authentication mechanisms, and more, in a format that's both human-readable and machine-processable. This dual utility encourages a design-first approach to API development, ensuring that the API's design is clear and agreed upon before implementation proceeds.

To integrate Swagger with Django Rest Framework, the `django-rest-swagger` package can be utilized. This package leverages the introspection capabilities of Django Rest Framework to automatically generate a Swagger-enabled API frontend, where users can explore the complete API documentation and interact with the API by sending requests and viewing responses directly through the browser.

Setting Up Swagger in Your Django Project

To set up Swagger documentation for your Django Rest Framework project, follow these steps:

1. Install the `django-rest-swagger` package using pip:

```
1  pip install django-rest-swagger
```

2. Add `'rest_framework_swagger'` to the `INSTALLED_APPS` setting in your Django project's `settings.py` file.

3. Include the Swagger URLs in your project's `urls.py` file:

```
1  from rest_framework_swagger.views import get_swagger_view
2
3  schema_view = get_swagger_view(title='API Documentation')
4
5  urlpatterns = [
6      url(r'^docs/$', schema_view),
7  ]
```

Once configured, navigating to `<your_domain>/docs/` will display the auto-generated API documentation, allowing developers and API consumers to interact with the API endpoints directly.

Advantages of Using Swagger

- **Interactive Documentation:** Swagger provides an interactive API console, which makes it easier for developers and API consumers to understand how the API works and to test it directly from the browser.

- **Standardized:** By adhering to the OpenAPI Specification, Swagger ensures that the API documentation is standardized and consistent across different projects.

276

- **Design-first Approach:** Swagger encourages developers to think about the design of the API first, leading to more predictable and cohesive APIs.

- **Automated Generation:** The ability to automatically generate documentation from the codebase reduces manual efforts and helps in keeping the documentation and API implementation in sync.

Best Practices for Documenting Your API with Swagger

- Ensure that all API endpoints are thoroughly documented, including descriptions of their parameters, request bodies, response bodies, status codes, and error messages.

- Use clear and concise language in your descriptions to enhance understandability.

- Regularly update the documentation to reflect any changes in the API.

- Leverage Swagger's annotation capabilities to enrich your API documentation and provide additional context where necessary.

Swagger offers an effective and efficient way to document RESTful APIs. By integrating Swagger into your Django Rest Framework project, you can improve developer productivity, enhance API usability, and ensure a smoother API development and consumption experience. The tools and practices discussed in this section will help you build comprehensive, interactive, and user-friendly API documentation that aligns with both your project's needs and industry standards.

9.11 Testing RESTful APIs with Django Rest Framework

Testing is a critical component of developing RESTful APIs with Django Rest Framework (DRF). It ensures the reliability, performance, and security of the APIs you develop. This section will discuss strategies and techniques for effectively testing RESTful APIs constructed with DRF.

To begin with, Django provides a powerful set of tools in its testing framework that can be extended to test APIs created with DRF. These tools include the TestCase class from Django's django.test module, which is designed for creating test cases for Django applications, and APIClient from DRF's rest_framework.test module, which extends Django's TestCase to provide a specific client for API interactions.

Let's start with a simple test scenario. Assume we have an API endpoint that allows users to retrieve a list of blog posts. The method to test this endpoint could look like the following:

```
from rest_framework.test import APITestCase
from django.urls import reverse
from .models import BlogPost
from rest_framework import status

class BlogPostAPITests(APITestCase):

    def test_view_blog_posts(self):
        url = reverse('blogpost-list')
        response = self.client.get(url, format='json')
        self.assertEqual(response.status_code, status.HTTP_200_OK)
```

This test case uses the APITestCase class and the APIClient's get method to send an HTTP GET request to the API endpoint. The reverse function from Django's django.urls module is used to dynamically generate the URL for the blog post list endpoint, which is named blogpost-list in this example. The response status code is then checked to ensure that the request was successful (status.HTTP_200_OK).

For APIs that require authentication and permissions, DRF's testing framework allows you to simulate authenticated requests by using the force_authenticate method. Here's an example:

```
from django.contrib.auth.models import User

def test_create_blog_post(self):
    self.user = User.objects.create_user(username='testuser', password='
        testpassword')
    self.client.force_authenticate(user=self.user)
    url = reverse('blogpost-create')
    data = {'title': 'New Blog Post', 'content': 'Content of the new blog post.'}
    response = self.client.post(url, data, format='json')
    self.assertEqual(response.status_code, status.HTTP_201_CREATED)
    self.client.logout()
```

In this example, a user is created and authenticated using the force_authenticate method. Then, an HTTP POST request is sent to the API endpoint responsible for creating a new blog post. The test

278

checks if the blog post is created successfully by looking at the HTTP status code in the response.

Additionally, testing DRF APIs is not limited to simple CRUD operations. Complex functionalities such as pagination, filtering, and sorting can also be tested. For instance, to test pagination, you can insert a number of records into the database and then send a GET request to an endpoint that returns a paginated response. You would then verify that the response contains the correct number of records per page and includes pagination metadata, like the total number of pages.

Furthermore, testing throttling and other security practices involves configuring the throttle rates and then performing requests to the API to ensure that the request limits are enforced properly. This is done by surpassing the number of allowed requests within a specified time window and verifying that the server returns a 429 Too Many Requests status code.

Effective testing also encompasses ensuring the accuracy of serialized data. Serializers in DRF convert complex data such as querysets and model instances into Python datatypes that can then be easily rendered into JSON, XML, or other content types. Tests can verify that the serialized data matches the expected format and content. For example, you might test that a serializer accurately represents a model instance's fields and their values in the API's response.

In summary, testing RESTful APIs built with Django Rest Framework is an essential practice that demands thoroughness and attention to detail. By leveraging Django's test framework and DRF's extensions for API testing, developers can write robust tests that cover a wide range of scenarios, from simple CRUD operations to complex business logic, authentication, and permissions. Through rigorous testing practices, developers can ensure their APIs are reliable, secure, and performant, critical qualities for the success of any application relying on web APIs.

9.12 Throttling, Permissions, and Other Security Practices

In this section, we will discuss the implementation of throttling, permissions, and other vital security practices within the Django Rest Framework (DRF). These mechanisms are crucial for maintaining the integrity, confidentiality, and availability of web APIs. Throttling helps control the rate of requests a user can make to an API within a given timeframe, thereby preventing abuse and ensuring that the service remains available to all users. Permissions determine what actions an authenticated user can perform. Additional security practices include handling Cross-Origin Resource Sharing (CORS) and employing secure communication channels.

Throttling

Throttling in DRF is configurable and allows for fine-grained control over how many requests each user or IP address can make. It is a preventive measure to avoid unintentional or deliberate denial of service attacks. To implement throttling, DRF provides several classes, but the most commonly used are `ScopedRateThrottle` and `AnonRateThrottle`. The former applies to authenticated users, while the latter pertains to anonymous requests.

An example of setting up throttling is as follows:

```
REST_FRAMEWORK = {
    'DEFAULT_THROTTLE_CLASSES': [
        'rest_framework.throttling.AnonRateThrottle',
        'rest_framework.throttling.UserRateThrottle'
    ],
    'DEFAULT_THROTTLE_RATES': {
        'anon': '100/day',
        'user': '1000/day'
    }
}
```

This configuration in the Django settings file means anonymous users can make up to 100 requests per day, and authenticated users can make up to 1000 requests per day.

Permissions

Permissions in DRF are used to grant or deny access to different parts of an API based on the requesting user. DRF provides a wide range of permission classes, but permissions can also be custom-built as needed. Permissions are evaluated at the view level and can be applied globally or specifically to individual views.

By default, DRF allows unrestricted access to any request. However, it is vital to restrict access to sensitive information. For instance, using the permissions class IsAuthenticated, you can ensure that only authenticated users can access a view:

```
from rest_framework.permissions import IsAuthenticated
from rest_framework.response import Response
from rest_framework.views import APIView

class ExampleView(APIView):
    permission_classes = [IsAuthenticated]

    def get(self, request, format=None):
        content = {'message': 'Hello, World!'}
        return Response(content)
```

This simple example shows how to restrict access to a view for authenticated users only.

Cross-Origin Resource Sharing (CORS)

CORS is a security feature that restricts web applications from making requests to APIs hosted on different origins. However, APIs often need to be accessed from web applications running on other domains. To handle this securely, DRF can be configured to accept requests from trusted origins by using middleware that adds the appropriate CORS headers to the response.

To enable CORS, you can use packages such as django-cors-headers which allow you to define allowed origins and other CORS-related settings in your Django project's settings file:

```
CORS_ALLOWED_ORIGINS = [
    "https://www.example.com",
    "https://sub.example.com",
]

CORS_ALLOW_METHODS = [
    "DELETE",
    "GET",
    "OPTIONS",
    "PATCH",
    "POST",
    "PUT",
]
```

Secure Communication Channels

Ensuring that all communication between the client and server occurs over a secure channel is paramount. Utilizing HTTPS, which encrypts data in transit, can prevent man-in-the-middle attacks and protect sensitive information from being intercepted. Django and DRF do not directly handle HTTPS redirection, but this can be managed at the web server or load balancer level. Additionally, setting the SECURE_SSL_REDIRECT setting in Django to True enforces that all HTTP requests are redirected to HTTPS.

Implementing throttling, permissions, CORS, and secure communication protocols are essential aspects of building secure and reliable APIs with Django Rest Framework. By taking these considerations into account, developers can safeguard their applications against common security threats and ensure a secure experience for end-users.

9.13   Optimizing API Performance and Response Times

Optimizing API performance and response times is crucial for maintaining a high-quality user experience in web and mobile applications. Efficiently designed APIs can handle high volumes of requests while minimizing latency, thereby ensuring that applications remain responsive and reliable. This section will discuss various strategies and techniques for improving the performance of RESTful APIs developed with Django REST Framework (DRF).

Firstly, efficient database queries are fundamental to optimizing API performance. Django ORM, utilized by DRF for database interactions, allows for complex queries to be executed with minimal code. However, improperly managed queries can lead to excessive database load, significantly affecting API response times. To mitigate this, developers should make judicious use of select_related and prefetch_related methods provided by Django ORM. These methods optimize database access by reducing the number of queries executed during request handling.

```
from django.db import models

class Author(models.Model):
    name = models.CharField(max_length=100)
```

```
6   class Book(models.Model):
7       title = models.CharField(max_length=100)
8       author = models.ForeignKey(Author, on_delete=models.CASCADE)
```

When fetching books along with their authors, using `select_related` will perform a single joined query instead of a separate query for each book's author, thus improving performance.

```
1   books = Book.objects.select_related('author').all()
```

Secondly, API response times can be significantly improved by caching. Caching stores the results of expensive calculations or queries so that subsequent requests can be served faster. Django offers various caching mechanisms that can be leveraged within DRF. The simplest form of caching involves storing entire API responses, allowing identical requests to be served without re-executing the entire view logic.

```
1   from django.core.cache import cache
2
3   def book_list(request):
4       if 'book_list' in cache:
5           # Fetch the cached response
6           return cache.get('book_list')
7       else:
8           books = Book.objects.all()
9           response = render_to_response('book_list.html', {'books': books})
10          # Cache the response for future requests
11          cache.set('book_list', response, timeout=300)
12          return response
```

Thirdly, pagination is another effective technique for improving API performance, particularly when dealing with large datasets. By limiting the number of records returned in a single response, pagination reduces the load on the server and the amount of data transmitted over the network. DRF provides built-in support for pagination, enabling developers to easily add pagination to their API views.

Next, throttling ensures that a single user or client cannot overwhelm the API by sending too many requests in a short timeframe. Implementing throttling protects the API from abuse and helps maintain a consistent level of performance for all users. DRF includes a flexible throttling mechanism that can be customized based on the application's requirements.

```
1   REST_FRAMEWORK = {
2       'DEFAULT_THROTTLE_CLASSES': [
3           'rest_framework.throttling.AnonRateThrottle',
4           'rest_framework.throttling.UserRateThrottle'
5       ],
6       'DEFAULT_THROTTLE_RATES': {
7           'anon': '100/day',
```

```
8        'user': '1000/day'
9      }
10 }
```

Finally, optimizing API performance also involves diligent monitoring and profiling to identify bottlenecks. Tools such as Django Debug Toolbar and Silk can be integrated into a Django project to provide detailed insights into database queries, API call performance, and resource utilization. By regularly analyzing this data, developers can make informed decisions on where optimizations are most needed.

Optimizing API performance and response times is a multifaceted task that involves efficient database querying, caching, pagination, throttling, and continuous monitoring. By applying these strategies within Django and Django REST Framework, developers can build robust and high-performing APIs that enhance the user experience of web and mobile applications.

9.14 Advanced Topics: Hyperlinked APIs and Custom Fields

In this section, we will discuss two advanced concepts in RESTful API design with Django Rest Framework (DRF): hyperlinked APIs and custom fields. These features contribute to building more navigable and flexible APIs, enhancing the client's interaction with the API resources.

Hyperlinked APIs are an extension of the Representational State Transfer (REST) architectural style, promoting the use of hyperlinks for resource identification and navigation. Instead of relying solely on primary keys and explicit URLs, hyperlinked APIs leverage Uniform Resource Identifiers (URIs) to link between resources, offering a more web-friendly approach to API design. This technique makes APIs more discoverable and self-descriptive, as clients can navigate between resources through hyperlinks, akin to browsing web pages.

Implementing hyperlinked APIs in DRF requires the use of `HyperlinkedModelSerializer` instead of the traditional `ModelSerializer`. This serializer automatically generates URL fields in place of foreign keys, linking resources together. Consider the following example:

```
1 from rest_framework import serializers
2 from .models import Author, Book
3
```

```
 4   class AuthorSerializer(serializers.HyperlinkedModelSerializer):
 5       class Meta:
 6           model = Author
 7           fields = ['url', 'name', 'book_set']
 8
 9   class BookSerializer(serializers.HyperlinkedModelSerializer):
10       class Meta:
11           model = Book
12           fields = ['url', 'title', 'author']
```

In the above code, AuthorSerializer and BookSerializer use HyperlinkedModelSerializer, which automatically includes a 'url' field. The 'book_set' field in the AuthorSerializer leverages Django's reverse relationships, providing a hyperlink to navigate from an author to their associated books.

Now, let's turn our attention to **Custom Fields**. Custom fields in DRF allow for more control over how data is represented. This feature is particularly useful when the default field types do not meet your requirements, or when you want to present the data in a non-standard format. Implementing a custom field typically involves subclassing one of DRF's field classes and overriding methods to define serialization and deserialization logic.

For instance, if we want to create a custom field that serializes a datetime object to a more readable format, we could do the following:

```
1   from rest_framework import serializers
2   import datetime
3
4   class ReadableDateField(serializers.Field):
5       def to_representation(self, value):
6           return value.strftime('%B %d, %Y')
7
8       def to_internal_value(self, data):
9           return datetime.datetime.strptime(data, '%B %d, %Y')
```

In this custom field, to_representation method transforms the datetime object into a more user-friendly string format, while to_internal_value parses the string back to a datetime object. This field can then be used in a serializer like so:

```
1   class EventSerializer(serializers.ModelSerializer):
2       date = ReadableDateField()
3
4       class Meta:
5           model = Event
6           fields = ['name', 'date']
```

Hyperlinked APIs and custom fields are instrumental in enhancing the functionality and user experience of RESTful APIs developed with

Django Rest Framework. Hyperlinked APIs improve discoverability and navigability, making the API more intuitive and aligned with web standards. On the other hand, custom fields provide the flexibility needed to meet specific data representation requirements, enabling developers to tailor the API output to the client's needs. Together, these advanced features promote the development of robust, user-friendly, and scalable web APIs.

9.15   Deploying Your API: Best Practices and Considerations

Deploying a RESTful API developed using Django Rest Framework (DRF) involves more than merely transferring code to a server. It encompasses several best practices and considerations to ensure the API's reliability, security, and performance in a production environment. This section will discuss pertinent topics such as choosing an appropriate deployment environment, securing the API, optimizing performance, and maintaining API versioning. Additionally, we will touch upon the importance of monitoring and logging for ongoing operations.

Choosing the Right Deployment Environment: The selection of an environment for deploying your API is crucial. Cloud platforms like AWS, Google Cloud Platform, and Azure offer managed services that can significantly reduce the overhead of deploying and managing Django applications. Docker containers paired with orchestration tools such as Kubernetes facilitate the deployment, scaling, and management of your application in various environments, ensuring consistency across development, testing, and production.

Securing Your API: Security is paramount in the deployment phase. Implement HTTPS to encrypt data in transit, protecting it from interception and tampering. Django Rest Framework provides mechanisms for securing your API, including various authentication schemes such as token-based authentication and OAuth2. Ensure that permissions are correctly implemented to grant access only to the right entities. Additionally, consider using Throttling to protect your API against brute force attacks or misuse.

```
1   # Example of implementing Token Authentication in Django Rest Framework
2   from rest_framework.authentication import TokenAuthentication
3   from rest_framework.permissions import IsAuthenticated
4   from myapp.models import MyModel
```

```
5   from myapp.serializers import MyModelSerializer
6   from rest_framework import viewsets
7
8   class MyModelViewSet(viewsets.ModelViewSet):
9       queryset = MyModel.objects.all()
10      serializer_class = MyModelSerializer
11      authentication_classes = (TokenAuthentication,)
12      permission_classes = (IsAuthenticated,)
```

Performance Optimization: Optimizing the performance of your API involves several strategies. Efficient database querying is crucial; use Django's ORM capabilities to reduce unnecessary database hits. Implement caching strategies to store frequently requested data, reducing the load on your database and improving response times. Django's cache framework supports various backends such as Memcached or Redis. Pagination is another vital aspect of performance, preventing large dataset transfers by splitting them into manageable chunks.

API Versioning: API versioning ensures backward compatibility and scaffolds the evolution of your API without disrupting existing clients. Versioning can be implemented through URL paths, query parameters, or custom headers. Django Rest Framework provides built-in support for namespace versioning, allowing you to encapsulate versions within your URL configurations seamlessly.

```
1   # Example of URL namespace versioning in Django
2   from django.urls import path, include
3
4   urlpatterns = [
5       path('api/v1/', include('myapp.api.v1.urls')),
6       path('api/v2/', include('myapp.api.v2.urls')),
7   ]
```

Monitoring and Logging: Once deployed, it is essential to monitor your API to ensure its availability and performance. Tools like Sentry, New Relic, or Prometheus can provide real-time monitoring and alerting for your applications. Logging is equally important for diagnosing issues. Django's built-in logging framework can be configured to log various events, which can be leveraged for troubleshooting.

Deploying a RESTful API with Django Rest Framework successfully into production is a multifaceted process involving careful planning and execution. By adhering to best practices in security, performance optimization, and versioning, and employing robust monitoring and logging mechanisms, you can ensure a seamless, efficient, and secure operational environment for your API. Always remain agile and open to adopting new technologies and methodologies that can further enhance the deployment and management of your Django applications.

Chapter 10

Testing and Debugging in Django

Testing and debugging are critical components of the Django development process, ensuring code quality and application stability. This chapter explores the framework's built-in tools for creating and executing tests, covering unit and integration testing to assess individual components and their interactions within the application. It also dives into debugging techniques and tools that help identify issues in the development and production environments. Emphasizing the importance of a systematic approach to testing and debugging, this chapter equips developers with the skills to build robust Django applications that perform reliably under various scenarios.

10.1   Introduction to Testing in Django

Testing is an integral part of the development process in Django, as it ensures that the application behaves as expected and that code changes do not introduce regressions. Django provides a comprehensive test framework that simplifies the creation, execution, and management of tests. This section will discuss the types of tests typically used in Django applications, the significance of testing, and the basic setup necessary for writing and running tests.

Testing can be broadly categorized into several types depending on the scope and purpose of the test. These include:

- Unit tests, which test individual units of code in isolation from the rest of the system.

- Integration tests, which verify that different components of the application work together as expected.

- Functional tests, which test the application from the end-user's perspective.

- Regression tests, which ensure that previously developed and tested software still performs after a change.

- Performance tests, which evaluate the responsiveness and stability of the application under a particular workload.

The Django testing framework primarily focuses on unit and integration tests, providing a powerful toolset for testing the models, views, forms, templates, and other parts of a Django application. The framework is built on top of Python's standard 'unittest' module, extending it with application-specific features that allow developers to simulate requests, insert test data into the database, and inspect the output of Django views.

To use Django's testing framework, tests are written as Python classes that inherit from 'django.test.TestCase'. This class provides a rich set of utilities for test execution and database transaction management. When tests are run, Django creates a separate test database to ensure that test execution does not interfere with the application's production data. This test database is destroyed at the end of the test run, ensuring a clean state for subsequent test executions.

A basic example of a Django unit test might look something like this:

```
1  from django.test import TestCase
2  from myapp.models import MyModel
3
4  class MyModelTest(TestCase):
5      def test_str_representation(self):
6          entry = MyModel(name="Test name")
7          self.assertEqual(str(entry), "Test name")
```

Running tests in Django is straightforward. Developers can use the 'manage.py test' command to execute all or selected tests. Django discovers tests in any file named with the pattern 'test*.py' under the applications of the Django project.

The importance of testing can hardly be overstated. A well-designed test suite can catch bugs early in the development process, prevent regressions, facilitate refactoring, and act as documentation for the codebase. By adopting a disciplined approach to testing, teams can ensure that their Django applications perform reliably under different scenarios and withstand the test of time.

In later sections, we will explore in greater detail how to write and organize tests for Django models, views, forms, and templates, as well as how to employ more advanced techniques like mocking and integration testing. With a comprehensive understanding of Django's testing framework, developers are well-equipped to build high-quality web applications that are both robust and maintainable.

10.2   Setting Up Your Testing Environment

Setting up a proper testing environment is a foundational step in embracing a rigorous and methodical testing approach within Django development. This setup involves configuring several components that facilitate the creation, execution, and assessment of test cases. Ensuring this environment closely mirrors the production setting or as closely as possible within the constraints of development is paramount.

The first step involves the modification of settings dedicated to the testing environment in the Django project's settings.py file. It's advisable to create a separate Python module, test_settings.py, which imports the base configurations from settings.py and overrides certain parameters to tailor the environment for testing. These overrides may include configuring a separate database for testing purposes, tweaking logging levels, and adjusting any third-party application settings that could influence test outcomes. For instance, setting up a SQLite database for testing can dramatically increase test execution speed due to its in-memory capabilities:

```
1   from .settings import *
2
3   # Configure a separate database for testing
4   DATABASES = {
5       'default': {
6           'ENGINE': 'django.db.backends.sqlite3',
7           'NAME': ':memory:',
8       }
9   }
```

```
10
11   # Reduce logging output during the testing
12   LOGGING['loggers']['django']['level'] = 'WARNING'
```

After configuring the test settings, the DATABASES snippet redirects the test suite to use an in-memory SQLite database, ensuring tests run swiftly and do not interfere with the development or production databases.

To utilize this testing configuration, command line argument --settings can be passed to the manage.py test command, specifying the path to the test_settings.py module:

```
python manage.py test --settings=your_project.settings.test_settings
```

The next step is to acquaint oneself with Django's test runner, which discovers and executes test cases. Django's testing framework is built atop Python's unittest framework, providing a rich set of features for organizing tests, including test discovery, fixtures, and assertions specific to Django's components. Leveraging django.test.TestCase as the base class for your test cases is recommended as it wraps each test in a transaction and rolls back changes after each test to ensure a clean state:

```
1   from django.test import TestCase
2   from .models import YourModel
3
4   class YourModelTest(TestCase):
5       def test_str_representation(self):
6           entry = YourModel(name="Test Name")
7           self.assertEqual(str(entry), "Test Name")
```

In addition to setting up the environment, incorporating continuous integration (CI) tools into your workflow can significantly enhance the testing process. Services such as Travis CI, GitHub Actions, or GitLab CI/CD can be configured to automatically run your test suite against multiple environments whenever changes are pushed to the repository. This not only ensures your application is tested across different configurations but also instills confidence in the stability and reliability of the codebase with each change.

Finally, preparing fixtures or using factories (with libraries like Factory Boy) for generating test data is essential for efficient and meaningful tests. Fixtures provide pre-defined data sets that can be loaded into the test database, ensuring consistency across test runs and simplifying the setup for complex test scenarios:

```
1  from django.core.management import call_command
2  from django.test import TestCase
3
4  class LoadFixtureTest(TestCase):
5      fixtures = ['test_data.json']
6
7      def setUp(self):
8          # Load fixture
9          call_command('loaddata', 'test_data.json', verbosity=0)
10
11     def test_fixture_loaded(self):
12         self.assertEqual(YourModel.objects.count(), expected_count)
```

Setting up a testing environment tailored for Django applications involves configuring an isolated database, adjusting settings specifically for testing, and understanding the utilization of Django's test framework. Coupled with the integration of CI tools and efficient data generation strategies, this setup provides a solid foundation for developing robust, error-free Django applications. It streamlines the testing process, enabling developers to focus on writing meaningful tests that contribute significantly to the application's quality and long-term maintenance.

10.3 Writing Your First Test: Unit Tests and Test Cases

In this section, we will discuss how to write effective unit tests in Django. Unit testing is a software testing method where individual components of a software are tested to determine if they are fit for use. Django, being a high-level Python web framework, encourages the use of unit testing to ensure components behave as expected under various conditions.

To begin writing unit tests in Django, one must first understand Django's test framework which extends Python's standard unittest library. Django's TestCase class in the `django.test` module is specifically designed for testing Django web applications. It provides a range of tools to simulate web requests, insert test data, and inspect your application's output.

```
1  from django.test import TestCase
2  from .models import YourModel
3
4  class YourModelTest(TestCase):
5      def test_string_representation(self):
6          entry = YourModel(name="My test entry")
7          self.assertEqual(str(entry), entry.name)
```

In the example above, a simple test case is defined for testing the string representation of a Django model YourModel. It illustrates how to create an instance of the model, set its attributes, and verify that its string representation matches expected output. This is a basic unit test structure that verifies a single aspect of the component under test.

It is essential to ensure that unit tests are isolated and do not depend on external systems or the state of the database. Django provides a test database that is completely separate from the production database to guarantee that tests remain isolated. The test database is created automatically when the test suite runs and is destroyed afterwards.

To run the tests, use the manage.py script with the test command:

```
$ python manage.py test
```

This command will discover and run all tests in the Django project. The output will indicate whether each test passed or failed, providing detailed information on failures to aid in debugging.

For more complex assertions, Django's TestCase class offers a wide array of assertion methods such as assertEqual, assertTrue, assertFalse, and assertRaises. These methods help verify the correctness of your application's behavior in a flexible manner.

At this point, it's important to understand the significance of testing not just the 'happy path' but also edge cases and failure modes. For example, testing how your model behaves with invalid data or how your view functions react to incorrect inputs can reveal potential bugs that would not be discovered by testing only the expected behavior.

```
1  def test_model_with_invalid_data(self):
2      with self.assertRaises(ValueError):
3          YourModel.objects.create(name=None)
```

The above test case uses assertRaises to ensure that creating a YourModel instance with invalid data raises a ValueError. This is crucial for maintaining robustness and reliability in your application's components.

Writing unit tests is a vital practice in Django development. It offers a systematic approach to verifying that individual components perform correctly in isolation. By leveraging Django's built-in testing tools and adhering to best practices, developers can significantly improve the quality and stability of their web applications.

10.4 Testing Django Models

Testing models in Django is crucial as they form the backbone of any application, directly interacting with the database. This section will discuss the importance of testing models and present a systematic approach to writing tests that ensure the integrity and expected behavior of the models in a Django application.

Models in Django represent the data structure. Proper testing ensures that the application handles data accurately and maintains consistency, especially when the application undergoes changes or scales. Tests can verify field validations, default values, methods within the models, and the relationships between different models.

Let's start with setting up the infrastructure for testing models. In a Django project, tests are typically written in a file named tests.py within each application folder. However, for larger projects, it is advisable to create a dedicated tests directory, organizing tests into different files for clarity and maintainability.

```
from django.test import TestCase
from .models import MyModel

class MyModelTest(TestCase):
    @classmethod
    def setUpTestData(cls):
        MyModel.objects.create(field1='test', field2=True)
```

The setUpTestData class method is used to set up any objects that will be used across different test methods. It is executed once for the entire test case, before all test methods. This is efficient when testing models as it reduces database operations.

Now, consider testing the simplest aspect: model instantiation. This checks if a model instance can be created and saved into the database correctly.

```
def test_model_instantiation(self):
    instance = MyModel.objects.get(field1='test')
    self.assertIsInstance(instance, MyModel)
```

Beyond instantiation, model methods should be thoroughly tested to ensure their correctness. Suppose MyModel has a method is_valid that checks certain conditions. A test would look as follows:

```
def test_model_method(self):
    instance = MyModel.objects.get(field1='test')
    self.assertTrue(instance.is_valid())
```

295

Field validation is another critical area. Django models often use validators to enforce database integrity and business logic at the model level. It is important to test that these validations are working as expected.

```
from django.core.exceptions import ValidationError

def test_field_validation(self):
    instance = MyModel(field1='', field2=False)
    with self.assertRaises(ValidationError):
        instance.full_clean()
```

In the example above, `full_clean` is called to manually trigger validation checks, expecting it to raise a `ValidationError` due to field requirements not being met.

Relational fields, such as ForeignKey and ManyToMany fields, express database relationships. Testing these involves creating instances of related models and ensuring relationships are correctly established and accessed.

```
from .models import RelatedModel

def test_model_relationships(self):
    related_instance = RelatedModel.objects.create(name='Related')
    instance = MyModel.objects.get(field1='test')
    instance.related_field = related_instance
    instance.save()

    self.assertEqual(instance.related_field.name, 'Related')
```

Finally, testing model signals (if any) involves checking that signals are correctly dispatched and received under specific model actions (such as saving or deleting).

Testing Django models is a fundamental practice that ensures the application's data integrity and stability. By systematically testing model instantiation, field validations, custom methods, and relationships, developers can confidently make changes and enhancements to the application, knowing that their data structures are solid and reliable. Ensuring comprehensive coverage of model tests contributes significantly to the overall quality of Django applications.

10.5   Testing Views and URL Configuration

Testing views and URL configuration in Django involves verifying that the correct view is called for a given URL and that the view behaves as expected under various conditions. This is crucial for ensuring that web applications correctly resolve URLs and return the appropriate content to the user.

Firstly, let's discuss how to craft tests for Django views. Django provides a `Client` class in `django.test` which simulates a user interacting with the application. Using the `Client` instance, tests can make requests to the application and receive a response object, which can be inspected to verify behavior.

```
from django.test import TestCase, Client
from django.urls import reverse

class ViewTest(TestCase):
    def setUp(self):
        # Setup run before every test method.
        self.client = Client()

    def test_index_view(self):
        response = self.client.get(reverse('index'))
        self.assertEqual(response.status_code, 200)
        self.assertContains(response, "Welcome to the Index Page")
```

In the example above, a test case is created for testing an index view. The `setUp` method initializes a `Client` instance before each test. The `test_index_view` method uses this client to simulate a GET request to the URL named 'index'. The response is then checked to ensure it has a status code of 200 (HTTP OK) and contains the expected text.

Next, testing URL configuration involves ensuring that URLs map to the correct view functions. Django's `resolve` function can be used in tests to verify this mapping. This function is part of Django's URL resolver system and when given a path, it determines which view is called.

```
from django.urls import resolve
from .views import index

class URLTest(TestCase):
    def test_index_url(self):
        resolver = resolve('/')
        self.assertEqual(resolver.func, index)
```

In the snippet above, the `test_index_url` method uses the `resolve` function to check that the root URL ('/') correctly resolves to the `index` view function.

For thorough testing, it's advisable to also verify that views handle errors appropriately. For instance, testing how your application responds to a request for a nonexistent item should yield a 404 status code. Similarly, testing for the correct handling of form submissions, both with valid and invalid data, ensures robustness in user interactions.

```
1  def test_404_error_view(self):
2      response = self.client.get('/nonexistentpath/')
3      self.assertEqual(response.status_code, 404)
```

In this example, the test expects accessing an undefined path returns a 404 status code indicating that the requested resource was not found.

Furthermore, when testing views that require authentication, the Client class provides methods like login() and logout() to simulate authenticated sessions. This allows testing behavior both when a user is authenticated, and when they are not, ensuring that views correctly manage access control.

Effective testing of views and URL configuration in Django requires a comprehensive approach, examining how views are resolved from URLs, how they handle various HTTP methods, their behavior under different circumstances (including error conditions), and their interaction with Django's authentication mechanisms. Adhering to these testing practices not only improves the reliability of the application but also contributes significantly to its security and usability.

10.6   Testing Forms and Form Validation

In this section, we will discuss how to test forms and form validation in Django, which is crucial for ensuring that user input is processed correctly and securely. Django's forms system abstracts form creation and handling, providing a powerful set of tools for both simple and complex data processing tasks. Therefore, writing tests for forms is essential to validate that these tasks are carried out properly under various conditions.

Testing forms involves verifying that they not only accept valid data but also reject invalid data appropriately, ensuring that any data processing logic tied to forms is executed correctly. This encompasses testing field validations, custom validation methods, and the form's behavior within views.

First, let's examine how to create a simple test for form validation. Assuming we have a form MyForm with several fields, our goal is to test whether the form validates the data correctly. Here's a basic example using Django's TestCase.

```
1  from django.test import TestCase
2  from .forms import MyForm
3
4  class TestMyForm(TestCase):
5
6      def test_form_validity(self):
7          form_data = {'field1': 'valid_data', 'field2': 'valid_data'}
8          form = MyForm(data=form_data)
9          self.assertTrue(form.is_valid())
```

In the example above, `form_data` is a dictionary representing the data we're submitting to the form. The `is_valid()` method checks if the data satisfies all the field requirements and custom validations, returning True if so and False otherwise.

Testing forms also involves verifying the behavior of invalid data submissions. This often includes checking error messages that are added to the form's errors attribute when validation fails. Continuing with the `MyForm` example:

```
1  def test_form_invalidity(self):
2      form_data = {'field1': '', 'field2': 'valid_data'}
3      form = MyForm(data=form_data)
4      self.assertFalse(form.is_valid())
5      self.assertIn('field1', form.errors)
```

Here, `form_data` contains deliberately invalid data for `field1`. After asserting that the form is not valid, the test checks that `field1` is listed within the form's errors, indicating that the specified validation check was triggered.

Furthermore, when testing custom validation methods within a form, ensure to include scenarios that both pass and fail the validation rules. Suppose `MyForm` has a custom validator that requires `field2`'s value to be a specific format or value. You would test this custom logic explicitly:

```
1  def test_custom_validation(self):
2      valid_data = {'field1': 'data', 'field2': 'special_format'}
3      invalid_data = {'field1': 'data', 'field2': 'wrong_format'}
4      self.assertTrue(MyForm(data=valid_data).is_valid())
5      self.assertFalse(MyForm(data=invalid_data).is_valid())
```

For forms integrated within views, testing involves simulating HTTP requests with test client and asserting on the responses. Consider a scenario where a form submission takes place in a view. You want to test the view's behavior when handling both valid and invalid form submissions.

```
1  from django.urls import reverse
```

```
 2
 3   class TestFormView(TestCase):
 4
 5       def test_view_with_valid_form(self):
 6           response = self.client.post(reverse('form_view'), {'field1': 'data', 'field2
                 ': 'valid_data'})
 7           self.assertEqual(response.status_code, 302) # assuming a redirect occurs
                 after a successful submission
 8
 9       def test_view_with_invalid_form(self):
10           response = self.client.post(reverse('form_view'), {'field1': '', 'field2': '
                 data'})
11           self.form_errors = response.context['form'].errors
12           self.assertIn('field1', self.form_errors)
```

In testing views that handle forms, it's critical to examine not only the HTTP response codes but also the context variables passed to the templates, especially the form's error messages.

In summary, testing forms and form validation in Django covers writing unit tests for form validations, including tests for custom validation logic, and integration tests for form-processing views. Carefully designed tests ensure the reliability and security of form handling in Django applications, contributing to the overall quality of the web application.

10.7   Testing Template Rendering

Testing template rendering in Django involves ensuring that the templates render the expected HTML output given a certain set of contexts. Django's test framework provides a powerful set of tools for this purpose, leveraging the 'Client' class to simulate user requests and capture the response for analysis. This section will discuss how to write tests that verify the correctness of template rendering, including the use of context data, the correct use of templates, and the inclusion of expected content within the rendered HTML.

When testing template rendering, it's crucial to focus on the output that the end-user will see. This includes not only the correct visual elements but also the correct data being displayed. Django's testing tools allow developers to examine both aspects in detail.

```
1   from django.test import TestCase
2   from django.urls import reverse
3
4   class HomePageTest(TestCase):
5       def test_home_page_renders_correct_template(self):
6           response = self.client.get(reverse('home'))
7           self.assertTemplateUsed(response, 'home.html')
```

The above example demonstrates a basic test case that checks whether the 'home' view renders the 'home.html' template. The 'assertTemplateUsed' method is a powerful assertion that specifically checks for template use in the response. This is essential for verifying that views render templates as expected.

Additionally, testing the context data passed to templates is crucial for ensuring the correct display of dynamic content. The context data should be inspected to confirm that it contains the right values and types of data that the template expects.

```
1  def test_home_page_contains_welcome_message(self):
2      response = self.client.get(reverse('home'))
3      self.assertContains(response, 'Welcome to Our Site!')
```

In this example, 'assertContains' checks not only that the template was rendered but also that certain text - in this case, a welcome message - is present in the HTML content of the response. This method is invaluable for testing the presence of dynamic data within the rendered template.

To further refine template rendering tests, developers might need to test for the absence of certain elements or texts under specific conditions. This can be crucial for applications where the output varies significantly based on user interactions or other context factors.

```
1  def test_logged_out_user_cannot_see_profile_link(self):
2      response = self.client.get(reverse('home'))
3      self.assertNotContains(response, 'Profile')
```

The 'assertNotContains' method complements 'assertContains' by verifying that the rendered content does not include specific text or elements. This is particularly useful for testing conditional rendering logic within templates.

For complex applications, testing template rendering may also involve checking for the correct inheritance and inclusion of partial templates. Django templates can extend base templates and include partial templates, forming a hierarchy or composition of templates. Ensuring that the correct base templates are extended and the correct partials are included is as important as verifying the presence of specific content.

Testing template rendering is a critical aspect of developing reliable Django applications. It ensures not only that the correct templates are used but also that the templates are correctly populated with the required context data. Additionally, it verifies that the application's logic correctly handles various user states and conditions, affecting the rendered output. Employing Django's robust testing framework for template rendering tests empowers developers to build applications with confidence, knowing that their application will render correctly under a wide array of conditions.

10.8 Integration Testing: Testing the Application as a Whole

Integration testing in the context of Django applications serves as a critical step to verify that different components of the application work together as expected. Unlike unit testing, which isolates and tests individual units of code, integration testing focuses on the interactions between components, covering the flow of data across various modules and the system's overall functionality. This section will discuss the rationale, implementation, and best practices for conducting integration tests in Django applications to ensure comprehensive coverage and robustness of the web application.

Integration testing evaluates the application's performance, reliability, and behavior under real-world scenarios. It is performed after unit tests and before validation testing. The primary goal is to identify and address issues related to the integration of different parts of the application, such as database interactions, middleware, and third-party services. Django provides a set of tools and libraries specifically designed to facilitate the writing and execution of integration tests, leveraging the Django test client to simulate requests to the application and verify the responses.

To effectively implement integration tests in a Django application, follow these steps:

- Set up a dedicated testing environment that closely mirrors the production setup to ensure accurate results.

- Use Django's built-in TestCase class for creating integration tests, as it provides functionalities essential for integration testing, such as setting up a test database and the ability to execute requests against the application.

- Employ Django's test client within your tests to simulate HTTP requests to the application's views. This allows for the testing of endpoints' responses, including status codes, headers, and content.

- Verify the interaction between different components, such as the rendering of templates with the correct context, the proper functioning of middleware, and the integration with databases and external APIs.

- Ensure that transactions and data creation in the test database are accurately rolled back or removed after each test to maintain test isolation and prevent test pollution.

Consider the following example that demonstrates an integration test for a Django application, where we test a simple view that retrieves a list of objects from the database and renders them on a page:

```
1   from django.test import TestCase
2   from django.urls import reverse
3   from .models import MyModel
4
5   class MyModelListViewTest(TestCase):
6
7       @classmethod
8       def setUpTestData(cls):
9           # Set up data for the whole TestCase
10          number_of_my_models = 5
11          for my_model_num in range(number_of_my_models):
12              MyModel.objects.create(name=f'Test {my_model_num}')
13
14      def test_view_url_exists_at_desired_location(self):
15          response = self.client.get('/mymodels/')
16          self.assertEqual(response.status_code, 200)
17
18      def test_view_url_accessible_by_name(self):
19          response = self.client.get(reverse('my-models-list'))
20          self.assertEqual(response.status_code, 200)
21
22      def test_view_uses_correct_template(self):
23          response = self.client.get(reverse('my-models-list'))
24          self.assertEqual(response.status_code, 200)
25          self.assertTemplateUsed(response, 'app/my_model_list.html')
26
27      def test_pagination_is_five(self):
28          response = self.client.get(reverse('my-models-list'))
29          self.assertTrue('is_paginated' in response.context)
30          self.assertTrue(response.context['is_paginated'] == True)
31          self.assertEqual(len(response.context['my_model_list']), 5)
```

This example illustrates the process of setting up a test case, executing HTTP requests, and asserting conditions about the responses and application behavior. It leverages Django's test framework features,

303

such as the test client and the `TestCase` class's utilities, to perform comprehensive integration testing.

To enhance the effectiveness of your integration tests, consider the following best practices:

- Keep tests focused and avoid testing external services directly. Use mocking to simulate interactions with external systems where possible.

- Regularly review and update your integration tests to cover new features and changes in the application's codebase.

- Organize tests logically and name them descriptively to make it easier for other developers to understand the purpose and coverage of each test.

- Integrate testing into the continuous integration/continuous deployment (CI/CD) workflow to ensure tests are automatically run and issues are identified early in the development process.

Integration testing is a vital component of the testing strategy for Django applications. It complements unit testing by covering the interactions between different parts of the application and ensuring the system works together as a whole. By following the recommended practices and leveraging Django's testing tools, developers can build more reliable, robust, and maintainable web applications.

10.9   Using Mock Objects and Factories for Efficient Testing

Testing in Django aims to ensure that each component of the application functions as expected under various conditions. However, simulating these conditions can sometimes be challenging, especially when dealing with external services, database interactions, or the need for setting up complex data structures. This is where mock objects and factories become invaluable tools in the developer's testing arsenal.

Mock objects are used to simulate real objects in your system, allowing you to mimic interactions with external systems or components without the overhead of setting up actual dependencies. Factories, on the other hand, help in generating data or model instances that can be used in tests, ensuring consistency and reducing the amount of boilerplate code. Together, these tools facilitate more efficient and effective testing practices in Django applications.

Understanding Mock Objects

Mock objects in Django tests are typically used through the unittest.mock module, which is a part of Python's standard library. It provides a powerful mechanism for replacing parts of your system under test with mock objects and configuring them to return predefined responses. This is particularly useful in unit testing, where the focus is on the functionality of individual units of code in isolation from their dependencies.

```
1  from unittest.mock import Mock, patch
2
3  def test_external_api_call():
4      with patch('path.to.external.service') as mock_service:
5          mock_service.return_value = Mock(status_code=200, data="Success")
6          response = call_external_service()
7          assert response.status_code == 200
```

In the example above, patch is used to replace the real external service with a mock object, which is then configured to simulate a successful API call. This approach allows testing the behavior of your code when interacting with the external service, without actually making a network request.

Using Factories for Data Generation

Factories are another critical tool for improving test efficiency in Django. They allow the creation of model instances for testing purposes, eliminating the need to manually set up each object. Libraries like Factory Boy integrate seamlessly with Django, providing a simple, declarative syntax for defining factories.

```
1   # Define a factory for your Django model
2   import factory
3   from .models import MyModel
4
5   class MyModelFactory(factory.django.DjangoModelFactory):
6       class Meta:
7           model = MyModel
8
9       field_one = 'Test data'
10      field_two = 123
11
12  # Using the factory in tests
```

305

```
13  def test_model_behavior():
14      test_instance = MyModelFactory(field_two=456)
15      assert test_instance.field_one == 'Test data'
16      assert test_instance.field_two == 456
```

In the above example, MyModelFactory is defined using Factory Boy, specifying the model and default values for its fields. In tests, this factory can then be used to create instances of MyModel, with the option to override default values as needed. This significantly simplifies the setup process for tests that depend on database records.

Best Practices for Using Mocks and Factories

While mock objects and factories greatly enhance testing efficiency, their usage should follow certain best practices to ensure tests remain reliable and maintainable:

- **Limit Mocks to External Dependencies:** Use mocks primarily for external dependencies or complex internals. Overuse of mocks for internal components can lead to tests that are too tightly coupled to the implementation details.

- **Prefer Factories for Data Models:** Whenever possible, use factories to create test data. Factories ensure data consistency and reduce the risk of tests failing due to data setup issues.

- **Clean Up After Tests:** Make sure that any data created with factories is cleaned up after tests, especially when using a real database. Django's TestCase class provides transaction rollback after each test to help with cleanup.

By integrating mock objects and factories into Django testing practices, developers can achieve more thorough, efficient, and manageable test suites. This not only accelerates the development process but also significantly enhances the reliability and robustness of the application.

10.10 Testing RESTful APIs with Django Rest Framework

Django Rest Framework (DRF) provides a powerful toolkit for building Web APIs. Testing these APIs is crucial to ensure they function correctly and efficiently under various scenarios. This section discusses techniques for testing RESTful APIs designed with Django Rest Framework, focusing on creating comprehensive test suites that cover request handling, response output, and error handling.

To start, testing DRF APIs requires an understanding of the 'APIClient' class provided by DRF. This client extends Django's 'Client' class, offering additional functionality specifically designed for testing APIs. It simplifies sending various types of HTTP requests, handling content types like JSON, and parsing responses.

Consider the following example to demonstrate how to use 'APIClient' to test a simple post creation API:

```
1   from rest_framework.test import APIClient
2   from django.urls import reverse
3   from rest_framework import status
4   from django.test import TestCase
5
6   class PostAPITestCase(TestCase):
7       def setUp(self):
8           self.client = APIClient()
9           self.post_url = reverse('post-list')
10          self.post_data = {'title': 'Test Post', 'content': 'Test Content'}
11
12      def test_create_post(self):
13          response = self.client.post(self.post_url, self.post_data, format='json')
14          self.assertEqual(response.status_code, status.HTTP_201_CREATED)
15          self.assertTrue('id' in response.json())
```

The 'APIClient' is instantiated in the 'setUp' method, ensuring it's available for all tests within the class. The 'test_create_post' method demonstrates submitting a POST request to the 'post-list' URL, which corresponds to an API endpoint for creating new posts. It sends data as JSON and verifies that the response status is 201 (CREATED). Further, it checks for the presence of an 'id' in the JSON response, indicating successful resource creation.

Error handling is another critical aspect of testing RESTful APIs. Ensuring that your API responds correctly to invalid data and authentication errors is vital. The following example shows how to test for a bad request response:

```
1   def test_create_post_with_invalid_data(self):
```

307

```
2    response = self.client.post(self.post_url, {}, format='json')
3    self.assertEqual(response.status_code, status.HTTP_400_BAD_REQUEST)
```

This test attempts to create a post without providing necessary data, expecting the API to return a 400 (BAD REQUEST) status code.

When testing APIs that require authentication, DRF's 'APIClient' allows you to easily authenticate requests either by setting the 'HTTP_AUTHORIZATION' header manually or by using convenience methods like 'force_authenticate' to simulate authenticated sessions:

```
1    from django.contrib.auth.models import User
2
3    def test_create_post_authenticated_user(self):
4        user = User.objects.create_user('testuser', 'test@example.com', 'testpassword')
5        self.client.force_authenticate(user=user)
6        response = self.client.post(self.post_url, self.post_data, format='json')
7        self.client.force_authenticate(user=None) # Reset authentication
8        self.assertEqual(response.status_code, status.HTTP_201_CREATED)
```

This test ensures that authenticated users can create posts, demonstrating the use of 'force_authenticate' to simulate a user session.

Finally, testing the response output is crucial for verifying that your API behaves as expected. This includes testing not just the status codes but also the structure of the JSON response and the values it contains. It ensures the client applications consuming your API can correctly parse and utilize the data provided.

```
1    def test_post_list(self):
2        self.client.post(self.post_url, self.post_data, format='json')
3        response = self.client.get(self.post_url, format='json')
4        self.assertEqual(response.status_code, status.HTTP_200_OK)
5        self.assertEqual(len(response.json()), 1)
6        post = response.json()[0]
7        self.assertEqual(post['title'], 'Test Post')
8        self.assertEqual(post['content'], 'Test Content')
```

In this test, after creating a post, a GET request is made to the 'post-list' URL. It verifies that the API returns a successful response containing the created post data. This ensures that the list endpoint correctly retrieves and serializes post objects.

In summary, testing RESTful APIs with Django Rest Framework involves sending various types of HTTP requests, handling authentication, and verifying both the HTTP response status and the content. Through comprehensive testing, developers can ensure their APIs are robust, performant, and secure.

10.11 Debugging Techniques in Django

Debugging is a crucial part of the development process in Django, as it enables developers to identify and rectify errors and issues in their applications efficiently. Django provides several tools and techniques for debugging, which can be broadly classified into logging, interactive debugging, and the use of external tools. This section will elaborate on these techniques, ensuring developers can utilize them effectively to maintain and enhance their applications.

Firstly, it's fundamental to understand the use of Django's logging framework. Django's logging module is built on Python's standard logging module, providing a versatile system for tracking events in your code. By configuring logging appropriately, developers can capture and record various levels of information, from critical errors to debug-level insights which are instrumental in troubleshooting issues. Here's a basic configuration example in Django's settings.py file:

```
LOGGING = {
    'version': 1,
    'disable_existing_loggers': False,
    'handlers': {
        'file': {
            'level': 'DEBUG',
            'class': 'logging.FileHandler',
            'filename': 'debug.log',
        },
    },
    'loggers': {
        'django': {
            'handlers': ['file'],
            'level': 'DEBUG',
            'propagate': True,
        },
    },
}
```

This setup directs DEBUG and higher-level messages to a file named 'debug.log', aiding in the post-mortem analysis of issues.

Aside from logging, interactive debuggers are invaluable in the real-time investigation of how code executes. One such debugger that integrates well with Django is the Django Debug Toolbar. It is a third-party extension that provides a detailed panel on each page of your development site showcasing timing, SQL queries, template usage information, and more. Installing and configuring it requires adding it to your installed apps and middleware in Django's settings.py file, followed by including its URLs in your project's urlconf. Here is an example configuration:

```
1   INSTALLED_APPS = [
2       ...
3       'debug_toolbar',
4       ...
5   ]
6
7   MIDDLEWARE = [
8       ...
9       'debug_toolbar.middleware.DebugToolbarMiddleware',
10      ...
11  ]
12
13  import debug_toolbar
14  urlpatterns = [
15      ...
16      path('__debug__/', include(debug_toolbar.urls)),
17  ]
```

For deeper code analysis, Python's built-in module pdb (Python Debugger) can be used within Django applications. By inserting 'import pdb; pdb.set_trace()' at any point in your Django code, execution will pause, allowing for interactive debugging in the console. This halts the server's response cycle, permitting the inspection of variables, stack traces, and command execution step-by-step.

Furthermore, external tools like Sentry can be integrated into Django projects to offer advanced error tracking and monitoring. Sentry provides real-time error logging with detailed reports, including stack traces and affected users, which helps developers identify and fix issues proactively. Configuration involves adding the 'sentry-sdk' package to your project and setting up a DSN (Data Source Name) in your settings.py file:

```
1   import sentry_sdk
2   from sentry_sdk.integrations.django import DjangoIntegration
3
4   sentry_sdk.init(
5       dsn="your_dsn_here",
6       integrations=[DjangoIntegration()]
7   )
```

This approach enhances error insight, particularly useful in production environments where debugging is otherwise constrained.

To conclude, effective debugging in Django involves a multi-faceted approach leveraging logging, interactive debug sessions, and the thoughtful integration of external tools. By combining detailed logging for post-mortem analysis, real-time insight from interactive debuggers, and advanced error tracking through services like Sentry, developers can identify, understand, and resolve issues more efficiently. Embracing these techniques will significantly contribute to the stability and

310

reliability of Django applications, fostering a robust development and operational environment.

10.12 Using Django's Logging Framework for Debugging

Django's built-in logging framework is a powerful tool for identifying and debugging potential issues in applications. It allows developers to track events occurring within a Django application, providing insights into its execution and highlighting any anomalies that could indicate errors or suboptimal performance.

The framework aligns with the python standard module `logging`, enabling a configurable and hierarchical logging system. This system permits the definition of loggers, handlers, and formatters which work together to capture and display log messages according to specified severities.

Configuring Django's Logging Framework

Django's logging configuration is typically set in the `settings.py` file of a Django project under the `LOGGING` dictionary. A fundamental logging setup might include configuring loggers for Django's own actions and for the application's custom actions. It may also define handlers for determining where to output log records, such as to console or to a file, and formatters to specify the format of the log messages.

A simple configuration example in `settings.py` could look like:

```
LOGGING = {
    'version': 1,
    'disable_existing_loggers': False,
    'handlers': {
        'console': {
            'level': 'DEBUG',
            'class': 'logging.StreamHandler',
        },
    },
    'loggers': {
        'django': {
            'handlers': ['console'],
            'level': 'DEBUG',
            'propagate': True,
        },
        'myapp': {
            'handlers': ['console'],
            'level': 'DEBUG',
            'propagate': False,
        },
    },
```

```
22  }
```

This configuration directs DEBUG and higher level messages from Django and a custom application named myapp to the console. It ensures important information regarding the application's execution is available during development and testing phases.

Creating and Using Loggers in Your Django Application

To utilize the logging framework within your Django application, you must import the logging module and define a logger using logging.getLogger(__name__) at the top of your Python file. This practice uses Python's convention of setting the logger's name to the module's name, facilitating the mapping of log messages to their source.

A basic usage example in a Django view could be:

```
1  import logging
2
3  logger = logging.getLogger(__name__)
4
5  def my_view(request):
6      logger.debug('Rendering my_view')
7      return render(request, 'my_template.html')
```

Here, a debug level log message is generated each time my_view is executed, assisting developers in tracing the view's invocation and rendering process.

Leveraging Django's Logging for Effective Debugging

Efficient debugging requires more than just capturing log messages; it necessitates strategic logging practices that provide context and facilitate the isolation of issues. Practical strategies include:

- Using varying log levels appropriately (DEBUG, INFO, WARN-ING, ERROR, CRITICAL) to communicate the severity and nature of events.

- Including contextual information in log messages, such as user ID or request data, to pinpoint the source of issues.

- Implementing custom log handlers or filters for advanced processing or filtering of log messages, like sending ERROR level messages to a monitoring service or email.

Incorporating Django's logging framework effectively into the development and debugging process empowers developers to monitor their

Django applications systematically. This capability is crucial for maintaining the reliability, performance, and security of Django applications across all stages of their development lifecycle.

10.13 Performance Testing: Identifying Bottlenecks

Performance testing is a critical aspect of web development, particularly in frameworks like Django, where applications can scale to handle high volumes of traffic. Its primary goal is to identify and eliminate bottlenecks that could impair the application's responsiveness or efficiency under load. In this context, a bottleneck refers to a point in the system where the flow of data is significantly slowed or halted, causing the system to underperform. Within Django projects, these bottlenecks can manifest in various components, including database queries, template rendering, middleware processing, and the communication between Django and its web server.

Identifying bottlenecks in a Django application involves a series of steps, starting with setting up an appropriate environment for performance testing. This setup should mimic the production environment as closely as possible to ensure realistic test results. Once the environment is prepared, developers can employ several tools and strategies to pinpoint the performance issues.

First, Django's Debug Toolbar is an indispensable tool for performance testing. It provides detailed information on the SQL queries generated by each request, including their execution time. This visibility allows developers to identify inefficient queries that need optimization, such as those causing N+1 query problems or those that could benefit from indexing.

```
1   # Example of enabling Django Debug Toolbar in settings.py
2   INSTALLED_APPS = [
3       ...
4       'debug_toolbar',
5       ...
6   ]
7
8   MIDDLEWARE = [
9       ...
10      'debug_toolbar.middleware.DebugToolbarMiddleware',
11      ...
12  ]
13
14  # Ensuring the toolbar is only enabled in a development environment
```

313

```
15   if DEBUG:
16       import socket
17       hostname, _, ips = socket.gethostbyname_ex(socket.gethostname())
18       INTERNAL_IPS = [ip[:-1] + "1" for ip in ips]
```

The Django testing framework itself is another vital resource for performance testing. Django tests, especially those marked with the `TransactionTestCase` class, can be used to simulate real-world loads and interactions with the database. Through these tests, developers can verify the application's behavior under stress conditions and assess the impact of optimization changes.

```
1   from django.test import TransactionTestCase
2   from myapp.models import MyModel
3
4   class PerformanceTestCase(TransactionTestCase):
5       def test_model_creation(self):
6           for _ in range(10000):
7               MyModel.objects.create(name='Test')
```

Django's cache framework can also play a significant role in mitigating performance bottlenecks. Effective use of caching can drastically reduce database access times and the load on the server by storing frequently requested data in a readily accessible location. Testing various caching strategies and configurations can reveal opportunities to enhance application performance.

Testing external APIs and third-party services is crucial for identifying bottlenecks outside of the Django application itself. Tools such as Locust or Apache JMeter enable developers to simulate thousands of users interacting with the application, providing insights into how external services respond under heavy load and how these responses impact the overall performance.

Name	# reqs	# fails		Avg	Min	Max	Median		req/s	failures/s
GET /api/external-service	50000	0(0.00%)		67	50	230	60		150.00	0.00
Total		50000		0(0.00%)						
				/						

Finally, continuous monitoring and logging of performance metrics in production can help detect new bottlenecks as they emerge. Django's logging framework can be configured to capture detailed performance data, and integrating with services like New Relic or Datadog can provide real-time monitoring and alerting for performance anomalies.

314

Optimizing a Django application for performance is an ongoing process. It requires vigilance, regular testing, and a commitment to refining the codebase. By identifying and addressing bottlenecks, developers can ensure that their applications remain fast, responsive, and capable of scaling to meet user demand.

10.14 Security Testing: Identifying Vulnerabilities

Security testing in the context of Django applications plays a pivotal role in safeguarding against potential breaches and attacks which can compromise data integrity and privacy. This process encompasses the identification and remediation of vulnerabilities within the application's codebase, dependencies, and deployment configurations. In this section, we will discuss key aspects of security testing, focusing on methodologies that developers can employ to detect and mitigate risks effectively.

Firstly, it is essential to understand the common vulnerabilities in web applications, as outlined by the Open Web Application Security Project (OWASP). Among these, the most critical issues include injection flaws, such as SQL injection; cross-site scripting (XSS); broken authentication; and insecure direct object references. Having a baseline knowledge of these vulnerabilities provides a solid foundation for developing a targeted testing strategy.

In Django, security testing can be approached systematically through both automated and manual testing procedures. Automated testing tools, such as security scanners and linters, can swiftly identify known vulnerabilities in dependencies and static code. For instance, using a tool like Bandit specifically designed for Python, developers can automate the detection of security-related issues in their code. An example command to run Bandit over a Django project might look like this:

```
1   $ bandit -r path/to/your/django/project
```

The output will list potential security issues flagged by the tool, which might look something like this:

```
Path: path/to/your/file.py:LineNumber
Issue: [B101:assert_used] Use of assert detected.
```

315

While automated tools provide a broad sweep for detecting vulnerabilities, it is imperative not to solely rely on them. Manual security testing, such as code reviews and penetration testing, plays a crucial role in identifying complex vulnerabilities that automated tools might miss. Code reviews, conducted by peers or security specialists, can provide insights into security practices and logic errors that could lead to vulnerabilities.

Penetration testing, or pen testing, involves simulating cyber attacks on your application to identify exploitable vulnerabilities. This form of testing is critical for uncovering issues related to authentication, authorization, data validation, and session management. Although pen testing can be time-consuming and requires specialized knowledge, it offers a real-world examination of your application's security posture.

When performing security testing, it is also vital to consider the Django project's configuration settings. Django offers numerous built-in security features that are configurable through the project's settings. Developers must ensure that settings such as DEBUG are appropriately configured for the development and production environments to prevent leakage of sensitive data. Moreover, the SECURE_HSTS_SECONDS setting should be enabled to enforce strict HTTPS, minimizing the risk of man-in-the-middle attacks.

Security testing in Django applications is multifaceted, combining automated tools, manual testing techniques, and best practices in configuration. By conducting thorough security testing, developers can significantly reduce the surface area for potential attacks, thus ensuring that their applications remain resilient against security threats. Emphasizing regular and comprehensive testing throughout the development lifecycle is crucial to maintaining the integrity and trustworthiness of Django applications in the face of evolving security challenges.

10.15   Best Practices for Testing and Debugging Django Applications

In the practice of developing Django applications, adherence to a set of best practices for testing and debugging can significantly enhance the quality and reliability of the software. This section delineates a comprehensive guide to such practices, aimed at equipping developers with the knowledge to implement effective testing strategies and debugging techniques.

Automate Testing: Automation is key to an efficient and robust testing process. Django's testing framework supports automated tests, which can be run frequently during development to ensure that changes do not break existing functionality. Employ continuous integration (CI) tools to automatically run tests whenever code is pushed to a repository, ensuring issues are identified and addressed promptly.

- Utilize Django's built-in testing framework extensively to create unit and integration tests.

- Configure CI pipelines to include running Django tests.

Write Comprehensive Test Cases: Covering a wide spectrum of use cases is crucial. This involves writing tests not only for the expected behavior of your application but also for edge cases and failure modes.

```
1  from django.test import TestCase
2  from .models import YourModel
3
4  class YourModelTestCase(TestCase):
5      def test_model_str(self):
6          item = YourModel(name="Test Name")
7          self.assertEqual(str(item), item.name)
```

Use Mock Objects and Factories: Testing often requires working with objects that have complex dependencies. Using mock objects and factory methods helps in isolating tests by simulating interactions with database models or external services without requiring access to those resources during the testing phase.

```
1   from unittest.mock import patch
2   from django.test import TestCase
3   from .views import external_api_view
4
5   class TestExternalAPIView(TestCase):
6       @patch('yourapp.views.requests.get')
7       def test_external_api_view(self, mock_get):
8           mock_get.return_value.ok = True
9           response = self.client.get('/api/external/')
10          self.assertEqual(response.status_code, 200)
```

Leverage Django's Debugging Tools: When debugging, Django's in-built features such as the Django Debug Toolbar can provide valuable insights into SQL queries, performance metrics, and configuration details which are often critical in identifying performance bottlenecks or misconfigurations.

Implement Logging Strategically: Logging plays a pivotal role in monitoring and debugging live applications. Django's logging framework

317

offers a flexible way to capture and record a wide range of information about the application's behavior.

```
1   import logging
2
3   logger = logging.getLogger(__name__)
4
5   def my_view(request):
6       try:
7           # Your business logic here
8       except Exception as e:
9           logger.error('An error occurred', exc_info=True)
10          raise e
```

Prioritize Security Testing: Security vulnerabilities can compromise data integrity and privacy. Incorporate security testing into your development cycle to identify and fix vulnerabilities like Cross-Site Scripting (XSS), SQL Injection, and Cross-Site Request Forgery (CSRF).

- Regularly update Django and dependencies to their latest secure versions.

- Use tools such as Django's check command for identifying common security issues.

Opt for Integration Tests Over Unit Tests Where Applicable: While unit tests are important for testing individual components, integration tests assess how these components work together. This is particularly relevant in web development, where the interaction between models, views, and templates can be complex.

Document Your Testing Approach: Effective documentation of the testing strategy, including the rationale behind chosen methods and tools, ensures that the approach is transparent and reproducible by the development team and stakeholders.

The cultivation of a thorough understanding and implementation of these best practices is essential for the development of robust, efficient, and secure Django applications. Not only do these practices streamline the development process, but they also contribute to the creation of software that is dependable and maintains a high level of integrity and performance across its lifespan.

Chapter 11

Performance Optimization in Django Applications

Performance optimization is crucial for ensuring that Django applications can handle scale and deliver content efficiently to users. This chapter addresses key strategies for enhancing the performance of Django projects, including database optimization, effective use of the Django ORM, caching, and optimizing static and media file management. It also covers advanced topics such as asynchronous processing and deployment best practices for high-performance applications. By applying these techniques, developers can significantly improve the responsiveness and scalability of their Django applications, providing a better experience for end-users.

11.1 Understanding Performance Bottlenecks in Web Applications

Performance bottlenecks in web applications can significantly affect the user experience by causing slow page load times, unresponsive interfaces, and even system crashes under heavy load. Identifying and addressing these bottlenecks is crucial for maintaining a smooth and efficient user experience. In the context of Django applications, performance issues can arise from several areas, including the database layer, server-side processing, client-side processing, network latency, and resource loading.

The first step in addressing performance bottlenecks is identifying their root causes. In web applications, one common bottleneck is database interaction. The way queries are written and data is accessed can have a profound effect on performance. For example, excessive database hits due to unoptimized queries or failure to use Django's ORM efficiently can lead to increased load times. Additionally, the lack of proper indexing in the database can slow down query execution, especially for large datasets.

Another significant area of concern is inefficient code within the Django application itself. This can include complex algorithms that run in polynomial or exponential time complexity, improper use of data structures, or lack of code optimization techniques such as memoization. Moreover, not taking advantage of Django's features like query caching or not implementing asynchronous processing where applicable can add to the server response time, negatively impacting the overall application performance.

Network latency is also a critical factor that influences web application performance. The physical distance between the user and the web servers can cause delays in data transmission, affecting page load times. Additionally, not optimizing static assets and media files can result in slow loading times, as large files take longer to transfer over the network. Implementing techniques such as content delivery networks (CDNs), compression, and minification of CSS and JavaScript files can greatly reduce transmission time and improve the user experience.

On the client side, the performance of web applications can be affected by how efficiently the browser renders the page. Complex JavaScript code that leads to excessive DOM manipulation can slow down rendering times and make the interface feel sluggish. Similarly, heavy use of synchronous XMLHttpRequest (XHR) requests can block the main thread, making the application unresponsive. Leveraging modern front-end frameworks and optimizing client-side code are essential steps towards enhancing web application performance.

Caching is another powerful strategy that can be used to mitigate performance issues. Effective caching reduces the need to recalculate or fetch data that has not changed, saving valuable server resources and reducing load times. Django offers various caching mechanisms, such as per-view cache, template fragment caching, and database query caching, which can be strategically utilized to improve performance.

```
1  # Example of caching in Django
2  from django.views.decorators.cache import cache_page
3
4  @cache_page(60 * 15) # Cache the view for 15 minutes
5  def my_view(request):
6      # View code here...
7      return render(request, 'my_template.html')
```

Moreover, appropriate monitoring and logging are essential for continuously assessing the performance of a web application. Tools like Django Debug Toolbar can help developers identify slow queries, template rendering times, and other performance-related metrics during development, while application performance monitoring (APM) solutions can provide insights into production environments.

Understanding and addressing performance bottlenecks in web applications is a multidimensional challenge that requires a comprehensive approach. From database optimization, efficient code practices, and minimizing network latency, to leveraging caching and optimizing client-side processing, each aspect plays a crucial role in enhancing the performance of a Django application. By systematically identifying and mitigating these bottlenecks, developers can ensure that their applications are scalable, responsive, and capable of delivering a superior user experience.

11.2 Database Optimization Techniques in Django

Optimizing database interactions is pivotal for enhancing the performance of Django applications. As the volume of data and the number of users grow, poorly optimized database queries can substantially degrade the application's responsiveness and scalability. This section discusses various techniques to optimize database operations in Django, emphasizing models, queries, and indexes.

Normalization and Denormalization

Firstly, the database schema should be thoughtfully designed to balance normalization and denormalization. Normalization involves dividing a database into distinct parts to minimize data redundancy, which can facilitate data integrity and reduce the disk space usage.

However, excessive normalization can lead to an increased number of table joins, potentially slowing down query performance.

Denormalization, on the other hand, involves adding redundant data in one table based on values from another in order to speed up read operations. It reduces the need for complex joins but at the cost of increased data redundancy and potential complications in data consistency. Therefore, denormalizing selectively, particularly for data that is read frequently but updated less often, can be an effective approach.

Optimizing Django ORM Queries

The Django Object Relational Mapper (ORM) is a powerful tool for abstracting database operations. However, its misuse can lead to inefficient database queries. Understanding and employing the following strategies can significantly optimize ORM usage:

- `select_related` and `prefetch_related` method are essential for reducing the number of database queries made for related objects. `select_related` is used for querying data when there is a single-valued relationship (e.g., ForeignKey and OneToOne relationships), and it performs a SQL join, thus reducing the database hits by fetching related objects in a single query. `prefetch_related` is suitable for fetching multiple related objects (e.g., reverse ForeignKey or ManyToMany relationships) using a separate lookup for each relationship and then joining the results in Python, which can drastically reduce query counts when accessing related items.

```
1    # Example of select_related
2    from django.db import models
3
4    class Publisher(models.Model):
5        name = models.CharField(max_length=300)
6
7    class Book(models.Model):
8        title = models.CharField(max_length=300)
9        publisher = models.ForeignKey(Publisher, on_delete=models.CASCADE)
10
11   books = Book.objects.select_related('publisher').all()
12
13   # Example of prefetch_related
14   class Author(models.Model):
15       name = models.CharField(max_length=300)
16       books = models.ManyToManyField(Book)
17
18   authors = Author.objects.prefetch_related('books').all()
```

- Using `only()` and `defer()` methods to limit the fields fetched from the database can significantly reduce the volume of data transferred, thereby improving performance for queries accessing large models.

- The `annotate()` function permits aggregate operations directly in querysets, which can reduce the need for extra Python processing and minimize the number of database queries.

- Efficient indexing and use of `exists()` to check for record existence without loading objects into memory can also significantly enhance performance.

Database Indexing

Proper indexing is crucial in database optimization. Indexes accelerate the retrieval of rows from a table and are paramount in queries involving filtering, JOIN operations, or aggregation. However, it is essential to strike a balance as each index consumes additional disk space and slows down write operations due to the need for index updates.

Django allows defining database indexes in the model's Meta class using the `indexes` option. Composite indexes, which are indexes on multiple columns, can also be defined and are particularly useful for optimizing queries that filter or sort on several columns simultaneously.

```
1  class Book(models.Model):
2      title = models.CharField(max_length=300)
3      published_date = models.DateField()
4      class Meta:
5          indexes = [
6              models.Index(fields=['title', 'published_date']),
7          ]
```

Concurrent Access Handling

In high-concurrency environments, handling locking and transaction management effectively is crucial for avoiding deadlocks and maintaining data integrity. Django's transaction management API provides tools for managing database transactions to ensure atomicity of operations, which is vital for applications requiring high levels of data consistency. Use of `select_for_update()` in Django ORM queries ensures that a lock is acquired on selected rows until the transaction is complete, preventing concurrent modifications.

Optimizing database interactions in Django applications requires a comprehensive approach involving thoughtful database schema design, judicious use of ORM features like select_related, prefetch_related, only(), and defer(), careful management of indexes, and effective handling of concurrent access. By applying these techniques, developers can significantly improve the performance and scalability of Django applications.

11.3 Query Optimization: Reducing Database Hits

Optimizing queries is paramount in enhancing the performance of Django applications. The goal is to reduce the number of database hits necessary to fulfill a request, thereby decreasing the response time of the application. This optimization involves refining how information is accessed and manipulated using Django's Object Relational Mapper (ORM). This section will discuss several strategies for reducing database hits, including selecting related objects in a single query, deferring the loading of unnecessary fields, using aggregates and annotations, and optimizing querysets by understanding Django's query execution.

Firstly, the use of select_related and prefetch_related methods can significantly reduce the number of database queries. select_related is used when we have a single-valued relationship, like a ForeignKey or a OneToOneField association. It works by creating a SQL join and including the fields of the related object in the SELECT statement. For example:

```
from django.db import models

class Author(models.Model):
    name = models.CharField(max_length=100)

class Book(models.Model):
    title = models.CharField(max_length=100)
    author = models.ForeignKey(Author, on_delete=models.CASCADE)

# Using select_related to minimize database hits
books = Book.objects.select_related('author').all()
for book in books:
    print(book.author.name)
```

This code snippet efficiently fetches all books along with their associated authors in a single database query. Contrast this with fetching books and then hitting the database again for each author, which is significantly less efficient.

prefetch_related, on the other hand, is suitable for prefetching many-to-many and reverse ForeignKey relationships. It performs a separate lookup for each relationship and does the joining in Python, which can be more efficient than select_related in cases of complex relationships or when fetching many objects.

Another strategy is deferring the loading of fields that are not immediately necessary using the defer and only methods. This can be particularly useful for models with fields that contain large amounts of data, such as text fields or binary fields. defer delays the loading of specified fields until they are explicitly accessed, while only loads only the specified fields, deferring all others.

```
1  # Using defer
2  Book.objects.defer("summary")
3
4  # Using only
5  Book.objects.only("title", "author")
```

Leveraging aggregates and annotations provided by Django's ORM can also enhance query performance by performing calculations directly in the database. Aggregate functions compute a summary value over a queryset, while annotate adds a calculated field to each object in a queryset.

```
1  from django.db.models import Count
2
3  # Using annotate to add a book count to each author
4  authors = Author.objects.annotate(book_count=Count('book'))
5  for author in authors:
6      print(author.name, author.book_count)
```

Finally, understanding how Django's ORM executes queries enables developers to write more efficient code. A key aspect of this is realizing that querysets are lazy, meaning they are not executed until they are explicitly evaluated. Judicious use of the filter and exclude methods in constructing querysets can minimize the amount of data transferred and processed, as can limiting the number of results using [:limit] slicing.

Optimizing database queries not only reduces the load on the database server but also significantly improves the overall performance and scalability of a Django application. By conscientiously applying these strategies, developers can enhance the efficiency with which their applications access and manipulate data, thereby providing a more responsive user experience.

11.4 Caching Strategies for Django Applications

In this section, we will discuss caching strategies that are essential for enhancing the performance of Django applications. Caching refers to the process of storing copies of files or results of expensive computations in a temporary storage location for fast access upon subsequent requests. Utilizing caching effectively can significantly reduce database query time, server response time, and overall page load time, thereby improving the user experience.

Django provides a robust caching framework that supports various caching methods, including in-memory caching, file-based caching, database caching, and distributed caching using Memcached or Redis. Selecting the appropriate caching strategy depends on the specific requirements and resources available for your project.

In-memory caching is the simplest form of caching available in Django. It keeps the cache in the RAM of the server where your Django application is running. While it is fast and efficient for single-server setups, it does not scale well for applications deployed in a distributed environment across multiple servers.

To set up in-memory caching, you would configure your settings.py file as follows:

```
CACHES = {
    'default': {
        'BACKEND': 'django.core.cache.backends.locmem.LocMemCache',
        'LOCATION': 'unique-snowflake',
    }
}
```

File-based caching stores the cache on the file system of the server. It is a straightforward approach that works well for small to medium-sized projects. File-based caching can be a good option when shared memory is limited.

Configuration for file-based caching in the settings.py file would look like this:

```
1  CACHES = {
2      'default': {
3          'BACKEND': 'django.core.cache.backends.filebased.FileBasedCache',
4          'LOCATION': '/path/to/django_cache',
5      }
6  }
```

Database caching uses your project's database as a backend for storing cache data. This method is particularly useful when you already have a scalable database infrastructure in place and prefer to utilize it for caching as well.

To use database caching, you first need to create a cache table in your database:

```
1  python manage.py createcachetable
```

Then, configure your settings.py file as follows:

```
1  CACHES = {
2      'default': {
3          'BACKEND': 'django.core.cache.backends.db.DatabaseCache',
4          'LOCATION': 'my_cache_table',
5      }
6  }
```

Distributed caching, with Memcached or Redis, allows for cache data to be stored across multiple servers. This is ideal for high-traffic sites that require scalability and performance optimization across a distributed system.

For Memcached:

```
1  CACHES = {
2      'default': {
3          'BACKEND': 'django.core.cache.backends.memcached.MemcachedCache',
4          'LOCATION': ['127.0.0.1:11211', '192.168.0.100:11211'],
5      }
6  }
```

For Redis:

```
1  CACHES = {
2      'default': {
3          'BACKEND': 'django_redis.cache.RedisCache',
4          'LOCATION': 'redis://127.0.0.1:6379/1',
5          'OPTIONS': {
6              'CLIENT_CLASS': 'django_redis.client.DefaultClient',
7          },
8      },
9  }
```

Regardless of the caching method chosen, it is crucial to implement cache invalidation strategies effectively. Cache invalidation ensures that the cache does not serve stale data. Django provides mechanisms like per-view cache, template fragment caching, and low-level cache API for fine-grained control over what gets cached and for how long.

Selecting the right caching strategy and configuring it correctly is key to maximizing the performance benefits in Django applications. The choice of caching method should align with the application's architecture, anticipated load, and deployment environment. By implementing caching, developers can significantly enhance the user experience by reducing page load times and improving the scalability of their applications.

11.5   Optimizing Django Views and URL Routing

Optimizing Django views and URL routing is essential for improving the performance of Django applications. This section will discuss strategies to enhance efficiency by optimizing views and URL patterns, which are crucial for handling client requests swiftly and reducing server response times.

View Optimization focuses on refining the logic within Django views, which handle HTTP requests and return responses. An optimized view minimizes database queries, streamlines data processing, and utilizes caching when appropriate.

Firstly, ensuring that database queries in views are optimized is vital. Django's Object-Relational Mapping (ORM) allows for lazy loading, meaning queries are not executed until their data is accessed. Developers can leverage `select_related` and `prefetch_related` methods to reduce the number of database hits. For example, using `select_related` for foreign key relationships can significantly cut down on query counts by joining related tables in a single database query.

```
1  from django.shortcuts import render
2  from .models import Author
3
4  def author_detail_view(request, author_id):
5      author = Author.objects.select_related('book').get(id=author_id)
6      return render(request, 'author_detail.html', {'author': author})
```

Secondly, minimizing the logic and computation in views can enhance performance. Offloading heavy computations to background tasks or optimizing algorithms can reduce the load time of views. Utilizing Django's caching framework can also cache expensive computations in views, thus speeding up response times for subsequent requests.

URL Routing Optimization involves efficiently managing the URL dispatcher for faster matching of URLs to their corresponding views. Django's URL dispatcher allows URLs to be defined in a modular and hierarchical manner, but inefficient patterns can lead to slower request processing.

Avoiding overly complex regular expressions in URL patterns can reduce the time it takes for Django to match a request URL to the correct view. Using simpler expressions or segmenting URLs into include() statements for app-specific URL configurations can improve the match-making process.

```
from django.urls import path, include

urlpatterns = [
    path('admin/', admin.site.urls),
    path('blog/', include('blog.urls')),
    path('users/', include('users.urls')),
]
```

Furthermore, ordering URL patterns judiciously is another optimization technique. Django processes URL patterns in the order they are listed, so placing the most frequently accessed URLs at the beginning of the list can reduce match times.

Asynchronous Views, introduced in Django 3.1, allow for asynchronous handling of requests and can further optimize performance by allowing for non-blocking IO operations. Asynchronous views are particularly beneficial for IO-bound operations such as making external API calls or handling file uploads.

```
from django.http import JsonResponse
from asgiref.sync import sync_to_async
import httpx

async def fetch_user_data(request):
    async with httpx.AsyncClient() as client:
        response = await client.get('https://api.example.com/user')
        return JsonResponse(response.json())
```

In summary, optimizing Django views and URL routing plays a critical role in enhancing the performance of Django applications. Efficiently executing database queries, minimizing view logic, caching view outputs, simplifying URL patterns, and leveraging asynchronous views are key strategies. By implementing these practices, developers can achieve faster response times, reduced server load, and a more scalable application.

11.6   Template Optimization Techniques

Template optimization is an essential aspect of enhancing the performance of Django applications. It involves refining the template rendering process to decrease the load time and improve the user experience. Django templates are a powerful feature for generating HTML dynamically, but without careful optimization, they can become a bottleneck in your application's performance.

First and foremost, it is crucial to understand the impact of template inheritance on rendering time. Django templates allow for base templates to be extended by child templates. While this is a powerful feature for avoiding code duplication and ensuring consistency across your application, excessive or improper use of template inheritance can lead to increased rendering times. To optimize template inheritance, developers should:

- Limit the depth of inheritance chains. Deeply nested templates can significantly increase rendering time as each layer adds overhead. Aim for a shallow inheritance hierarchy.

- Use includes for static content that does not need to be overridden. This can reduce the processing required to render a template.

Another vital technique for optimizing Django templates is the judicious use of template tags and filters. These are executed each time a template is rendered, and complex tags or filters can add significant overhead. Consider the following optimization strategies:

- Evaluate the necessity of custom template tags and filters. If the logic can be implemented more efficiently in a view or model, it might be preferable to do so.

- Optimize the implementation of custom tags and filters. Ensure that they perform their operations as efficiently as possible, avoiding expensive computations or database queries.

Caching is another powerful technique for improving the performance of template rendering. Django offers several levels of caching, including the ability to cache entire templates or portions of templates. When used appropriately, caching can drastically reduce the time required to render templates that contain data which does not change frequently. Implement template caching by:

- Utilizing the \cache template tag around blocks of the template that are expensive to render and change infrequently.

- Using template fragment caching to cache specific parts of a template independently, allowing for fine-grained control over what gets cached and for how long.

Precompiling templates can also contribute to performance gains. Django automatically compiles templates the first time they are rendered. However, for templates that are used frequently, precompiling them as part of the deployment process can save valuable time. This can be accomplished by using management commands or third-party tools designed for Django template precompilation.

Finally, minimizing template logic and focusing on data presentation can further enhance performance. Business logic should reside in views or models, not in templates. This separation of concerns not only adheres to best practices in software design but also reduces the complexity and rendering time of templates. Templates should be kept as simple and light as possible, delegating heavier computations to views or the database layer where they can be more efficiently processed.

Optimizing Django templates involves a multifaceted approach that includes managing template inheritance efficiently, optimizing template tags and filters, leveraging caching mechanisms, precompiling templates, and minimizing template logic. By applying these techniques, developers can significantly reduce template rendering times, contributing to faster page loads and a smoother user experience in Django applications.

11.7 Static Files and Media Management

In the context of web development, static files and media are essential components that contribute to the functionality and aesthetics of web applications. For Django applications, efficient management and delivery of these files are crucial for optimizing performance. This section will discuss strategies for managing static files and media in Django, including the configuration of static file storage, the use of CDNs for media delivery, and compression techniques for minimizing file sizes.

Django defines static files as those that do not change or require processing, such as CSS, JavaScript, and images. Media files, on the other hand, are typically user-uploaded content such as photos and documents. The management of these resources affects the loading time of web pages and, consequently, the user experience and search engine ranking of the application.

Let's start with the configuration of static files in Django. The first step involves setting the STATIC_URL and STATIC_ROOT settings in the project's settings.py file. STATIC_URL defines the URL to use when referring to static files in templates, whereas STATIC_ROOT specifies the directory where these files will be collected using the collectstatic command. It's important to differentiate between STATIC_ROOT and STATICFILES_DIRS; the latter is a list of additional directories where Django will search for static files, in addition to each application's static directory.

To efficiently serve media files, configuring MEDIA_URL and MEDIA_ROOT is essential. MEDIA_ROOT indicates the server's filesystem path where media files should be stored, and MEDIA_URL is the URL that serves these files. In production, serving media files directly from Django is not recommended due to performance implications. Instead, a more scalable approach involves using a web server like Nginx or a cloud-based storage solution such as Amazon S3 to serve media files.

Using a Content Delivery Network (CDN) can significantly enhance the delivery of static and media files. CDNs distribute the files across multiple, geographically dispersed servers, reducing the distance between the server and the end-user, and therefore, decreasing the load time. Integrating a CDN with Django can be achieved by modifying the STATIC_URL and MEDIA_URL settings to point to the CDN's URL. Furthermore, several Django packages simplify this integration and handle complexities such as file versioning and invalidating cached files on the CDN.

File compression is another effective technique for improving the performance of static and media management. Compression reduces file sizes, leading to faster transfer rates and loading times. Django's `django.contrib.staticfiles` app supports automatic compression of static files such as CSS and JavaScript using tools like `django-compressor` or `django-pipeline`. These tools can combine multiple files into one, minify CSS and JavaScript, and even compile languages like Sass and LESS to their CSS equivalents.

Moreover, optimizing images is vital for reducing load times, especially for media-heavy applications. Techniques include resizing images to their maximum display dimensions, using efficient image formats (e.g., WebP instead of JPEG or PNG), and leveraging lazy loading to delay the loading of images until they are needed. Several Django packages, like `django-imagekit`, automate these image optimization processes.

Lastly, it's critical to implement appropriate caching mechanisms for static and media files to avoid unnecessary requests to the server. Setting long-lived HTTP cache headers for static files can instruct browsers and CDNs to cache these files for extended periods. Django provides mechanisms for adding these headers and integrates with the web server's configurations to manage cache directives efficiently.

Effective static files and media management is a key aspect of performance optimization in Django applications. By carefully configuring storage settings, utilizing CDNs for content delivery, applying compression and optimization techniques, and implementing caching strategies, developers can ensure that static and media files are served efficiently. These actions collectively contribute to faster page load times, improved user experience, and enhanced overall performance of Django applications.

11.8 Using Asynchronous Views and Tasks

Asynchronous programming has gained significant importance in the field of web development, particularly when dealing with I/O-bound and high-latency operations. Django, being a robust web framework, provides support for asynchronous views and tasks to enhance the performance and scalability of applications. This section will discuss the implementation of asynchronous views in Django, leveraging asynchronous task queues for background tasks, and best practices for employing these features effectively.

Asynchronous Views in Django

Django introduced support for asynchronous views from version 3.1, allowing developers to write asynchronous code using the 'async def' syntax. This non-blocking approach is particularly useful in handling long-running I/O operations without halting the execution of other code, thus improving the throughput of the application.

To implement an asynchronous view in Django, you modify a standard view function to an async function. Here is an example:

```
from django.http import JsonResponse
import httpx

async def get_external_data(request):
    async with httpx.AsyncClient() as client:
        response = await client.get('https://api.example.com/data')
        return JsonResponse(response.json())
```

This asynchronous view performs an HTTP GET request to an external API. The 'await' keyword is used to wait for the network operation to complete without blocking the server's execution flow. This is especially beneficial when your Django application has to make multiple external API calls or deal with slow database queries.

Asynchronous Task Queues with Celery

While asynchronous views improve responsiveness and efficiency in handling HTTP requests, Django applications often require executing background tasks such as sending emails, processing images, or running heavy computations. For such scenarios, Django can integrate with asynchronous task queues like Celery.

Celery is a distributed task queue system that allows for the execution of tasks asynchronously with real-time processing. It supports scheduling and can work with multiple workers, making it a powerful tool for background task processing in Django.

Here is how to create an asynchronous task with Celery in a Django application:

```
from celery import shared_task

@shared_task
def process_data(data_id):
    # Logic to process data
    pass
```

This task can be called asynchronously from anywhere within your Django project:

```
1  from .tasks import process_data
2
3  process_data.delay(data_id)
```

The '.delay()' method is used to execute the task asynchronously. Celery takes care of queuing the task and executing it with a worker without blocking the main application flow.

Best Practices for Asynchronous Programming in Django

To effectively use asynchronous features in Django, developers must follow certain best practices:

- Use asynchronous views for I/O-bound operations, such as accessing APIs, reading or writing to external databases, or handling files.

- Limit the use of synchronous Django ORM operations within asynchronous code. If necessary, wrap these calls with 'sync_to_async' to prevent blocking the event loop.

- Ensure that any third-party libraries used within asynchronous code are compatible with async/await. If not, consider using alternative libraries that provide asynchronous support.

- Utilize Celery or similar distributed task queues for executing long-running or CPU-bound tasks outside the request/response cycle.

- Monitor the performance and scalability of your application with asynchronous features enabled. It may require tuning of the worker processes and threads based on the workload.

Leveraging asynchronous views and tasks in Django applications can significantly improve performance, especially for I/O-bound operations. By following the best practices outlined, developers can ensure that their Django applications are both efficient and scalable. Asynchronous programming requires a different mindset and careful handling, but when used appropriately, it opens up new possibilities for optimizing web application performance.

11.9 API Performance Optimization with Django Rest Framework

API performance optimization is essential in building responsive and scalable Django applications. Django Rest Framework (DRF) provides a powerful toolkit for building web APIs, but its performance can suffer if not properly optimized. This section will discuss strategies for improving the efficiency of APIs developed with Django Rest Framework.

To begin with, it is important to understand the impact of database interactions on API performance. Django ORM, while abstracting complex SQL queries, can lead to inefficient database hits if not used carefully. One common pitfall is the N+1 query problem, where an individual query is made for each item in a queryset to access related objects. Utilizing the `select_related` and `prefetch_related` methods provided by Django ORM can drastically reduce the number of database queries needed for fetching related objects.

```
from django.db import models

class Author(models.Model):
    name = models.CharField(max_length=100)

class Book(models.Model):
    title = models.CharField(max_length=100)
    author = models.ForeignKey(Author, on_delete=models.CASCADE)
```

By using `select_related` and `prefetch_related` in our queries, we can efficiently retrieve all related objects in a single or minimal number of database hits.

Serialization in DRF can also significantly impact performance. When returning large datasets, it is crucial to optimize serializer classes. Limit the fields that are serialized and consider flattening data structures where possible to reduce the amount of nested serialization, as deeply nested objects can be expensive to serialize.

Another effective strategy for optimizing DRF APIs is implementing caching. Caching can be applied at various levels within an application, but endpoint-level caching is particularly effective for APIs. DRF provides simple mechanisms to cache entire responses, ensuring that subsequent requests to the same endpoint can be served quickly without hitting the database or re-processing data.

```
from rest_framework.response import Response
from rest_framework.decorators import api_view
from django.core.cache import cache
```

```
 4
 5   @api_view(['GET'])
 6   def book_list(request):
 7       if 'books' in cache:
 8           # Return cached response
 9           return Response(cache.get('books'))
10       else:
11           books = Book.objects.all()
12           serialized_books = BookSerializer(books, many=True).data
13           cache.set('books', serialized_books, timeout=300)
14           return Response(serialized_books)
```

Throttling and pagination are additional tools that can be employed to limit the load on your server and improve the client's experience by controlling the rate of API requests and the volume of data sent in a single response, respectively. DRF provides built-in support for both features, allowing for easy integration into your API views.

Finally, asynchronous processing can be a game-changer for API performance. Django 3.1 and newer versions support asynchronous views, and Django Rest Framework can be used in conjunction with Django's asynchronous capabilities to handle long-running operations or high volume, concurrent requests without blocking the server's main thread.

```
1   from rest_framework.response import Response
2   from rest_framework.decorators import api_view
3
4   @api_view(['GET'])
5   async def async_view(request):
6       # Perform some asynchronous I/O operation
7       data = await some_async_io_operation()
8       return Response(data)
```

In sum, optimizing an API with Django Rest Framework involves careful consideration of database interactions, the efficiency of serialization, the strategic use of caching, and the leveraging of Django's asynchronous capabilities. By applying these strategies, developers can vastly improve the scalability and responsiveness of their Django applications, enhancing the end-user experience.

The performance of Django Rest Framework APIs is not solely dependent on correct coding practices but also on a deep understanding of underlying mechanisms and thoughtful application architecture. Continuous performance monitoring and regular optimizations based on observed metrics and logs are essential practices for maintaining high-performing APIs.

11.10   Front-end Optimization Techniques for Django Projects

Front-end optimization in Django projects involves a multitude of strategies aimed at reducing load times and improving the interaction experience for end-users. These techniques span from the minimization and compression of static files to the strategic loading of resources and beyond. Implementing these optimizations ensures that the Django application feels responsive and delivers content efficiently, which is crucial for user retention and satisfaction.

The first area of focus in front-end optimization is the minimization of CSS, JavaScript, and HTML. The rationale behind this technique is straightforward: smaller files load faster over the network. Minimization removes unnecessary characters from code files without changing their functionality. This includes whitespace, line breaks, comments, and block delimiters. Code examples before and after minimization clearly illustrate its impact:

```
1  /* Before Minimization */
2  function helloWorld() {
3      console.log("Hello, world!");
4  }
5
6  /* After Minimization */
7  function helloWorld(){console.log("Hello, world!");}
```

Further, combining multiple CSS or JavaScript files into single files reduces the number of HTTP requests that a browser needs to make. A single, combined file can be loaded once and cached, rather than fetching multiple files individually. This technique, however, should be balanced with the practice of splitting code into chunks that are loaded on demand, which can reduce the initial load time for web pages.

Caching is another pivotal aspect of front-end performance. By setting appropriate cache-control headers for static assets, repeated visits to a page can load much faster as the browser can retrieve the assets from its cache instead of making new requests to the server. Here is a Django setting that configures caching for static files:

```
1  STATICFILES_STORAGE = 'django.contrib.staticfiles.storage.CachedStaticFilesStorage'
```

Next, the optimization of images plays a significant role. This involves serving scaled images, using modern, efficient formats, and lazy loading off-screen images until they are needed. For instance, converting images to formats like WebP can significantly reduce their filesize without compromising quality. Lazy loading, on the other hand, can be implemented using JavaScript or with the loading="lazy" attribute in the <img> tag, which tells modern browsers to delay loading these images until they are about to enter the viewport.

Using content delivery networks (CDNs) to serve static files is a strategy that considerably decreases load times for users regardless of their geographical location. CDNs distribute your content across multiple servers around the world, ensuring that requests are routed to the nearest server.

To further reduce load times, consider implementing server push, a feature of HTTP/2. With server push, servers can send critical resources to the client before the browser explicitly requests them. This preemptive action can eliminate round-trip delays and speed up the page load process.

Finally, the front-end optimization process involves regular auditing using tools like Google's PageSpeed Insights. These tools provide actionable feedback and quantifiable metrics on the performance of a web page, highlighting areas for improvement. Continuously monitoring performance after implementing optimizations is essential for maintaining and improving upon the initial gains.

The successful application of these front-end optimization techniques within Django projects results in significantly improved user experience, reduced server load, and enhanced SEO as page speed is a ranking factor for search engines. By focusing on efficient content delivery and streamlined user interaction, developers can ensure their Django applications are not only functional but also competitive in the fast-paced realm of web development.

11.11 Securing Your Django Application from Common Performance Issues

In this section, we will discuss securing Django applications from common performance pitfalls. Performance is not solely about speed and efficiency; it also encompasses the stability and reliability of your application under load. Security aspects, when overlooked, can intro-duce performance bottlenecks, making the application susceptible to various issues. As such, addressing these concerns is paramount for maintaining optimal performance.

One critical aspect of securing Django applications is validating and sanitizing input. This process involves ensuring that all incoming data, whether from user forms, API calls, or any external source, is correctly formatted and harmless before it is processed or stored. Incorrectly handled input can lead to SQL injection, cross-site scripting (XSS), and other vulnerabilities which not only compromise security but also degrade performance as they can lead to unnecessary database queries and server load.

```
1  from django.core.validators import validate_email
2  from django.core.exceptions import ValidationError
3
4  def validate_user_input(email):
5      try:
6          validate_email(email)
7      except ValidationError:
8          return False
9      return True
```

This example demonstrates a simple input validation in Django. By val-idating emails before processing them, we reduce the risk of injection attacks which can cause performance issues by overloading the servers or triggering unnecessary processes.

Session management is another crucial area for maintaining perfor-mance while keeping the application secure. Django session handling is highly efficient, but misconfiguration can lead to vulnerabilities and performance degradation. For instance, storing session data in a database without regular cleanup can result in the database size grow-ing exponentially, which slows down response times. It is essential to periodically clear expired sessions and consider storing session data in cached memory or other fast-access data storage solutions for high-traffic applications.

```
1  SESSION_ENGINE = 'django.contrib.sessions.backends.cache'
2  SESSION_CACHE_ALIAS = 'default'
```

This configuration snippet tells Django to store session data in cache rather than in the database. It is a simple change that can have a profound impact on performance, especially for applications with a large user base.

Caching is a well-established method for enhancing performance, but it must be implemented with security considerations in mind. Caching dynamic content without proper controls can lead to privacy violations or data leakage, as users might receive content intended for others. Implement caching strategies that are context-aware and invalidate cache entries when the underlying data changes or when user sessions end.

```
from django.core.cache import cache

def cache_user_profile(user_id):
    key = f"user_profile_{user_id}"
    user_profile = cache.get(key)
    if user_profile is None:
        user_profile = retrieve_user_profile_from_db(user_id)
        cache.set(key, user_profile, timeout=120)
    return user_profile
```

Here, caching is implemented carefully to ensure that user profiles are stored and retrieved securely, avoiding serving cached data to the wrong user. Furthermore, specifying a timeout for cached data helps in maintaining the freshness of data, which is essential for both performance and security.

Lastly, regular security audits and performance profiling are essential practices. They help in identifying and addressing vulnerabilities that could be exploited to degrade performance. Tools like Django Debug Toolbar can be used to profile views and SQL queries, identifying slow database queries and inefficient code that might not only slow down the application but also expose it to security threats such as denial of service attacks.

Securing a Django application from common performance issues involves a multifaceted approach that includes proper input validation, efficient session management, secure and intelligent caching, and regular auditing. By integrating these security measures, developers can significantly enhance both the security and the performance of Django applications, ensuring a reliable and efficient user experience.

11.12 Monitoring and Logging for Performance Issues

Monitoring and logging in Django applications are critical processes for identifying and resolving performance bottlenecks. These processes

341

enable developers to gain insight into the runtime behavior of their applications, understand how different components interact, and pinpoint inefficiencies that could impact application performance. This section will discuss key concepts, tools, and practices for effective monitoring and logging that can help in enhancing the performance of Django applications.

Effective monitoring of Django applications involves tracking various metrics and events that reflect the health and performance of the application. Key metrics include response times, database query performance, error rates, and server resource usage, such as CPU and memory consumption. Events, on the other hand, include exceptions, user-generated actions, and system-level occurrences that could influence the application's performance.

The Django framework comes with built-in capabilities for logging, which can be extended and customized based on the application's requirements. The logging module in Django, configured in the `settings.py` file, allows developers to capture and record various types of information, including debug messages, information on system activities, warnings, and errors. Effective logging practice in Django involves:

- Defining loggers for different components of the application.

- Setting appropriate logging levels (e.g., DEBUG, INFO, WARNING, ERROR) to control the granularity of the logged information.

- Configuring handlers to specify where to direct the logging output (e.g., console, files, external monitoring services).

- Using formatters to define the format of log messages, ensuring that they contain relevant information for troubleshooting (e.g., timestamps, logger names, message levels).

For example, configuring logging in Django might involve adding the following to your `settings.py` file:

```
1  LOGGING = {
2      'version': 1,
3      'disable_existing_loggers': False,
4      'handlers': {
5          'console': {
6              'level': 'INFO',
7              'class': 'logging.StreamHandler',
8          },
```

```
 9      },
10      'loggers': {
11          'django': {
12              'handlers': ['console'],
13              'level': 'INFO',
14              'propagate': True,
15          },
16      },
17  }
```

Monitoring and logging for performance issues also involve utilizing third-party tools and services that offer advanced analytics, alerting, and visualization capabilities. Tools such as Datadog, Sentry, and New Relic integrate seamlessly with Django and offer real-time monitoring and alerting for performance anomalies. They provide dashboards that visualize metrics and logs, making it easier to understand application behavior and identify bottlenecks.

In addition to automated monitoring and logging, regular performance testing and profiling can help in identifying potential issues before they impact end-users. Django's testing framework and various Python profiling tools (e.g., cProfile, Py-Spy) can be used to simulate traffic, analyze request lifecycles, and pinpoint resource-intensive code paths.

To maintain optimal performance, the monitoring and logging setup should be reviewed and updated regularly as the application evolves. This includes revisiting logging levels, updating metrics to monitor based on new features, and integrating new tools that may offer better insights or performance.

Effective monitoring and logging are indispensable for maintaining and improving the performance of Django applications. By leveraging Django's built-in capabilities, configuring appropriate logging levels and handlers, and utilizing advanced third-party monitoring tools, developers can gain deep insights into their applications' behavior, identify performance bottlenecks, and implement targeted optimizations to ensure a seamless and efficient user experience.

11.13 Tools and Frameworks for Django Performance Testing

Performance testing is a critical phase in the development cycle of web applications, providing insights into the application's scalability, stability, and speed under various conditions. For Django applications,

343

several tools and frameworks are instrumental in identifying performance bottlenecks and ensuring the application can handle expected loads efficiently. This section will discuss key tools and frameworks that are vital for performance testing in Django.

First on the list is Django's built-in testing framework, which includes a suite of tools for writing and executing tests. It is designed to test the internal logic of your applications, but with some extensions, it can be adapted for performance testing. For instance, using Django's `Client` class within test cases allows developers to measure response times for various requests, making it a simple yet effective tool for preliminary performance assessments.

```
1   from django.test import TestCase
2   from django.test.client import Client
3
4   class PerformanceTest(TestCase):
5       def test_response_time(self):
6           client = Client()
7           response = client.get('/your-url/')
8           self.assertLess(response.elapsed.total_seconds(), 0.5)
```

However, for more comprehensive performance testing, developers turn to specialized tools. One such tool is Locust, an open-source load testing tool written in Python. It allows you to write test scenarios in straightforward Python code and simulate millions of simultaneous users. Locust is highly valued for its versatility and precise control over test cases, making it ideal for Django applications where Python is the primary language.

```
1   from locust import HttpUser, task, between
2
3   class WebsiteUser(HttpUser):
4       wait_time = between(1, 5)
5
6       @task
7       def view_item(self):
8           self.client.get("/item/1/")
```

Another pivotal tool is Apache JMeter, a Java-based load testing tool capable of analyzing and measuring the performance of web applications. JMeter is highly versatile, allowing for load, stress, and functional testing. It supports various server types, including HTTP/HTTPS, making it suitable for Django applications. Although it requires Java, its extensive features and community support make it a popular choice among developers for detailed performance analysis.

```
Test Plan
    Thread Group
        HTTP Request
```

344

```
Server Name: www.yoursite.com
Path: /your-path/
Listener
```

For Django applications specifically, Silk is a profiling tool that intercepts and stores HTTP requests and database queries made by your application. It offers a user-friendly interface to analyze these requests and queries, helping developers identify slow queries and endpoints quickly. Silk is integrated directly into the Django application, making it incredibly convenient for ongoing performance monitoring during development.

```
1  MIDDLEWARE = [
2      'silk.middleware.SilkyMiddleware',
3      ...
4  ]
5
6  SILKY_PYTHON_PROFILER = True
```

Lastly, Django-Debug-Toolbar is an invaluable tool for developers during the local development phase. It provides a detailed panel with debug information about the current request/response cycle, including SQL queries, template render times, and cache usage. This tool helps in identifying inefficient database queries and optimizing them without leaving the development environment.

```
1  INSTALLED_APPS = [
2      ...
3      'debug_toolbar',
4  ]
5
6  MIDDLEWARE = [
7      ...
8      'debug_toolbar.middleware.DebugToolbarMiddleware',
9  ]
```

Applying these tools and frameworks systematically can significantly enhance the performance of Django applications. By identifying bottlenecks early in the development cycle, developers can take corrective measures to optimize the application, ensuring that it can withstand the demands of real-world usage. Performance testing should, therefore, be an integral part of any Django development process, facilitated by the effective use of these tools and frameworks.

11.14 Deploying Django Applications for High Performance

Deploying Django applications for high performance involves an assessment and finely tuned configuration of both the application environment and the hosting infrastructure. This section will discuss strategies to enhance performance through deployment best practices, focusing on aspects such as application server configuration, database setup, static files management, and the use of a Content Delivery Network (CDN).

In the context of application servers, Django applications are commonly served using a combination of Gunicorn or uWSGI and Nginx. Gunicorn acts as the WSGI HTTP Server for UNIX, providing a powerful interface between web applications and web servers. To configure Gunicorn for high performance, it is critical to adjust the number of worker processes according to the server's CPU cores. For instance, if a server has 4 CPU cores, configuring Gunicorn with at least 4 worker processes is recommended to utilize the CPU efficiently.

```
1  # Example configuration for Gunicorn with 4 worker processes
2  gunicorn my_django_project.wsgi:application --workers 4
```

For Nginx, configuring it as a reverse proxy for Gunicorn enhances performance by delegating tasks such as serving static files and handling client connections. This setup reduces the load on Gunicorn, allowing it to focus on running the Django application. Nginx can be configured to cache static content and compress responses, further reducing response times.

Database setup is another critical factor in deploying Django applications. Using PostgreSQL or MySQL with connection pooling can significantly reduce connection overhead. Django supports persistent connections to databases, which can be enabled in the DATABASES setting by configuring 'CONN_MAX_AGE' with a positive integer (the persistence duration in seconds).

```
1  # Example configuration for persistent database connections in Django settings.py
2  DATABASES = {
3      'default': {
4          'ENGINE': 'django.db.backends.postgresql',
5          'NAME': 'mydatabase',
6          'USER': 'mydatabaseuser',
7          'PASSWORD': 'mypassword',
8          'HOST': 'localhost',
9          'PORT': '',
10         'CONN_MAX_AGE': 600, # 10 minutes of persistent connection
```

```
11       }
12   }
```

Managing static files and media effectively is pivotal for performance. Django's `collectstatic` command gathers static files from each of your applications (and any other places you specify) into a single location that is easily servable by web servers like Nginx. Moreover, configuring Nginx to serve static files directly, without involving Django, can boost response times significantly.

Utilizing a CDN for serving static and media files can dramatically improve application performance, especially for users geographically distant from the server. A CDN distributes your content across multiple, globally dispersed servers, reducing the latency by serving the content from the location nearest to the user.

Lastly, ensuring the Django application runs in a production-ready environment is essential for high performance. This includes setting `DEBUG` to `False` in Django settings and utilizing Django's security and performance recommendations such as database query optimization, cache framework, and asynchronous processing where appropriate.

Implementing these deployment strategies can significantly enhance the performance of a Django application. By carefully configuring the application server, database, static file handling, and using a CDN, developers can ensure their applications are prepared to handle high traffic volumes efficiently and deliver a fast, responsive user experience.

11.15   Case Studies: Real-world Django Performance Optimization

This section will discuss real-world case studies highlighting the application of performance optimization techniques in Django applications. These cases illustrate how specific strategies and practices can significantly enhance application performance, providing insights into effective optimization in various contexts.

Case Study 1: Database Optimization for E-commerce Platform

An e-commerce platform experienced slow page loads and timeouts during high-traffic events. The primary bottleneck was traced to inefficient database queries and excessive number of database hits per request. To address these issues, the development team implemented several optimization strategies.

First, they employed Django's `select_related` and `prefetch_related` query optimization methods to reduce the number of database queries. This was particularly effective for product listing pages where multiple related models were accessed.

```
1   from django.db import models
2
3   class Product(models.Model):
4       # Product fields
5
6   class ProductReview(models.Model):
7       product = models.ForeignKey(Product, on_delete=models.CASCADE)
8       # Review fields
9
10  # Before Optimization
11  products = Product.objects.all()
12  for product in products:
13      reviews = product.productreview_set.all()
14
15  # After Optimization
16  from django.db.models import Prefetch
17  prefetched_reviews = Prefetch('productreview_set')
18  products = Product.objects.prefetch_related(prefetched_reviews)
```

Additionally, indexing critical fields and employing database query caching significantly improved query execution time. This not only accelerated page loading times but also enhanced the overall user experience during peak load periods.

Case Study 2: Caching Strategy for News Publishing Website

A high-traffic news website built with Django struggled with serving dynamic content quickly to its users. The application's performance was hindered by repetitive rendering of templates and fetching similar data sets from the database for each request.

The solution implemented involved a comprehensive caching strategy using Django's built-in caching framework. Critical views delivering news articles and homepage content were cached at both the view and template levels. This approach vastly reduced the need for database access and template rendering, thereby decreasing response times significantly.

```
1   from django.views.decorators.cache import cache_page
2
3   @cache_page(60 * 15)  # Cache page for 15 minutes
4   def index(request):
5       # View logic
```

The team also utilized Django's LowLevelCache API for granular caching of frequently accessed but rarely modified objects, such as configuration settings and top menu items.

Case Study 3: Asynchronous Tasks for Social Media Analytics Tool

A social media analytics tool built on Django experienced performance issues due to synchronous execution of computationally intensive tasks, such as data aggregation and analysis. This not only slowed down request handling but also led to a poor user experience during data processing operations.

The development team tackled this challenge by integrating Django with Celery, an asynchronous task queue based on distributed message passing. Heavy computations and data processing tasks were moved out of the request-response cycle and executed asynchronously.

```
from celery import shared_task


@shared_task
def aggregate_social_media_data():
    # Data aggregation logic
```

This approach allowed the web application to respond to user requests promptly while handling resource-intensive tasks in the background. By decoupling data processing from request handling, the application achieved significant improvements in responsiveness and scalability.

These case studies highlight the importance of targeted performance optimization strategies in large-scale Django applications. From database optimization, caching strategies, to asynchronous task execution, the effective application of Django's features and external tools can lead to substantial improvements in application performance. Developers are encouraged to consider these techniques and tailor them to their specific application context to achieve optimal performance.

Chapter 12

Deployment and Scaling Django Applications

Deploying and scaling Django applications involves moving projects from the development environment to production-ready platforms, ensuring they are optimized to handle increased load and traffic. This chapter discusses various deployment options, from traditional servers to cloud-based solutions, and the configuration necessary to secure and optimize Django applications for production. It addresses the challenges of scaling web applications horizontally and vertically to accommodate growth, and the use of load balancers, caching, and database replication techniques. By mastering deployment and scaling strategies, developers can ensure their Django applications remain robust, secure, and highly available as they grow.

12.1 Overview of Django Application Deployment

Deploying a Django application is a critical step in the development life cycle, marking the transition from a development environment to a production setting. This process entails preparing the application to run efficiently and securely in a live environment, accessible by end-users. Deployment is a multifaceted operation that incorporates various stages, including configuring the application for the production

351

environment, selecting an appropriate deployment platform, setting up a web server, and ensuring that static and media files are correctly served. This section will discuss the key considerations and steps involved in deploying Django applications.

Firstly, the importance of separating development settings from production settings cannot be overstated. It is crucial to have different configurations for these environments to ensure security and optimize performance. Production settings should disable debug mode, use secure database connections, employ encryption for transmitting data, and configure logging appropriately. This separation can be achieved through the use of environment variables or separate settings files in Django.

Second, choosing the right deployment environment is vital for the success and scalability of the application. The application's requirements, traffic expectations, and available resources will guide the selection process. Virtual Private Servers (VPS), Platform as a Service (PaaS) solutions, and serverless architectures each have their advantages and limitations. VPS options offer control and flexibility but require more setup and maintenance effort. PaaS solutions, such as Heroku or Google App Engine, provide ease of use and scalability but at a higher cost and with less control. Serverless architectures, on the other hand, allow developers to build applications that scale automatically with usage, though they can introduce complexity in state management and architecture.

For Django applications, the web server acts as a gateway between the application and the internet. Django is typically deployed with a Web Server Gateway Interface (WSGI) server, such as Gunicorn or uWSGI, which serves as a link between the Django application and the web server, like Nginx or Apache. The WSGI server handles HTTP requests and communicates with Django, while the web server manages client connections and serves static files. The configuration of the WSGI server and the web server is critical for performance, security, and reliability.

```
1  # Example Gunicorn command to start a Django application
2  gunicorn myproject.wsgi:application --bind 0.0.0.0:8000 --workers 3
```

Additionally, managing static and media files in a production environment is another key aspect of deployment. In development, Django conveniently serves these files automatically, but in production, it is recommended to configure a web server like Nginx to serve these files.

This setup reduces the load on the application server and improves response times for static content.

Proper database configuration is a cornerstone of deploying Django applications. Using persistent connections, optimizing database queries, and selecting the appropriate database backend are essential for better performance and scalability. For high-traffic applications, employing database replication and sharding techniques could be necessary to distribute the load and ensure high availability.

Security is another significant aspect of deploying Django applications. This includes setting up HTTPS, configuring security middleware options in Django, preventing Cross-Site Scripting (XSS) and Cross-Site Request Forgery (CSRF) attacks, and ensuring that user data is protected. Django provides a robust set of built-in tools and libraries to help secure applications, but it is essential to stay informed about new vulnerabilities and apply security patches promptly.

Finally, the importance of monitoring and logging cannot be overstressed. Effective logging provides insights into the application's performance and helps identify issues early. Tools such as Sentry, Logstash, and Prometheus can be integrated with Django to enable comprehensive monitoring and logging, facilitating proactive application management.

Deploying a Django application is a comprehensive process that encompasses configuring the application for production, choosing the correct deployment environment, setting up web and WSGI servers, managing static and media files, optimizing database configurations, securing the application, and implementing effective monitoring and logging. By meticulously following best practices in each of these areas, developers can ensure that their Django applications are secure, efficient, and scalable in a production environment.

12.2 Choosing a Deployment Environment: VPS, PaaS, and Serverless

When deploying Django applications, selecting the right environment is crucial for optimal performance, security, and scalability. The choice between Virtual Private Server (VPS), Platform as a Service (PaaS), and Serverless computing depends on various factors, including application requirements, budget constraints, and technical expertise. This section will discuss each deployment option and their implications for Django applications.

Virtual Private Server (VPS): A VPS provides a dedicated portion of a physical server's resources, including CPU time, memory, and disk space, isolated for your use. This setup offers greater control over the server environment, allowing for custom configurations tailored to the specific needs of your Django application. Deploying a Django application on a VPS requires a thorough understanding of server management, security configurations, and network settings.

The process typically involves setting up a web server, such as Nginx or Apache, configuring the server block or virtual host to serve the Django application, and ensuring the database backend is properly installed and configured. Security considerations, including setting up firewall rules and secure shell (SSH) access, are also paramount. For Django applications, a WSGI server like Gunicorn or uWSGI acts as the interface between the web server and the Python application.

Platform as a Service (PaaS): PaaS offerings, such as Heroku, Google App Engine, and AWS Elastic Beanstalk, abstract much of the infrastructure management away from the developer. These platforms automatically handle the deployment, server provisioning, scaling, and security. Opting for a PaaS solution means developers can focus more on application development rather than server management.

Deploying a Django application to a PaaS environment often involves configuring the application for the specific platform, which may include setting up environment variables, defining resource requirements, and customizing the application to work with the platform's provided services, like databases and email services. PaaS platforms typically offer integrated scaling options, making it easier to scale applications based on demand.

Serverless Computing: Serverless architectures offer a further abstraction, where developers are charged based on the execution of functions in response to events. This model eliminates the need to manage servers or specify resource requirements upfront. Serverless platforms like AWS Lambda, Google Cloud Functions, and Azure Functions can automatically scale from a few requests per day to thousands per second.

While Django is not inherently designed for serverless architectures, it can be adapted using a gateway interface or an adaptation layer, such as Zappa, which packages Django applications into a format suitable for serverless platforms. This approach can significantly reduce operational costs for applications with variable traffic and can speed up deployment processes. However, it may introduce complexities in managing stateful connections, like those to databases, and can lead to cold start issues, where the initial request after a period of inactivity suffers from a higher response time.

Conclusion: The choice of deployment environment for a Django application should be guided by the application's specific requirements, expected traffic patterns, and the team's technical capabilities. VPS solutions offer the most control but require significant server management knowledge. PaaS services reduce the operational burden but may come with higher costs and less flexibility. Serverless computing offers the highest level of abstraction, ideal for applications with highly variable traffic, though it may introduce certain architectural complexities. Each of these environments has its strengths and challenges, and the choice between them should align with the strategic goals of the application development and deployment process.

12.3 Setting Up a Production Environment for Django

Setting up a production environment for Django applications involves a series of crucial steps designed to ensure that applications run efficiently, securely, and reliably. Unlike a development environment, where ease of use and accessibility for a single developer is often prioritized, a production environment must be optimized for performance, security, and scalability. This entails configuring web servers, database servers, static and media files, and ensuring secure communication between these components. This section will discuss the necessary steps to prepare a Django application for a production environment.

Let's start with the web server configuration. Django applications can be served using various Web Server Gateway Interface (WSGI) servers like Gunicorn or uWSGI, coupled with a web server like Nginx or Apache serving as a reverse proxy. This setup ensures that the Django application can handle multiple simultaneous requests efficiently and securely.

```
1  # Sample Gunicorn command to start a Django project
2  gunicorn myproject.wsgi:application --bind 0.0.0.0:8000
```

This command starts a Gunicorn server instance for a Django project named myproject, listening on all interfaces at port 8000. It highlights the importance of separating the concerns of handling HTTP traffic and application logic by having a dedicated WSGI HTTP server.

For the reverse proxy setup using Nginx, the configuration directs the HTTP traffic to the WSGI server serving the Django application. The following snippet demonstrates a basic Nginx server block configuration, forwarding traffic to a Gunicorn server instance:

```
server {
    listen 80;
    server_name example.com;

    location / {
        proxy_pass http://127.0.0.1:8000;
        proxy_set_header Host $host;
        proxy_set_header X-Real-IP $remote_addr;
    }
}
```

This Nginx configuration listens for HTTP traffic on port 80 for the domain example.com, and forwards requests to the Gunicorn server running at 127.0.0.1:8000. It also configures headers to ensure the Django application receives the original host and client IP address, which is necessary for certain applications and analytics.

Database servers play a critical role in production environments. It is advisable to use a dedicated database server, such as PostgreSQL, which offers robust features and strong compliance with ACID (Atomicity, Consistency, Isolation, Durability) properties. Configuring a separate database server involves installing the database software, creating a database user with necessary permissions, and configuring network access if the database server is not hosted on the same machine as the Django application.

The management of static and media files in production is markedly different from development. Django's collectstatic command gathers static files from all applications in the project into a single location that can be efficiently served by a web server. For media files, a common practice is to configure a dedicated directory accessible by the web server, with proper access controls to ensure files are served securely.

```
# Collect static files in Django
./manage.py collectstatic
```

Implementing SSL/TLS for secure communications between the client, web server, and database server is paramount. Certificates can be

obtained from certificate authorities (CA) like Let's Encrypt and configured on the web server to ensure that all data transmitted is encrypted,
protecting sensitive information from being intercepted during transmission.

Finally, environment settings in Django's `settings.py` must be adjusted for production. Debug mode should be disabled (`DEBUG =
False`), and Django's `ALLOWED_HOSTS` setting must be configured to
accept requests only from specific domains or IP addresses. Security settings such as `SECURE_SSL_REDIRECT`, `CSRF_COOKIE_SECURE`, and
`SESSION_COOKIE_SECURE` should be enabled to enhance the security
posture of the Django application.

Setting up a production environment for a Django application requires
careful planning and execution. By ensuring the correct configuration
of web and database servers, managing static and media files appropriately, and implementing necessary security measures, developers can
create a robust, secure, and scalable production environment suitable
for handling real-world traffic and workloads.

12.4   Configuring Django for Production

When transitioning a Django application from a development environment to a production setting, several critical configurations must
be addressed to ensure the application's security, performance, and
reliability. This section will discuss key settings and considerations
necessary to prepare a Django project for production. The focus will
be on the Django settings module, commonly found as `settings.py`,
which plays a crucial role in this transition.

Firstly, it's essential to differentiate between the `DEBUG` mode in Django.
In a development environment, `DEBUG` is typically set to `True` to provide detailed error reports and debugging information. However, for
production:

```
1  DEBUG = False
```

Setting `DEBUG` to `False` is critical for security and performance reasons.
Additionally, it is important to configure the `ALLOWED_HOSTS` setting,
which defines a list of strings representing the host/domain names that
this Django site can serve. This is a security measure to prevent HTTP
Host header attacks:

```
1  ALLOWED_HOSTS = ['yourdomain.com', 'www.yourdomain.com']
```

Database configuration is another critical aspect of setting up Django for production. While SQLite can suffice for development, production environments usually require a more robust database system like PostgreSQL, MySQL, or Oracle. Django's database settings should be meticulously configured to ensure secure and efficient database access. For instance, using PostgreSQL:

```
1  DATABASES = {
2      'default': {
3          'ENGINE': 'django.db.backends.postgresql',
4          'NAME': 'mydatabase',
5          'USER': 'mydatabaseuser',
6          'PASSWORD': 'mypassword',
7          'HOST': 'localhost',
8          'PORT': '5432',
9      }
10 }
```

Securely managing static and media files is essential in a production environment. Django provides STATIC_ROOT and MEDIA_ROOT settings to define the file system path to static and media files, respectively. For example:

```
1  STATIC_ROOT = '/var/www/yourdomain.com/static/'
2  MEDIA_ROOT = '/var/www/yourdomain.com/media/'
```

Furthermore, configuring secure connections is imperative. Implementing HTTPS by setting SECURE_SSL_REDIRECT to True forces all non-HTTPS connections to be redirected to HTTPS:

```
1  SECURE_SSL_REDIRECT = True
```

Additionally, setting CSRF_COOKIE_SECURE and SESSION_COOKIE_SECURE to True ensures that CSRF and session cookies are only sent over HTTPS connections, which is a crucial measure for preventing man-in-the-middle attacks:

```
1  CSRF_COOKIE_SECURE = True
2  SESSION_COOKIE_SECURE = True
```

Caching is an effective strategy to enhance the performance of a Django application. Configuring caching mechanisms, whether using Django's built-in caching framework or external caching systems like Memcached or Redis, can significantly reduce database query times and server response times. An example of setting up Memcached with Django might look like this:

```
1   CACHES = {
2       'default': {
3           'BACKEND': 'django.core.cache.backends.memcached.MemcachedCache',
4           'LOCATION': '127.0.0.1:11211',
5       }
6   }
```

Lastly, logging configuration should not be overlooked. Properly set up logging can aid in monitoring the application's health and debugging issues swiftly. Django's LOGGING configuration allows for comprehensive logging strategies, including file-based logging, console logging, and integration with external logging services:

```
1    LOGGING = {
2        'version': 1,
3        'disable_existing_loggers': False,
4        'handlers': {
5            'file': {
6                'level': 'ERROR',
7                'class': 'logging.FileHandler',
8                'filename': '/path/to/django/errors.log',
9            },
10       },
11       'loggers': {
12           'django': {
13               'handlers': ['file'],
14               'level': 'ERROR',
15               'propagate': True,
16           },
17       },
18   }
```

Configuring a Django application for production involves careful consideration and adjustment of various settings related to security, performance, and reliability. By meticulously configuring the DEBUG mode, database settings, static and media file management, secure connections, caching strategies, and logging, developers can ensure that their Django applications are optimized for the challenges of a production environment.

12.5   Deploying Django with WSGI and ASGI Servers

Deploying Django applications requires an understanding of the Web Server Gateway Interface (WSGI) and Asynchronous Server Gateway Interface (ASGI) servers. These interfaces serve as a bridge between Django applications and the web server, ensuring that Python applications can communicate fluently with web protocols. This section will discuss the deployment process using both WSGI and ASGI servers, highlighting their differences, configurations, and when to use one over the other.

WSGI has been the standard for Python web application deployment for many years. It is designed for synchronous processing of requests, which means it handles one request at a time per process. Django, by default, supports WSGI and it is suitable for applications that do not require handling long-lived connections such as WebSockets.

To deploy Django with a WSGI server, the application needs to be configured with a WSGI application module. Django automatically generates a file named `wsgi.py` in the project directory, which contains the application callable that the server uses to communicate with the Django application. The following code snippet demonstrates how to use the `wsgi.py` file with a popular WSGI server, Gunicorn:

```
1  gunicorn myproject.wsgi:application --bind 0.0.0.0:8000
```

This command starts Gunicorn on port 8000 and uses the `wsgi.py` file from the Django project named `myproject` to serve the application. Gunicorn is highly configurable, and various options such as the number of worker processes can be adjusted based on the anticipated load.

In contrast to WSGI, ASGI is designed to support asynchronous processing, allowing Django applications to handle long-lived connections, such as those needed for WebSockets, HTTP/2, and other real-time features. ASGI is an evolving standard and has gained traction with the rise of asynchronous frameworks in Python.

Deploying Django with an ASGI server entails configuring an ASGI application module. Django applications targeting ASGI must include an `asgi.py` file in the project directory, similar to the `wsgi.py` file but tailored for asynchronous protocols. The `asgi.py` module contains the ASGI application callable for the server. An example deployment using Daphne, an ASGI server, is shown below:

```
1  daphne myproject.asgi:application --bind 0.0.0.0:8000
```

This command starts the Daphne server on port 8000, using the `asgi.py` file from the `myproject`. Daphne can handle both traditional HTTP requests and WebSocket connections, making it ideal for real-time Django applications.

The choice between WSGI and ASGI servers depends on the requirements of the Django application. For applications that primarily serve

HTML pages or handle RESTful APIs without the need for asynchronous processing, a WSGI server like Gunicorn may be sufficient. However, for applications that require real-time capabilities or handle long-lived connections, an ASGI server like Daphne or Uvicorn is recommended.

Configuring Django for ASGI also requires adjustments in settings and application architecture to take full advantage of asynchronous features. Django introduced ASGI support from version 3.0, allowing developers to write asynchronous views and middleware. Nonetheless, care must be taken to ensure compatibility with asynchronous database drivers and other asynchronous components to avoid blocking operations.

Deploying Django with WSGI or ASGI servers is a critical step in preparing applications for production. While WSGI servers offer simplicity and robustness for synchronous applications, ASGI servers cater to modern web applications requiring real-time features and asynchronous processing. Proper configuration of the Django application and the chosen server is essential for optimal performance, security, and scalability.

12.6 Working with Reverse Proxies and Load Balancers

Deploying Django applications for high availability and scalability often necessitates the use of reverse proxies and load balancers. These tools play a crucial role in managing incoming traffic and distributing it efficiently across multiple instances of an application. Understanding their functionality and configuration is essential for optimizing the performance and reliability of Django applications in production environments.

A reverse proxy acts as an intermediary for requests from clients seeking resources from servers. In the context of Django deployments, a reverse proxy can serve several purposes, such as terminating SSL connections, serving static files, compressing responses, and even caching. Its primary role, however, is to forward client requests to the Django application and send responses back to the client. This setup simplifies networking setup, enhances security, and can significantly improve the performance of web applications by offloading tasks from the application server.

361

```
1   # Example configuration snippet for Nginx reverse proxy
2   server {
3       listen 80;
4       server_name example.com;
5
6       location / {
7           proxy_pass http://localhost:8000;
8           proxy_set_header Host $host;
9           proxy_set_header X-Real-IP $remote_addr;
10          proxy_set_header X-Forwarded-For $proxy_add_x_forwarded_for;
11          proxy_set_header X-Forwarded-Proto $scheme;
12      }
13  }
```

In the above Nginx configuration, the reverse proxy listens for HTTP requests and forwards them to a Django application running on the same server on port 8000. The `proxy_set_header` directives ensure that the Django application can access the original request information, which is necessary for accurate request processing.

Load balancers, on the other hand, distribute incoming network traffic across multiple servers to ensure no single server becomes overwhelmed, thus improving the responsiveness of applications. They can operate at various layers of the OSI model, but for Django deployments, Layer 7 (application layer) load balancing is most relevant. This allows intelligent distribution of requests based on content, ensuring efficient use of resources and maintaining high availability.

- Load balancing algorithms (e.g., round-robin, least connections, IP hash) play a pivotal role in determining how traffic is distributed.

- Health checks ensure traffic is only directed to servers that are currently operational, enhancing the reliability of the application.

- Session persistence can be important for applications that require users to maintain a consistent session across multiple requests.

```
# Example of load balancer output
Server 1: Handling request
Server 2: Handling request
Server 1: Handling request
Server 3: Handling request
```

Integrating a load balancer with Django applications often involves configuring the load balancer to communicate with multiple instances of the application, possibly running on separate machines. This complicates session management and static file serving but can be managed through careful configuration of both Django and the load balancer.

Combining a reverse proxy with a load balancer presents a robust setup for serving Django applications. The reverse proxy can manage SSL termination, static and media files serving, and apply HTTP headers adjustments before the requests hit the load balancer, which then intelligently routes the requests to the best available application server. This layered approach not only maximizes the application's uptime but also bolsters its security and efficiency.

Successful implementation of reverse proxies and load balancers in Django deployments hinges on a deep understanding of both the operational environment and the specific requirements of the application. Properly configured, these components can significantly enhance the performance, reliability, and scalability of Django applications, making them indispensable tools in the arsenal of Django developers aiming for production-level quality and efficiency.

12.7 Static and Media File Management in Production

Managing static and media files in a Django production environment is critical for the application's performance and scalability. Static files include CSS, JavaScript, and images that are not dynamically generated, and typically remain unchanged. Media files, on the other hand, refer to user-uploaded content, which can vary and grow over time. Proper management of these files is essential to ensure fast load times and efficient use of resources.

Django's collectstatic command is a key tool in the management of static files. When run, it collects all static files from each of your applications (and any other places you specify) into a single, centralized location that can easily be served by web servers or a Content Delivery Network (CDN). This process is crucial in production settings, where performance is optimized by serving static files separately from Django.

```
1  python manage.py collectstatic
```

This command should be part of your deployment process, ensuring that any changes to static files are made available in your production environment. In a Dockerized environment, this step can be included in the Dockerfile, while in a CI/CD pipeline, it could be part of a script that runs after a successful build.

In regards to serving these files, a common practice is to configure a dedicated web server such as Nginx or Apache to serve static and media files. This approach offloads the work from Django, enabling it to focus solely on dynamic content generation. Configuring these web servers necessitates proper settings to specify the location from which to serve the files:

```
1   location /static/ {
2       alias /path/to/static/files;
3   }
4
5   location /media/ {
6       alias /path/to/media/files;
7   }
```

When scalability and global reach are considerations, utilizing a CDN for static file distribution is recommended. CDNs can dramatically reduce load times by caching static files in multiple locations around the world, ensuring that these files are served from a location closest to the user. Integration of a CDN into a Django project involves updating the STATIC_URL and possibly the MEDIA_URL settings to point to the CDN.

Handling media files in production also requires careful consideration of storage and scalability. For small projects, serving media files directly from the same server may suffice, but this quickly becomes impractical as scale increases. Cloud storage services like Amazon S3 or Google Cloud Storage offer a solution, providing scalable, secure, and accessible file storage. Integrating these services with Django can be achieved through packages such as django-storages, which abstracts over the differences between different storage backends and provides a unified API for file operations.

```
1   pip install django-storages
2   pip install boto3 # For Amazon S3
```

Configuration of django-storages for use with a cloud storage service requires setting the appropriate storage backend and supplying necessary authentication credentials and permissions. Each storage backend has its specific settings, but typically, you will at least need to define the DEFAULT_FILE_STORAGE setting to point to the right backend and set up authentication keys.

```
1   # settings.py
2   DEFAULT_FILE_STORAGE = 'storages.backends.s3boto3.S3Boto3Storage'
3   AWS_ACCESS_KEY_ID = 'your-access-key'
4   AWS_SECRET_ACCESS_KEY = 'your-secret-key'
5   AWS_STORAGE_BUCKET_NAME = 'your-bucket-name'
```

In summary, efficient static and media file management in Django applications is facilitated through the use of the `collectstatic` command, proper configuration of web servers, integration with CDNs for global content delivery, and leveraging cloud storage solutions for media files. These strategies collectively enhance the performance, scalability, and user experience of your Django applications in production environments.

12.8 Database Deployment and Scaling Strategies

Deploying and scaling databases for Django applications is a critical aspect of ensuring application performance and reliability as user base and data volumes grow. This section will discuss strategies for deploying databases in a production environment and methods for scaling them to handle increased load.

Initially, deploying a database involves choosing the right database engine that matches the application's needs in terms of data structure complexity, transaction rates, and scalability requirements. Django supports several databases out of the box, including PostgreSQL, MySQL, SQLite, and Oracle. For most production applications, PostgreSQL is recommended due to its robustness, feature set, and compatibility with Django's ORM.

For deployment, the database should be installed on a server that is optimized for its workload. This means allocating sufficient memory, CPU resources, and disk space. It also involves configuring the database with appropriate settings for connection pooling, cache sizing, and query optimization. These configurations are crucial for maintaining fast response times and reducing load on the database server.

In the context of scaling, there are generally two approaches: vertical scaling and horizontal scaling.

Vertical scaling involves increasing the capacity of the existing database server by adding more CPU, RAM, or storage. While this is the simplest method of scaling, it has its limitations as there is a maximum to how much a single server's resources can be increased.

Example of vertical scaling:
Upgrading a database server from 4 cores and 16GB RAM to 8 cores and 32GB RAM.

Horizontal scaling, on the other hand, involves distributing the database load across multiple servers or instances. This can be achieved through techniques such as database sharding, where different portions of the database are stored on different servers, and replication, where copies of the database are kept in sync across multiple servers.

```
1   # Example of a database sharding logic in pseudo-code
2   if userId <= 1000:
3      connect to databaseServer1
4   elif userId <= 2000:
5      connect to databaseServer2
6   else:
7      connect to databaseServer3
```

For load distribution, Read replicas can be particularly effective. This involves creating copies of the database that are read-only and can handle read queries, thereby reducing the load on the primary database that handles both read and write operations.

- Primary Database - Handles all write operations and critical read operations

- Read Replica - Serves high-volume read requests to reduce load on the primary database

Ensuring database resilience and high availability is also critical. This can be achieved through a combination of replication for data redundancy, automated failover processes to switch to backup servers in the case of a primary server failure, and regular backup procedures to recover from data loss scenarios.

Algorithm 1: Pseudocode for setting up a highly available database

---

input : A database that needs to be made highly available
output: A resilient, highly available database setup
1 replicate database to multiple servers;
2 configure automatic failover to standby servers;
3 schedule regular backups;
4 monitor servers and replication lag;

Primary DBRead ReplicaRead Replica 2

Finally, monitoring and fine-tuning the database system is an ongoing process. This involves tracking key performance metrics such as query times, error rates, and server resource utilization. Based on these metrics, adjustments to configuration settings, resource allocations, and scaling strategies may be made to optimize performance and cost-efficiency.

In summary, deploying and scaling databases for Django applications involves careful planning and execution. It requires selecting the appropriate database engine, configuring and optimizing the database server, implementing scaling strategies such as vertical scaling, horizontal scaling, and read replicas, ensuring high availability and resilience, and continuously monitoring and fine-tuning the system. By following these strategies, developers can ensure their Django applications are supported by a robust and scalable database infrastructure.

12.9 Implementing Caching for High Traffic Django Applications

Implementing caching in Django applications is a critical strategy for enhancing performance and scalability, particularly in environments experiencing high traffic. Caching refers to the process of storing copies of files or computational results in a temporary storage location for faster access upon future requests. This section will discuss the various caching strategies available in Django, how to configure them, and best practices for their use in production environments.

Django provides a robust caching framework that supports several caching methods: per-site cache, per-view cache, and low-level cache API. Developers can also choose between different backends like Memcached, Redis, filesystem caching, local memory caching, or custom caching backends to suit their application's needs.

Configuring Django's Caching System

To utilize Django's caching, it is mandatory to first configure the caching backend. This is done in the settings.py file of a Django project. Consider an example where Memcached is used as the caching backend:

```
1  CACHES = {
2      'default': {
3          'BACKEND': 'django.core.cache.backends.memcached.MemcachedCache',
4          'LOCATION': '127.0.0.1:11211',
```

```
5        }
6    }
```

In the example above, the CACHES setting is a dictionary that defines the cache backend to use ('BACKEND') and its location ('LOCATION'). For different caching backends, the 'BACKEND' value would change accordingly and may require additional parameters.

Per-Site and Per-View Caching

For applications where most content remains static or changes infrequently, per-site caching offers a convenient approach. It caches the entire site, serving saved responses for each request. While effective for sites with mostly static content, it is less suitable for dynamic sites where content changes based on user interaction.

Per-view caching provides finer control by caching the output of specific views. A view can be cached by using the @cache_page decorator:

```
1    from django.views.decorators.cache import cache_page
2
3    @cache_page(60 * 15) # Cache for 15 minutes
4    def my_view(request):
5        ...
```

This decorator caches the output of the my_view function for 15 minutes, reducing database load and improving response times for repeated requests.

Low-level Cache API

For maximum control over what is cached, Django offers a low-level caching API. This approach allows caching of specific objects or querysets rather than entire views or the site. The following is an example of using the low-level cache API:

```
1    from django.core.cache import cache
2
3    def expensive_query():
4        if cache.get('my_key'):
5            return cache.get('my_key')
6        else:
7            result = perform_expensive_query()
8            cache.set('my_key', result, timeout=300) # Cache for 5 minutes
9            return result
```

This technique is particularly useful for caching heavy computations, database queries, or API calls that do not need to be executed on each request.

Best Practices for Caching in Production

When deploying a Django application to a production environment, it is essential to follow best practices for caching:

- Choose the caching backend based on application needs and available infrastructure. Memcached and Redis are popular choices for their performance and ease of use.

- Use per-view caching judiciously, particularly for dynamic content that changes based on user interactions or real-time data updates.

- Leverage the low-level cache API for granular control over cached data, especially for optimizing expensive operations.

- Regularly invalidate cached data to prevent serving outdated or incorrect information. Django's cache framework includes mechanisms for timeout and explicit invalidation, but developers should design their caching strategy to align with the application's data update patterns.

- Consider browser and HTTP caching in conjunction with Django's server-side caching to reduce server load and further improve user experience.

Caching is a powerful tool in Django's arsenal for improving the performance and scalability of web applications. By thoughtfully applying the caching strategies and best practices outlined above, developers can significantly enhance the responsiveness and throughput of Django applications, particularly in high-traffic scenarios.

12.10 Securing Your Django Application for Production

Securing a Django application for production requires meticulous attention to detail across multiple layers of the application stack. First and foremost, it is essential to ensure that the Django's settings.py file is appropriately configured to leverage Django's built-in security features. This includes setting DEBUG to False, configuring ALLOWED_HOSTS, using secure cookie settings, and implementing HTTPS.

To start, setting DEBUG to False in production is crucial. When DEBUG is set to True, Django displays detailed error pages that could inadvertently reveal sensitive information about the application, such as file paths or configuration settings, to potential attackers. The ALLOWED_HOSTS setting defines a list of IP addresses or domain names that Django can serve. This prevents HTTP Host header attacks, where attackers attempt to manipulate the Host header to cause cache poisoning or redirect users to malicious sites.

Secure cookie settings are also vital for protecting session and csrf tokens from being intercepted or manipulated. This involves setting the SESSION_COOKIE_SECURE and CSRF_COOKIE_SECURE to True, which ensures that cookies are only sent over HTTPS connections. Additionally, setting X_FRAME_OPTIONS to 'DENY' protects against clickjacking attacks by preventing the site from being framed by third parties.

Implementing HTTPS across the entire application is non-negotiable for production environments. HTTPS encrypts data in transit between the client and server, safeguarding against man-in-the-middle attacks. Django applications can enforce HTTPS by setting SECURE_SSL_REDIRECT to True, which redirects all HTTP requests to HTTPS.

Beyond the Django-specific settings, using environment variables for sensitive information, such as database credentials or API keys, ensures that this critical data is not hard-coded into the application's source code. Libraries like django-environ can be used to facilitate this practice.

Database security is another crucial aspect. Using Django's built-in ORM (Object-Relational Mapping) helps prevent SQL injection attacks by safely parameterizing queries. Regularly updating Django and all dependencies is also critical to protect against known vulnerabilities.

Authentication and authorization mechanisms provided by Django, such as the user authentication system and permission-based access control, should be thoroughly implemented and customized when necessary. Implementing custom user models when the project begins allows for flexibility in user authentication methods, including integration with third-party providers.

Rate limiting on login and other sensitive endpoints can thwart brute-force attacks. Django-ratelimit or custom middleware can be utilized to implement rate limiting based on IP addresses or user accounts.

Content Security Policy (CSP) headers add an additional layer of protection by controlling the resources the browser is allowed to load for the page. Libraries like django-csp assist in adding CSP headers to Django applications.

Securing a Django application also extends to its deployment environment. Ensuring that the server software is up-to-date, using a WSGI server like Gunicorn behind a properly configured HTTP server like Nginx, and securing the server with firewalls are all practices that contribute to the overall security of the application.

Lastly, continuous monitoring and logging of security-related events are imperative for identifying and responding to security incidents promptly. Django's logging framework can be configured to log security-sensitive actions, while external tools can monitor and alert on suspicious activity.

Securing a Django application for production is a comprehensive undertaking that touches every part of the application and its environment. By meticulously implementing Django's security features, following best practices for web security, and continuously monitoring for new vulnerabilities or attacks, developers can significantly reduce the risk of security breaches in their Django applications.

12.11 Continuous Integration and Continuous Deployment (CI/CD) for Django

Continuous Integration (CI) and Continuous Deployment (CD) are practices in software development designed to improve code quality and facilitate automated deployment, respectively. Implementing CI/CD for Django applications streamlines the process of integrating changes, testing, and deploying applications to production environments automatically, ensuring that the application remains reliable, scalable, and secure over time.

Continuous Integration emphasizes the frequent integration of code changes into a shared repository. Each integration is automatically verified by building the project and running a series of tests, a practice that helps in identifying and addressing errors quickly, improving code quality, and reducing the time needed to release new software updates. For a Django application, this involves setting up a CI pipeline that automatically runs unit tests, integration tests, and other static analysis tools (like linting) whenever changes are pushed to the codebase.

On the other hand, Continuous Deployment extends Continuous Integration by automatically deploying all code changes to a production or staging environment after the build stage. This means that every successful build can be deployed to users automatically, ensuring that the deployment process is not bottlenecked by manual reviews and operations. This process involves configuring the CI/CD pipeline to deploy the Django application to a server or cloud environment, ensuring that the latest version of the application is always available to users.

To implement CI/CD for Django applications, developers often rely on CI/CD platforms such as Jenkins, GitLab CI/CD, GitHub Actions, or CircleCI. These platforms provide tools and infrastructure to automatically build, test, and deploy applications based on predefined workflows and triggers, such as pushing code to a specific branch in the version control system.

```
1   # Example GitHub Actions workflow for a Django application
2
3   name: Django CI/CD Pipeline
4
5   on:
6     push:
7       branches: [ master ]
8     pull_request:
9       branches: [ master ]
10
11  jobs:
12    build:
13      runs-on: ubuntu-latest
14
15      steps:
16      - uses: actions/checkout@v2
17      - name: Set up Python
18        uses: actions/setup-python@v2
19        with:
20          python-version: 3.8
21      - name: Install dependencies
22        run: |
23          python -m pip install --upgrade pip
24          pip install -r requirements.txt
25      - name: Run tests
26        run: |
27          python manage.py test
28      - name: Deploy to Production
29        if: github.ref == 'refs/heads/master' && github.event_name == 'push'
30        run: |
31          # Add deployment scripts here
```

This example GitHub Actions workflow demonstrates a basic CI/CD pipeline for a Django project. It triggers on every push or pull request to the master branch, sets up the Python environment, installs dependencies, runs tests, and—conditional on the push event being to the master branch—runs a deployment script.

Key steps in setting up CI/CD for Django include:

- Configuring the Django application for production environments, including setting appropriate environment variables, database configurations, and static/media file handling.

- Writing comprehensive test suites covering unit tests, integration tests, and end-to-end tests to validate the functionality and reliability of the application.

- Automating the deployment process, which might involve configuring the server, setting up a database, and managing static and media files efficiently. This often includes automating migrations, bundling static assets, and applying security configurations without human intervention.

- Monitoring and maintaining the CI/CD pipeline to ensure that it is updated with respect to changes in the application architecture or the deployment environment.

Implementing CI/CD for Django applications not only ensures a systematic approach to code integration, testing, and deployment but also emphasizes the importance of quality, automation, and rapid delivery in the modern web development lifecycle. By adopting CI/CD practices, developers can significantly reduce manual errors, improve application stability, and enhance the user experience by delivering updates more frequently and reliably.

This comprehensive section on implementing CI/CD for Django applications is crafted to assist developers in understanding the importance, setup, and maintenance of CI/CD pipelines, specifically tailored for Django projects. It covers the definition and benefits of CI/CD, a practical example using GitHub Actions, and key considerations for successfully integrating continuous integration and deployment into Django application development workflows.

12.12 Monitoring and Logging Django Applications in Production

Monitoring and logging are indispensable aspects of maintaining the health and performance of Django applications in production. Effective logging practices provide insight into the application's behavior, catch unexpected errors, and track down issues that users encounter. Monitoring, on the other hand, involves observing the application's performance in real-time to ensure that it meets the required service level objectives and responses efficiently to varying loads.

In the context of Django applications, logging is handled through Django's logging module, which is a configuration wrapper around Python's built-in logging module. This module allows developers to declare loggers, handlers, filters, and formatters in the Django settings file, providing a granular level of control over both what is logged and where it is logged to.

```
LOGGING = {
    'version': 1,
    'disable_existing_loggers': False,
    'handlers': {
        'file': {
            'level': 'DEBUG',
            'class': 'logging.FileHandler',
            'filename': '/path/to/django/debug.log',
        },
    },
    'loggers': {
        'django': {
            'handlers': ['file'],
            'level': 'DEBUG',
            'propagate': True,
        },
    },
}
```

In this configuration, Django logs all debug messages to a file at the specified path. Adjusting the level to INFO, WARNING, ERROR, or CRITICAL can reduce or increase the verbosity of the log output depending on the production needs.

For monitoring, several third-party services and tools can be integrated with Django applications. Popular options include New Relic, Datadog, and Prometheus. These services offer extensive insights into application performance, such as response times, throughput, error rates, and more. To integrate Django with these services, developers often use middleware or external libraries provided by the monitoring service. For example, integrating Django with Prometheus can be achieved using the django-prometheus library.

```
1   INSTALLED_APPS = [
2       ...
3       'django_prometheus',
4       ...
5   ]
6
7   MIDDLEWARE = [
8       ...
9       'django_prometheus.middleware.PrometheusBeforeMiddleware',
10      'django_prometheus.middleware.PrometheusAfterMiddleware',
11      ...
12  ]
```

With these configurations, every request and response is tracked, providing metrics that can be visualized and alerted on through the Prometheus platform.

Combining monitoring and logging gives a comprehensive overview of an application's health and performance. It enables developers to detect and diagnose problems early, often before they impact users. However, it also requires careful consideration of what data to collect to ensure that the logs and metrics are both useful and manageable. Excessive logging can lead to large volumes of data that are difficult to analyze, while insufficient logging can leave gaps in understanding how the application behaves under certain conditions.

- Emphasize critical paths in the application flow where performance and errors should be closely monitored.

- Utilize structured logging to make log analysis simpler and more productive.

- Establish monitoring thresholds and alerts based on performance baselines and key metrics.

- Secure and manage log data to comply with data protection regulations, ensuring that sensitive information is not inadvertently logged.

Effective monitoring and logging strategies are key to maintaining the reliability and performance of Django applications in production. By leveraging Django's built-in logging capabilities and integrating with monitoring tools, developers can ensure a high level of observability, facilitating prompt detection and resolution of issues. This, paired with a strategic selection of what data to log and monitor, allows for the efficient operation of Django applications at scale.

12.13 Scaling Django Applications Horizontally and Vertically

Scaling a Django application to accommodate growing numbers of requests is a critical aspect of maintaining performance and providing a seamless user experience. This entails increasing the application's capacity to handle requests either by adding more resources to the existing infrastructure (vertical scaling) or by adding more instances of the application (horizontal scaling). Both strategies have their distinct advantages and scenarios where they are most effective.

Vertical scaling, also known as scaling up, involves enhancing the capabilities of the existing server by adding more CPU, RAM, or storage. This approach is straightforward and can yield immediate performance improvements without significant changes to the application's architecture or the deployment process. However, vertical scaling is limited by the maximum capacity of a single machine, and at some point, the cost of upgrading hardware becomes prohibitively expensive. Moreover, it does not provide fault tolerance; if the server fails, the entire application becomes unavailable.

Horizontal scaling, or scaling out, refers to adding more servers to handle the load, distributing the traffic among multiple instances of the same application. This strategy requires the application to be stateless so that each request can be processed by any server, necessitating the use of shared session stores and databases accessible by all instances. Horizontal scaling offers the benefit of practically unlimited capacity as new servers can be added as needed. It also increases fault tolerance, as the failure of a single server does not affect the overall availability of the application.

To implement vertical scaling in a Django application, one must ensure that the application and the database server it connects to can utilize the added resources effectively. This may involve configuring the database to use additional memory for caching and optimizing the application settings to handle more concurrent connections.

In contrast, horizontal scaling requires a more systematic approach to manage multiple instances of the application. This involves configuring a load balancer to distribute incoming requests among the servers. Django's built-in functionalities support distributed environments, making it easier to scale applications horizontally. Sessions can be stored in a distributed cache like Redis or Memcached, or in a centralized database, allowing user sessions to persist across requests to different servers. Static files can be served through a content delivery network (CDN), ensuring quick access regardless of the server handling the request.

Implementing horizontal scaling effectively often includes adopting practices such as continuous integration and continuous deployment (CI/CD), containerization with tools like Docker, and orchestration with Kubernetes or Docker Swarm. These tools and practices facilitate the deployment, management, and scaling of containerized application instances across multiple servers.

Algorithm 2: Pseudocode for Distributing Incoming Requests Using a Load Balancer

---

    Data: IncomingRequest
    Result: Distribute IncomingRequest among ServerInstances
1 **begin**
2   LoadBalancer ← InitializeLoadBalancer(ServerInstances)
3   **while** *True* **do**
4   IncomingRequest ← ReceiveRequest()
5   SelectedServer ←
           LoadBalancer.SelectServer(IncomingRequest)
6   RouteRequest(SelectedServer, IncomingRequest)

Both vertical and horizontal scaling have implications for database performance. Database queries can become a bottleneck as the load increases. It is crucial to optimize query performance by using indexes, denormalizing data where necessary, and implementing read replicas for distributing read queries across multiple servers. In some cases, it might be beneficial to adopt a multi-database architecture, where different types of data are stored in distinct databases optimized for specific access patterns.

It is important for developers to monitor the performance of their Django applications continuously and to consider both vertical and horizontal scaling strategies as part of their overall performance optimization and scaling plan. By understanding the advantages and limitations of each approach, developers can make informed decisions about how best to scale their applications in response to increasing load.

12.14 Using CDN and Edge Computing for Global Scaling

Content Delivery Networks (CDNs) and Edge Computing have become vital components in the global scaling strategy for Django applications. These technologies play a crucial role in ensuring the delivery of content with high availability and performance, which is especially important for applications with a global user base. This section will discuss the integration of both CDN and Edge Computing for optimizing the deployment and scaling of Django applications on a global scale.

CDNs are distributed networks of servers that work collectively to provide fast delivery of Internet content. By caching content at various locations around the world, CDNs reduce the distance between the user and the content source, which significantly decreases the loading time for users regardless of their geographical location. When deploying a Django application at a global scale, utilizing a CDN can dramatically improve user experience by speeding up the loading time of static assets such as CSS files, JavaScript, and images.

To implement a CDN with a Django application, you will typically modify the application's settings to indicate where static and media files should be stored. By specifying a CDN's URL as the base URL for static and media files, you instruct Django to generate URLs for these assets that point to the CDN. For example:

```
STATIC_URL = 'https://<CDN_URL>/static/'
MEDIA_URL = 'https://<CDN_URL>/media/'
```

This configuration ensures that all static and media file URLs generated by Django will direct users to the cached versions on the CDN, thus reducing load times.

Edge Computing, on the other hand, refers to the practice of processing data closer to the location where it is generated or needed, instead of relying on a central data-processing warehouse. This is particularly beneficial for dynamic content and applications requiring real-time processing. For Django applications, Edge Computing can be employed to run application logic closer to the user, hence reducing latency and improving response times for dynamic content.

Integrating Edge Computing with Django involves deploying portions of the application or specific services at edge nodes provided by edge

378

computing services. These services often offer containerized environments where you can run your Django application components. For certain functionalities such as authentication, real-time data processing, or personalized content generation, running these components on edge nodes can significantly improve performance for users regardless of their location.

In practice, this might involve configuring a service to route requests for dynamic content to the closest edge node where the application logic is executed, and then seamlessly serving the result back to the user. This configuration could look something akin to a function deployed on an edge computing platform that interacts with the main Django application:

```
def edge_function(request):
    # Logic to process request at the edge
    # For example, generating personalized content
    personalized_content = generate_content_for_user(request.user)
    return JsonResponse(personalized_content)
```

Integrating CDN and Edge Computing requires careful planning of the application architecture. Specifically, developers must decide which components of the Django application are best suited for deployment at the edge. This often involves identifying parts of the application that benefit most from reduced latency, such as APIs for dynamic content, microservices for specific functionalities, or middleware services for authentication.

To complement the global scaling effort, it is also crucial to implement robust caching strategies. Caching at the edge can significantly reduce the need for each request to travel back to the origin server, further decreasing response times and reducing load on the central server. Django's cache framework can be configured to work with various backend caches, and when combined with Edge Computing, it provides a powerful way to cache both static and dynamic content close to the users.

Overall, the use of CDN and Edge Computing represents a paradigm shift in how Django applications are deployed and scaled globally. By leveraging these technologies, developers can ensure that their applications are not only capable of serving a global audience but do so with the responsiveness and efficiency that modern users demand. The key to successful implementation lies in a strategic architecture that optimizes content delivery and application logic processing through distributed networks, thus ensuring high performance, scalability, and a superior user experience across the globe.

12.15   Case Studies: Successful Deployment and Scaling Strategies

Deploying and scaling Django applications effectively require strategic planning and execution. This section examines real-world case studies that showcase successful deployment and scaling strategies. These examples provide valuable insights into the challenges faced during the scaling of web applications and the solutions implemented to overcome them.

Case Study 1: E-commerce Platform Scaling

An e-commerce platform started experiencing significant increases in traffic during holiday seasons. Initially, the application was deployed on a single server, causing performance bottlenecks and downtime during peak traffic periods. To address these challenges, the platform adopted a strategy for horizontal scaling and implemented several key changes.

First, they transitioned to using a cloud-based infrastructure as a service (IaaS) solution, allowing for easy addition of servers to distribute the load. They utilized `auto-scaling` groups to dynamically adjust the number of servers in response to traffic fluctuations.

Second, they deployed a load balancer to distribute incoming requests evenly across the available servers. This ensured that no single server became a performance bottleneck.

Third, static and media files were moved to a content delivery network (CDN), significantly reducing the load on the application servers and improving response times for end-users across different geographical locations.

Lastly, they implemented database replication, separating read and write operations. This allowed for scaling out the database layer by adding read replicas to handle the increased read operations, thus reducing the load on the primary database.

This multi-pronged approach to scaling effectively supported the e-commerce platform's growth, maintaining high availability and performance even during peak traffic.

Case Study 2: Social Media Application Handling Massive Data

A social media application with a rapidly growing user base faced challenges in managing and processing vast amounts of data in real-time. The application initially ran on a monolithic architecture, making it difficult to scale and update without significant downtime.

To overcome these challenges, the application was refactored into a microservices architecture. This refactoring allowed individual components of the application to be scaled independently based on demand.

For real-time data processing, the application utilized distributed task queues and message brokers. This enabled efficient handling of tasks such as updates to news feeds and notifications.

For data storage, the application leveraged sharding across multiple databases. This strategy allowed the data to be partitioned into smaller, more manageable chunks, reducing the load on any single database and improving query performance.

Caching strategies were also extensively employed to minimize database hits for frequently accessed data, thereby reducing response times and further lowering the server load.

These strategies collectively enabled the social media application to support a large user base and high volumes of data processing with minimal latency, providing a smooth user experience.

```
 1  # Sample Configuration for Auto-Scaling in Cloud Infrastructure
 2  autoscale_group:
 3    min_size: 2
 4    max_size: 100
 5    desired_capacity: 10
 6    health_check_type: EC2
 7    health_check_grace_period: 300
 8    launch_configuration:
 9      image_id: ami-123456
10      instance_type: t2.medium
11      security_groups: ["sg-123456"]
12      key_name: my-key-pair
```

These case studies illustrate the importance of adopting a comprehensive strategy for scaling Django applications. By utilizing cloud-based solutions, optimizing database performance, implementing caching, and adopting microservices where necessary, applications can achieve significant improvements in scalability and performance. Continuous monitoring and adjusting of these strategies in response to traffic patterns and growth is crucial for maintaining an efficient and reliable application infrastructure.